D1827331

Propping up the Performative School

Propping up the Performative School: A Critical Examination of the English Educational Paraprofessional

BY

JO BISHOP

University of Huddersfield, UK

United Kingdom – North America – Japan – India – Malaysia – China

Emerald Publishing Limited
Howard House, Wagon Lane, Bingley BD16 1WA, UK

First edition 2022

Copyright © 2022 Jo Bishop
Published under exclusive license by Emerald Publishing Limited.

Reprints and permissions service
Contact: permissions@emeraldinsight.com

No part of this book may be reproduced, stored in a retrieval system, transmitted in
any form or by any means electronic, mechanical, photocopying, recording or otherwise
without either the prior written permission of the publisher or a licence permitting
restricted copying issued in the UK by The Copyright Licensing Agency and in the USA
by The Copyright Clearance Center. Any opinions expressed in the chapters are those
of the authors. Whilst Emerald makes every effort to ensure the quality and accuracy of
its content, Emerald makes no representation implied or otherwise, as to the chapters'
suitability and application and disclaims any warranties, express or implied, to their use.

British Library Cataloguing in Publication Data
A catalogue record for this book is available from the British Library

ISBN: 978-1-83982-243-8 (Print)
ISBN: 978-1-83982-242-1 (Online)
ISBN: 978-1-83982-244-5 (Epub)

Printed and bound by CPI Group (UK) Ltd, Croydon, CR0 4YY

ISOQAR certified
Management System,
awarded to Emerald
for adherence to
Environmental
standard
ISO 14001:2004.

Certificate Number 1985
ISO 14001

INVESTOR IN PEOPLE

Endorsements for Propping Up the Performative School

This book shines a much-needed light on the often overseen and undervalued, yet ever present 'educational paraprofessional'. Using a policy focus and rich ethnographic data the author brings new theoretical and empirical insights into the analysis of the 'educational paraprofessional', while intricately highlighting the neglected but valid role that they occupy within the diversified and performance-driven English state school system. (Dr Lisa Russell, The University of Huddersfield).

This book provides a unique insight into the significant contribution that 'paraprofessionals' play in our children's education. The research demonstrates how these often 'hidden' school staff support young people holistically in the important transition to adulthood by working inside and outside of their school setting. As such to fundamentally question our conceptualisation of learning and the present English schooling system. (Dr Doug Martin, Carnegie School of Education, Leeds Beckett University).

This study brings to life the day-to-day lived experience of contemporary education. By exploring the under-researched role of 'paraprofessionals' it also helps us to reflect on their crucial role in supporting young people through crucial life transitions. The combination of policy analysis, ethnography, and theorising makes the book both engaging and enlightening. Highly recommended to all those interested in the field. (Nick Frost, Emeritus Professor of Social Work, Leeds Beckett University).

To Frank and Sheila – for all that you are and all that you do.

Contents

List of Tables and Figures

Tables

Figures

Abbreviations

ABI	Area Based Initiative
EPA	Educational Priority Area
BSF	Building Schools for the Future
BS	Behaviour Support
BSW	Behaviour Support Worker
CE	Compensatory Education
CPD	Continuing Professional Development
CWDC	Children's Workforce Development Council
DCSF	Department for Children, Schools and Families
DfE	Department for Education
DfEE	Department for Education and Employment
DES	Department of Education and Science
DfES	Department for Education and Skills
EAL	English as an Additional Language
EAZ	Education Action Zone
ECM	Every Child Matters
EiC	Excellence in Cities
FD	Foundation Degree
GCSE	General Certificate of Secondary Education
HLTA	Higher Level Teaching Assistant
HND	Higher National Diploma
HSO	Human Service Organisation
IE	Institutional Ethnography
LA	Local Authority
LEA	Local Education Authority
NEET	Not in Education, Employment or Training
NPM	New Public Management

NVQ	National Vocational Qualification
OFSTED	Office for Standards in Education
PFI	Private Finance Initiative
PL	Progress Leader
RAP	Raising Achievement Programme
SEU	Social Exclusion Unit
TA	Teaching Assistant
UK	United Kingdom
US/USA	United States of America
YM	Year Manager

About the Author

Jo Bishop is a Senior Lecturer in Childhood and Education Studies at the University of Huddersfield. She has worked in the English further and higher education sectors since the early 1990s teaching across a range of vocational and academic courses which prepare people for employment in schools, colleges, social care and youth work settings. Her current research interests lie in the enactment of policies which have resulted in a more diverse schools workforce. She has recently embarked on research which is looking at how processes and systems of pastoral care are conceived and implemented within an increasingly fragmented English school system.

Acknowledgements

I would like to convey a heartfelt thank you to the staff and pupils of *Priory Park High** in graciously giving up their time, answering my (many) questions and tolerating my presence, even on the busiest of days. I am in awe of the complexities and challenges that staff navigate in their desire to ensure that school is a positive experience for children and young people. To the support staff in particular, I hope this book has conveyed all that you do and the contribution that you make.

I would also like to express my thanks to those academic colleagues who have supported me throughout the writing of this book, particularly Robin Simmons who offered invaluable guidance at the proposal stage and Paul Thomas who provided feedback on draft chapters.

Earlier versions of some of this material have appeared in the *British Journal of Educational Research*, *69*(2), 197–216, 2021 and *Perspectives on and from Institutional Ethnography* published by Emerald.

---

*Pseudonyms have been used for the school and its staff named in this book.

Chapter 1

Introduction

This book is about the experiences and contribution of educational paraprofessionals. It tells the ethnographic story of one such group – learning mentors – working in an all-inclusive state secondary school in the North of England. Educational paraprofessionals are not widely researched as school-based ethnographies have tended to reflect the focal points pursued by educational research more generally, such as curriculum and pedagogy (Goldbart & Hustler, 2005). In taking this path, studies have traditionally examined the activities, experiences and perspectives of teachers and pupils (Bird, 1980; Denscombe, 1980; Willis, 1977; Woods, 1980) with less regard for other school-based roles. Where the focus has been outside of the classroom it has tended towards the upper echelons of the organisational structure as typified by Wolcott's (1973) seminal study of a school principal. This book sets out to broaden the parameters of a 'standard' school ethnography in going *beyond* both the classroom and the 'teacher/pupil' dichotomy. I argue that educational paraprofessionals are neglected but valid participants in schools, contributing a great deal to the education of young people albeit in less familiar and therefore more 'hidden' places than the traditional depiction of 'classroom'. Furthermore, I feel it imperative that school/educational ethnographies accurately reflect the diversity of *all staff* now present in English state schools and that their experiences are documented according to ethnographic conventions, rather than merely 'show-cased' through 'illustrative case studies' (Cruddas, 2005, p. 111) of particular practice communities.

What's in a Name? Defining 'Paraprofessional'

At this early stage it is useful to unpack the phrase 'paraprofessional' which is used frequently throughout this book. In general terms it describes workers who in some way occupy the margins of professional status within education and a number of other related occupational fields. As is often the case, it is possible to identify a cluster of terms which have come about with similar meanings premised as they are on shared experiences. Within an educational context, 'associate professional' was proposed at a time when there was a degree of optimism regarding the potential value that new and existing non-teaching roles could offer as part of

Propping up the Performative School: A Critical Examination of the English Educational Paraprofessional, 1–8
Copyright © 2022 by Jo Bishop
Published under exclusive licence by Emerald Publishing Limited
doi:10.1108/978-1-83982-242-120221001

a 'children and schools workforce' (Edmund & Price, 2009). Likewise, 'learning support worker' and 'para teacher' were used to describe similar roles and functions in post-16 educational settings (Bailey & Robson, 2004). Others note more critically how the term 'hybrid professional' has been utilised as a political means to inspire public confidence in less-qualified practitioners who have significantly lower salaries compared to teachers (Colley & Guery, 2015). In other human service organisations, the categorisation of 'Blue-Collar Professionalism' (McCann, Granter, Hyde, & Hassard, 2013) describes not only the liminal space occupied by paramedics but also conveys something about their struggle to achieve parity with other professional groups working in the English National Health Service.

Whilst these terms enable a useful overview of comparative titles, the older term 'paraprofessional' (Stanfield, 1973) is deemed to be the most appropriate to this particular discussion of educational workers because in using the prefix 'para' which signifies 'beside' or 'near', the worker is not identified by *negation* of their status (as with the terms non-professional or preprofessional), but rather as a *near*-professional, with no assumed expectation that they will necessarily move into a fully professional role. Moreover, the term paraprofessional is present in literature spanning both the time-frames and geo-political contexts covered in this book (see, e.g., Stewart, 1971 and Kerry, 2002, respectively). Thus having spent the last two decades researching both the concept and lived experiences of the 'educational paraprofessional' I am using the term to refer to any or all of the following: teaching assistants, higher level teaching assistants, learning mentors, behaviour support workers, inclusion workers, cover supervisors, parent support advisers and, I am sure, new titles still to come.[1] All of the above roles, whether temporary, now defunct, rebranded or continuing to endure, have at certain points in their varying histories been tasked with providing 'new' solutions to the seemingly intractable 'problems' of underachievement and disaffection within the state school system and are seen as continuing to play a fundamental role in pastoral and inclusion interventions in English school settings.

Their Presence and Roles in the Workforce

A recent school workforce census indicates that non-teaching staff with pupil support roles in English state-funded schools numbered 298,083, with just over 75,000 of these in secondary schools (DfE, 2018a). Behind these statistics is a story of policy evolution, policy borrowing and policy departures, all of which will be examined in the following chapters. But every story needs a starting point and in this case, it is 2001, when the then Secretary of State for Education, Estelle Morris, envisaged that 10 years on, schools would be 'rich in the number of trained adults [other than teachers] available to support learning to new high standards' (Department for Education and Skills, 2001a, p. 15). Just over a

---

[1]Exact numbers for each group are difficult to extrapolate as learning mentors come under the Teaching Assistant category and behaviour workers come under the category OSS (Other support staff) or BEHM (Behaviour Manager/Specialist).

decade later this prediction appears to have been confirmed with references to a 'diverse cast of "other adults" working in and around schools' (Ball, Maguire, & Braun, 2012, p. 2).

So what do educational paraprofessionals actually do? The titles referred to above give some idea of the area or responsibilities accorded to each role. For example, in secondary schools, teaching assistants tend to provide targeted support to individuals or small groups of learners and are predominantly classroom based. Learning mentors on the other hand provide interventions that take place outside of the classroom for children and young people deemed as having barriers to learning. Furthermore, in the early days of the role's implementation they were tasked with building relationships with families, communities and relevant agencies. It is worth noting that some commentators and schools do not make such distinctions in job title and use the term 'Teaching Assistant' generically to refer to those types of interventions mentioned above and others still (Tucker, 2009). Whilst distinctions can be made, it is also important to emphasise the overlapping nature of roles. For example, learning mentors can work with pupils deemed as having behavioural issues but this task could also be in the domain of the more recent behaviour support worker. Different avenues of support will often have a different underpinning philosophy and approach. Whilst *some* thought may have been given at both strategic and operational levels about how these roles sit alongside one another, it would be fair to say that this can often be overlooked in the frenetic and high-tempo pace of day-to-day school life, resulting in contradictory or confusing experiences for pupils on the receiving end of such interventions. Furthermore, the specifics of different paraprofessional roles will depend on *when* and *where* the role is implemented. For example, compared to other paraprofessional roles, teaching assistants have a considerable longevity having been a recognised part of the educational landscape certainly since the 1990s but established in embryonic form prior to that after the implementation of the Plowden Report in 1967 (Bartlett & Burton, 2020; Bishop, 2021). This provided the first documented reference to 'teaching aides' in English primary schools, a term often assumed to be imported as part of policy borrowing from the United States of America (USA or US) which at the time was expanding similar roles due to a drive for anti-poverty policies such as Head Start, a programme of early childhood intervention (Dunning, 2018; Lewis, 2004; Silver & Silver, 1991). There are earlier iterations still, 'classroom-based assistants' existed from the early 1960s (Clayton, 1993) and going back significantly further 'pupil-teachers' in the nineteenth century (Simmons, 2017). By contrast, learning mentors arrived much later (late twentieth/early twenty-first century) and initially only in those geographical areas covered by the policy which led to their implementation. This often piecemeal and arbitrary approach to the design and implementation of paraprofessional roles will become more apparent as the discussion progresses.

Another important point to consider is how educational paraprofessional roles are characterised. A cursory look at educational news media articles conjures up images of workers whose contribution is integral but whose visibility is questionable. Thus, paraprofessionals are described variously as: an 'auxiliary army' who are a 'force to be reckoned with' (Barker, 2008); the 'backroom brigade'

(Barton, 2010); part of the 'management engine' of a school (Woods, 2013) and 'unsung heroes' (Maddern, 2013). The paraprofessional workforce has traditionally been a feminised one and the most recent figures suggest this continues to be the case. In 2020/221 there were a total of 271,307 full time equivalent (fte) 'teaching assistants' (an official categorisation which includes learning mentors in this case) of which just over 248,000 were women. The category of 'Other Support Staff' which includes behaviour support workers shows a similar disparity with just over 34,000 fte women and 4,420 fte men (https://explore-education-statistics. service.gov.uk). Such demographics are reinforced by the salary which is usually 'term-time only', thereby assumed as a secondary income to that of a primary earner and a work arrangement which enables women to continue their own caring responsibilities during school holidays. Some of the newer paraprofessional roles suggest that this workforce is also becoming increasingly racialised (Bishop, 2021) for reasons which will be explained in due course. A more recent premise of paraprofessional roles is that they represent a 'stepping stone' or '*pre*professional' opportunity, providing experiences of educational and pastoral support work which will secure an individual's entry into teaching, social work and other allied professional training courses (Drury, 2013).

Despite paraprofessionals' now significant presence in the state school system, studies of their work and experiences tend to be small in number (Bishop, 2011; Bishop & Sanderson, 2017; Jones, Doveston, & Rose, 2009; Lee, 2011; Mansaray, 2006). Furthermore, after an initial period of optimism in the early 2000s regarding their potential contribution, it is their differential status that has ultimately served to reinforce a segmentation of functions between these occupational groups and their professionalised teaching counterparts (Edmund & Price, 2009). As stated above, this book focusses predominantly on the English learning mentor. It examines how this particular paraprofessional role was historically constructed and then continued to evolve through policy agendas enacted at the local level. The 'Learning Mentor' was conceived and implemented by the New Labour government (1997–2010). It drew in part on the rising popularity of youth mentoring which from the 1990s was utilised as a common approach to engage and work with young people not in education, employment or training (Colley, 2003a; Piper & Piper, 2000). This represents a further example of policy borrowing as such initiatives had been popular in the USA from the early 1980s[2] (Freedman, 1993; Philip, 2003). As will be explored further in the following chapter, the learning mentor formed one element in a series of social justice initiatives which underpinned this government's commitment to equity in schooling. However, this was an agenda which sat uneasily beside the acceptance and continuation of the quasi-market created within state education by their Conservative new-right predecessors (Thomson, 2020).

My own interest in work-based 'helping relationships' is long-standing. As a student of Social Care in the late 1980s, I observed and worked alongside

---

[2]Largely achieved through mass volunteer-based movements rather than the types of salaried positions under discussion here.

paraprofessionals attached to the Social Work profession. Their role was to support young people who, at just 16 years of age were preparing to leave the care system to embark on their adult lives. In the absence of a formal 'corporate parent' (a role not legislated in England until 2017), care leavers had only these more informal relationships with their residential key workers to rely upon in making their transition to independent living. Some years later, my focus shifted to state schools where I recognised similar skills and values being utilised by adults who were not teachers but nevertheless played a significant part in supporting pupils as they navigated their way through compulsory education. In one such example – which might be understood as a reconnaissance study – (Bishop, 2011) I aimed to ascertain how the work of learning mentors had developed some 8 years after the role was implemented. The data that this study generated indicated multiple, often contradictory ways in which learning mentors described their work, ranging from providing emotional support to vulnerable pupils, whilst monitoring more overtly institutional concerns like attendance, behaviour and ultimately attainment. What was also discernible was the degree of autonomy that some learning mentors were afforded in comparison to their professional teaching counterparts as shown in this extract below:

> Engaging with young people is my key focus. This takes me into all sorts of areas such as car mechanics, coaching rugby teams, gym work, routine building maintenance, visits to local businesses, etc. (cited in Bishop, 2011, p. 39)

I started to become intrigued by the tightrope that these workers were often required to walk in what I tentatively described as their 'dual role' of, on the one hand, engaging young people through the offering of emotional and social support whilst, on the other, meeting institutional imperatives of monitoring academic progress and attainment. I questioned what the personal impact of performing such a role might be and it was these ponderings that led to the ethnographic study of learning mentoring reported in this book (Bishop, 2017, 2021).

Since conducting the ethnography (2013–2015) the educational landscape has continued to evolve. There have been two changes of government with each one pursuing policies that have led to a more fragmented system of schooling in England (Ball, 2021; Mortimore, 2013). The existence of multi-academy trusts, free schools and faith schools alongside the now endangered community or 'maintained' school,[3] makes it more challenging than ever to build a coherent picture of the pastoral and inclusive interventions that schools adopt, not to mention the philosophies that underpin them. In more recent times, a period of policy paralysis has also taken place due in the first instance to the lengthy and at times seemingly intractable resolution of the United Kingdom's (UK) exit from the

---

[3]Community schools are state funded and have maintained their relationship with the local authority which employs the school staff, controls admissions, and owns the land and premises (Mortimore, 2013).

European Union, followed then by the outbreak and subsequent impact of the Covid 19 pandemic. Arguably, it is the latter which has given renewed attention to long-standing concerns regarding how socio-economic inequalities shape educational experiences and outcomes (Thomson, 2020). Not surprisingly, heroic characterisations of educational paraprofessionals emerged once again during this period with one study describing them as 'the mortar in the brickwork of our schools' (Moss, Webster, Harmey, & Bradbury, 2021, p. 30). Thus, it is a timely point to re-emphasise the important role played by educational paraprofessionals; to go beyond the 'headlines' and grasp an appreciation of the realities of their lived experiences as they continue to 'prop up' the education system in which they are situated.

Structure of the Book

Chapter 1 has set out the concept of the English educational paraprofessional by identifying a number of roles which come under this term; their presence in the school workforce and the ways in which their work and contribution has been characterised. A brief introduction has been given to the paraprofessional role of learning mentor, which forms the key focus of this book. The issues identified in this initial discussion will be picked up and examined further in the following chapters. A brief note for international readers: the focus on English, rather than UK educational policy and provisions in this book is due to the devolved nations (Scotland, Northern Ireland and Wales) pursuing their respective agendas to a greater or lesser extent.

Chapter 2 examines the political environment in which the learning mentor role was conceived. Particular attention is paid to the policy *Excellence in Cities* alongside other early intervention programmes and area-based initiatives both past and present. It also considers how the parallel agenda of 'remodelling' led to a restructuring of the teacher role. This involved (firstly) the reallocation of some teaching and learning tasks to more established paraprofessionals like teaching assistants and (secondly) the jettisoning of activities of a more pastoral nature to newly installed paraprofessional roles. For contextual purposes, broader policy agendas around social exclusion, a stated desire to abolish child poverty and the introduction of different working practices within the children and young people's workforce are also discussed in this chapter. This includes a brief introduction to the concepts of New Public Management (Hood, 1995) which has given rise to a system of 'performativity' (Ball, 2003; Elliot, 2001), both of which are returned to in Chapter 12 for further critical analysis. The final part of Chapter 2 sets out how the learning mentor role was constructed in both government literature and educational news media, highlighting the partial understandings of the role displayed by some teachers and school leaders. This discussion also considers academic critiques of learning mentorship/youth mentoring to ascertain their usefulness in developing a critical understanding of the role and the work activities associated with it.

Chapter 3 offers a wider geographical and temporal perspective in considering the pre-existence and rationale for paraprofessional roles akin to the learning mentor in another capitalist nation, the USA. Here, we delve into a rich histori-cal literature that offers accounts of ideologically driven, anti-poverty projects which desired to establish career trajectories for non-professional workers in the human and health services. This discussion also includes extracts from 'real-time' research studies which have proved invaluable in documenting who undertook paraprofessional roles and what their experiences were.

As might be expected from a discussion of methodology, Chapter 4 provides a commentary on the research design and methods employed in the ethnography including site selection, access and sampling; the consideration of ethical issues; methods employed and how the data were analysed and presented. However, the parameters of this discussion go much further in outlining how the study reported in this book was influenced by Institutional Ethnography (IE) (Smith, 2005) as a means to research marginalised work. In doing so it sets out how char-acteristics of IE were utilised as informing devices once in the field. Here I cover 'standpoint'; the 'relations of ruling' and the notion of the problematic; the iden-tification of texts; explicating the 'work knowledges' of different participants and the ability to distinguish between institutional and experiential accounts. Exam-ples of data which provide illustrations of these are presented throughout which will be of interest to readers regardless of whether they have an established or developing knowledge of IE. As such, this chapter may be accessed and read as a stand-alone section.

Chapters 5 through 9 represent the ethnographic study itself. Chapter 5 begins by introducing the setting in which the ethnography takes place. This starts with a brief history of the school, identifying key milestones and significant events in its evolution as a 'maintained', all-inclusive state secondary school. It then moves on to give a 'guided tour' of the school on a typical Monday morning, a 'story' which is based upon composite accounts written up over the fieldwork period. This device is a means to introduce the paraprofessionals who are the key actors in this ethnography so here we meet not only the learning mentor team who as stated above form the main focus of this book, but also the higher level teaching assistants (HLTAs), teaching assistants (TAs) and behaviour support workers, all of whom are considered as key informants. Included here are the learning and pastoral provisions that the paraprofessionals occupy, thereby setting out a useful contextual backdrop for the many issues that are identified and discussed in later chapter and re-emphasising the earlier point that this is an educational ethnogra-phy which focusses on what goes on *outside* of the mainstream classroom.

The key focus of Chapter 6 is in setting out the formal/official and what I have termed the 'seen' aspects of the learning mentor role. It provides an in-depth examination of the provisions they staff (namely Breakfast club and the mentor base) and the one-to-one interventions they are tasked with providing. In con-trast, Chapter 7 examines the unofficial or 'unseen' domain of the mentors' work, presenting a series of ad hoc, spontaneous and unofficial interventions which highlight the peripheral nature of their work and role. In doing so, this chap-ter captures the voices of young people gained in part through pupil data which evidence young people's understandings of the learning mentor role and how it differs from other staff roles. Chapter 7 also considers pupil agency through accounts of how pastoral systems are navigated and decisions made, regarding how and when they access support. To give further context to the mentor's work, this chapter also charts pupil experiences and perspectives on their educational experiences more generally.

The next two chapters set out how the learning mentor role is understood by those occupying other positions within the school hierarchy. Chapter 8 presents the views of three members of the Senior Leadership Team (the Headteacher, the Deputy Headteacher, Teacher and the Director of Pastoral Care) whose vary-ing understandings of the role become increasingly apparent as the chapter pro-gresses. Chapter 9 then turns to the Middle Management of the school looking at both the Progress Leader and the Year Manager positions. These two roles offer a useful means by which to understand how academic and pastoral functions within a school have been 'uncoupled', with those from a teaching background focussing on the academic 'progress' of pupils and those not being tasked with the management and monitoring of pupil attendance and engagement whilst addressing whatever issues might act as a hindrance to these. This chapter deals with questions of whether paraprofessionals like the learning mentor are able to meet the expectations of these two distinct managerial positions. Having consid-ered the views of senior and middle managers, Chapter 10 offers a 'right to reply' to the learning mentors by further examining how they manage, acquiesce and at times resist the official but often contradictory prescriptions of their work seen in the previous two chapters.

Chapter 11 provides an opportunity to examine how unique the mentors' experiences are in terms of the challenges they have faced both past and present. It does so by going back to the more established paraprofessionals (HLTAs and TAs) first introduced at the start of the ethnography. Through the accounts they provide, it is possible to identify shared experiences to the mentors when they were themselves entering schools as a new role, one decade earlier.

The final chapter draws out and discusses key issues identified in both the ethnography and supporting literature. It presents an overview of the construc-tion of the educational paraprofessional, drawing parallels between two policy agendas presented, albeit 50 years and two continents apart. It considers one important difference which is how performativity impacts on the educational paraprofessional in terms of both concept and practice. This leads to a discussion regarding the crucial question of how such 'helping relationships' develop and operate within the context of performance-based cultures. The final issue under consideration is what the enactment of the learning mentor and other parapro-fessional roles tells us about how practices previously conceived as 'pastoral' are evolving.

Chapter 2

The Wider Policy Context Giving Rise to Learning Mentors

> To overcome *economic and social disadvantage* and to make equality of opportunity a reality, we must strive to eliminate, and never excuse, underachievement in the most deprived parts of our country. *Educational attainment encourages aspiration and self-belief in the next generation,* and it is through family learning, as well as scholarship through formal schooling, that success will come. (David Blunkett, Secretary of State for Education 1999, cited in Bishop, 2011, p. 30, my emphasis)

> I say to the country in all honesty. You can have the education revolution, the health revolution, the welfare revolution. But it means hard choices. It means us all getting involved. And it means modernisation. And we need to bring a change to the way we treat each other. I tell you: a decent society is not based on rights. It is based on duty. Our duty to each other. To all should be given opportunity, from all responsibility demanded. (Tony Blair, Prime minister, Leader's speech, Brighton 1997)

The first few years of the New Labour administration witnessed the implementation of a genre of policies in which substantial funding was made available for a series of social justice initiatives. This not only signalled Labour's commitment to equity in schooling but was part of a wider social policy agenda which sought to reduce the levels of inequality that had increased as a result of Thatcherite policies (Thomson, 2020). The extracts above reveal two explicit agendas at play: in the first one by Blunkett, we can see that educational disparities were very much tied to wider economic and social disadvantage. This would lead to the implementation of early intervention programmes and area-based initiatives (ABIs) discussed in due course. However, this renewed investment came with conditions as seen in Blair's espousal of duty *and* responsibility, requiring communities,

Propping up the Performative School: A Critical Examination of the English Educational Paraprofessional, 9–27
Copyright © 2022 by Jo Bishop
Published under exclusive licence by Emerald Publishing Limited
doi:10.1108/978-1-83982-242-120221002

families and individuals to play their part in 'shoring up' the meritocratic ideals that the previous administration had put at risk.

This then was the political environment in which the learning mentor role was delivered, the components of which form the basis of the discussion for this chapter. First, I will focus on school-based initiatives, arguing that these can be helpfully understand as a revival in part of earlier influential projects. This first section also focusses on parallel programmes of raising standards and tackling the workload of the teaching profession which was itself going through profound changes. The school-based initiatives under discussion were part of a much wider policy context relating to children, young people and families; this will therefore form the second part of the chapter. In the third and final part, the discussion will narrow its focus to look in-depth at the learning mentor role, examining how it was conceived by policy innovators and correspondingly *received* by existing school personnel. In addition, the discussion will set out how both the role and its work was constructed through news media and academic accounts. Other concomitant agendas that impacted on the formation of the learning mentor role are also considered.

Area-based Initiatives: Back to the Future?

The election of the New Labour government in 1997 marked a sharp swing back to the introduction of ABIs not only in the areas of education, but also health, neighbourhood, and employment (Smith, Smith, & Smith, 2007). However, before focussing on those specific to this era, it is useful to look at their antecedents and determine the extent to which New Labour embarked on a programme of policy recycling.

In 1963, the Plowden Committee was set up to consider established and emerging views about the relationships between primary schools and social deprivation or disadvantage. The stubborn and enduring impact of poverty had a clear presence in the committee's thinking as illustrated in this draft formulation:

> The fact is that, with primary as with secondary [schools], the social changes of the last quarter of a century for all their pace and scope have passed some children by almost as if they had not happened .... People have been reshuffled in space against a backdrop which has remained obstinately the same. Divisions in society still exist. The poor are still poor. The children of the poor are still the children of the poor. (Working Party 2, March 1966, cited in Silver & Silver, 1991, p. 234)

Although formulations of this kind were not included in the final Plowden Report (1967), they remained principally through the linked concepts and strategies of 'positive discrimination' and 'educational priority areas' (EPAs). The latter provide an early example of ABIs with the proposal that economically and socially disadvantaged areas were to be identified and targeted with additional resources and innovative educational developments (Smith et al., 2007).

One such resource was the establishment of the teacher aide as previously noted in Chapter 1.

Pinpointing specific areas of England that became EPAs is challenging for a number of reasons. Firstly, the term 'area' applied not only to a particular local authority but also included individual schools. Secondly, criteria to establish an EPA was based on certain conditions being present at the level of both the individual/family *and* the environment. Thus, criteria encompassed parental occupation; size of families; state supplements in cash or kind; overcrowded and shared housing; poor school attendance and truancy; proportion of retarded, disturbed or handicapped [*sic.*] pupils; incomplete families [*sic.*], and children unable to speak English (Silver & Silver, 1991). In relation to environmental criteria, the Plowden committee referred to the prevalence of grim buildings in older cities and unappealing schools which failed to attract teachers and motivate pupils. Perhaps not surprisingly then, the EPA idea itself was eventually challenged due to its confusion between areas, schools and children, which were 'hopelessly entangled from the start' (Smith et al., 2007, p. 148). Nevertheless, it can be clarified that in the earlier days of scoping activities, committee members visited 75 schools in Bristol, Manchester, Oldham, Salford, Rochdale, Nottingham and County Durham (Silver & Silver, 1991). Furthermore, based on the Index of Multiple Deprivation (IMD) measures in 2004, many of the areas selected to become EPAs continue some 50 years later to be in the most disadvantaged 10% of areas in England (Smith et al., 2007).

The focus of Conservative new right Governments in the intervening years emphasised individual improvement along with a rejection if not outright denial of systematic and structural differences. However, by the early 1990s it was clear that the 'old' problems of poverty and social inequality had not gone away. A study undertaken for the then newly formed Office for Standards in Education (Ofsted) pointed out that 'the majority of schools in the most disadvantaged areas were also very poorly rated by Her Majesty's Inspectors' (Smith, 1994 cited in Smith et al., 2007, p. 143). Following on from this, the idea of focussing on particular areas or groups that had dominated the late 1960s/early 1970s were revived across a number of forums and, as can be seen in the following section, worked their way into the emerging thinking of the New Labour government (Martin, 2016; Smith et al., 2007).

New Labour School-specific Policies: 'Benefiting the Many and Not the Few'

The first policy under discussion, *Excellence in schools* (Department for Education and Employment, 1997) was published just over two months after Labour entered government. Described as a 'bedrock' document (Ball, 2008) it contained almost all of the key themes of New Labour's education policy which in relation to this discussion were: an attack on low standards in schools; a declaration of zero tolerance of under-performance and a stated aim that policies would be designed to benefit the many and not the few. *Excellence in schools* was designed and disseminated as an accessible policy document, presented in a highly visual, colour-coded format and made available at supermarket checkouts (Maguire, 2004 in Ball, 2008). It also introduced Education Action Zones (EAZs) – a pilot project which attempted to 'join-up' services working with families as a way to tackle poor educational outcomes in disadvantaged areas. EAZs were set up on the basis of partnerships usually formed between schools, their Local Education Authority (LEA) and other local organisations, 'especially from the business community' (Ofsted, 2003, p. 5). EAZs provide an illustration of how New Labour were attempting to learn how to adjust the market so that less advantaged communities were not left behind (Martin, 2016), however, interest and take-up by businesses was low and, by the admission of the scheme's own innovator Michael Barber (chief educational advisor to the government): 'we failed to design some programmes properly: educational action zones was the classic case' (Barber, 2007, p. 36).

EAZs were eventually incorporated into *Excellence in Cities* (DfES, 2001b) a policy initiative which carried the explicit intention to enable social engineering through schools as social organisations. Turning once again to Michael Barber who declared:

> Ultimately the programme should result in a complete re-engineering of secondary education. Instead of fitting students into systems as we did in the 20th century, we would build the system around the needs and aspirations of students. (cited in Elliott, 2001, pp. 194–195)

A further element implicit in this particular policy agenda was to make such schools more attractive 'to those parents who would otherwise abandon them' (Barber, 2007, p. 37) thus reconciling Tony Blair's emphasis on 'aspirant parents' with David Blunkett's desire for equity. Far wider in scope than Education Action Zones, EiC initially encompassed six English cities and urban conurbations of Inner London, Birmingham, Manchester/Salford, Liverpool/Knowsley, Sheffield/Rotherham and Leeds/Bradford. The initiative further evolved to form 'Excellence Clusters' targeting smaller pockets of disadvantage such as coastal towns and ex-mining communities (Bishop, 2011) and was also extended to primary schools (Lepkowska, 2004).

Excellence in Cities initially focussed on improving standards in secondary education by introducing several new strands of provision into schools. Extended opportunities were provided for those pupils perceived as 'Gifted and Talented' (particularly if they were from lower socio-economic backgrounds). Learning Support Units designed to remove disruptive students from classrooms and work intensively with pupils at risk of temporary or permanent exclusion were established (Naidoo & Muschamp, 2002). This was in part to reduce the overall number of permanent exclusions which had peaked in the mid-1990s due to schools attempting to 'off-roll' problematic pupils, eventually off-set by New Labour's move to incorporate national exclusion targets in institutional measures of performance (Gillies, 2016). Most relevant to this book however was the introduction of learning mentors and it was this new paraprofessional group that were trumpeted in government and educational news media circles as the most successful strand within the initiative (Bell, 2003; A. Hayward, personal communication with A Hayward, educational consultant interviewed, May 24, 2007; Kirkman, 2004; Stoney, 2005). The number and presence of learning mentors was significantly strengthened through EiC and by the mid-2000s, there were estimated to be between 12 and 14,000 working across the sector (Department for Education and Skills, 2005). Despite ring-fenced funding for EiC ending in 2008, the learning mentor role continued to exist in some local authority maintained schools, albeit in a rebranded form with examples including: 'pastoral officer', 'transition and child protection coordinator' and 'inclusive programmes manager' (Bishop, 2011).

Spotlight on the Teaching Profession in 'Driving Up Standards'

A corresponding policy document, *Schools Achieving Success* (Department for Education and Skills, 2001a) also played a significant part in influencing both the numbers and activities of paraprofessional staff working in schools (Andrews, 2006). Identifying the twin problems of teacher shortages and unsustainable teacher workloads this document argued that far greater flexibility was needed in relation to deployment of staff. In practical terms this meant the jettisoning of some responsibilities that had previously fallen within the domain of teachers with the promise of 20,000 more support (i.e., paraprofessional) staff in schools along with 10,000 more teachers (Ball, 2008; Department for Education and Skills, 2001a). This proposal was formalised through section 133 of the Education Act 2002 providing for the first time a regulatory framework for the role and deployment of support staff and leading to a national restructuring and remodelling of school staff, referred to as the 'remodelling agenda' (Department for Education and Skills, 2003a; Nathan, 2011). Teachers were no longer required to routinely undertake clerical and administrative tasks and also relinquished some aspects of their work defined in the Act as 'specified' to the Higher Level Teaching Assistant (HLTA), a role that was created partly in response to this changing policy climate. It is not possible to ascertain how far the work of learning mentors was directly linked to changes brought about under Section 133 as their work activities were often seen as falling outside of this 'specified work'. Nevertheless, the remodelling agenda was presented to support staff as a vehicle for recognising their skills and experience whilst also offering the potential to enhance their roles and provide a much-needed career structure (Department for Education and Skills, 2003a). On this last point, it is possible to confirm that learning mentors in one particular local authority did go on to be appointed in a range of 'new' pastoral leader posts bearing titles such as 'Pastoral Manager' and 'Inclusive Programmes Manager' (Bishop, 2011).

Although this is a book primarily about the experiences of educational paraprofessionals, it would be remiss to merely skip over how the changes set out above impacted on the teaching profession. Of relevance here is the term 'New Public Management' (Newman & Clarke, 1997) which from the late 1980s, signalled a move away from managing public services through traditional bureaucratic methods towards systems characterised by performance management; performance measurement and monitoring; an emphasis on 'outputs' (which involves the close control of behaviour to maximise efficiency) and, a distrust of traditional professionals (Hudson & Lowe, 2004; Mahoney & Hextall, 2001). This led to a far greater degree of monitoring and micro-management of their activities, in effect, the introduction of a new culture which has been termed 'performativity' within educational contexts (Ball, 2003; Jeffrey & Troman, 2012). Within an English context, the seeds of a performative culture were sown within the Conservative's Education Reform Act of 1988 (Perryman, 2012) but proceeded with a much firmer and confident resolve under New Labour (Elliott, 2001). Performativity has three distinct strands: the pervasive culture of targets and auditing; a regime of regulatory mechanisms and a general marketisation of the environment (Bright, 2012). It 'happens' via interventionist policies at both a macro and micro level. One example of the former is where the state, rather than 'de-regulating' and shifting towards privatisation (as it has with other areas of welfare provision), engages in processes of 're-regulating' (Ball, 2003), recasting itself as the evaluative state (Elliott, 2001). In this new guise its role is to prescribe the operating environment of schools and regulate their performance through a technology of audit: for example, inspections and the introduction of quasi-market mechanisms such as league tables – devices which serve to strengthen this 'indirect regulation of performance by central government' (Elliott, 2001, p.192). How the above interventionist policies have been experienced by the teaching profession, provides an understanding of how performativity is enacted at the micro level. For example, Ball (2003, p. 215) argues that it has resulted in a reconstruction of the self, changing not just what educators' do, but 'who we are' as illustrated here in the words of one teacher reported in a news media article:

> What happened to my creativity? What happened to my professional integrity? What happened to the fun in teaching and learning?. (*The Guardian*, 2001 cited in Ball, 2008, p. 51)

Ethnographic studies have also made a particularly strong contribution to charting the impact of performativity:

> [...] I feel [that] every time I do something intuitive I just feel guilty about it. 'Is this right ... does this cover what I am supposed to be covering ... should I be more structured?' ... of course it's multiplied by the fact that Ofsted is coming in because you get in a panic that you won't be able to justify yourself when they finally arrive. (Jeffrey & Woods, 1998, p. 118)

In Chapter 12, we will return to a discussion of performativity, but this time considering the extent and ways in which it impacts paraprofessional work and identity.

New Labour's Social Policy Agenda: The Identification and Elimination of Risk

So far I have set out the educational policy origins giving rise to the learning mentor role. The discussion will now move on to deal with the wider social policy agenda within which school-based social justice initiatives like *Excellence in Cities* and its predecessor, Education Action Zones were situated. Such initiatives were part of a broader policy strategy of tackling 'social exclusion', defined in UK government circles as:

> [...] a shorthand label for what can happen when individuals or areas suffer from a combination of linked problems such as unemployment, poor skills, low incomes, poor housing, high crime environments, bad health and family breakdown. (Social Exclusion Unit, 1999 cited in Peace, 2001, p. 27)

These issues were to be confronted through the establishment of the Social Exclusion Unit (SEU), a new cross-departmental group whose primary purpose was to lead policy thinking in tackling seemingly intractable social problems previously neglected due to the fact that 'no Whitehall department 'owned' them' (Blair, cited in Powell, 1999, p. 291). 'Social Exclusion' was (and remains) contested as both term and concept. Within a broader geographical context, the term was adopted by European policy makers during the 1980s as they struggled to describe innovative social policy in a way that avoided the stigma associated with concepts like 'poverty' and 'deprivation'. As French and English were the mandatory official languages for all European-Union-wide policy initiatives, the term was not only mutually recognisable in both languages ('*exclusion sociale*'/'social exclusion'), but offered a fresh alternative, something which was 'shiny and new' (Peace, 2001, p. 18). However, there is no monolithic pan-European definition of social exclusion but rather a range of national discourses which used the idea in a number of different ways (Levitas, 2005).

Within the UK, the adoption of the term was more than a simple rebranding exercise. Rather it signalled an ideological shift away from Labour's traditional and unconditional language of social justice, predicated on an understanding of how structural forces impact adversely on individuals and communities, towards an implication that human agency could and should play a greater part in addressing the issues identified in the definition of social exclusion above. This shift was evidenced by the Party's constitutional revision of Clause IV which, since its inception in 1918, had committed the party to social equality but now talked of 'the rights we enjoy reflect[ing] the duties we owe' (cited in Dean, 1999, p. 220). The subsequent adoption of a Third Way philosophy (Giddens, 1998) led to a mix of market combined with pubic interventionism (Martin, 2016). As party leader and eventual Prime minister, Blair presented this approach as necessary to modern day governance, coining the phrase 'what works' and in doing so emphasising pragmatism and downplaying ideology. Nonetheless New Labour's

1997 manifesto drew explicitly on a contractarian and thereby conditional discourse claiming a 'bond of trust' which it sought to forge with 'the broad majority of people who work hard, play by the rules [and] pay their dues' (cited in Dean, 1999, p. 220). As argued above, the short extract of Blair's speech presented at the outset of this chapter is heavily imbued with notions of duty and personal responsibility. These changes can also be understood as a result of competing discourses which had a profound impact on New Labour as both a party in opposition and in government (Levitas, 2005). Briefly these competing discourses were: a redistributionist discourse situated in a critical social policy which understands social exclusion as very much intertwined with poverty; a moral discourse which looks to cultural, rather than material explanations of poverty and finally a social integrationist discourse which sees inclusion primarily in terms of labour market attachment. Although the identification of these discourses is to act principally as an analytical device, Levitas (2005) reminds us that:

> [...] [A] discourse also constitutes ways of acting in the world ...
> [which] both opens up and closes down possibilities for action for
> ourselves. If we can make it stick, it does this for others too. (p. 3)

In examining how these permutations of social exclusion were reflected in policy, it is argued that New Labour drew heavily on both social integrationist and moral discourses for a 'discursive reconstruction of the self' (Levitas, 2005, p. 3) both of which became recurring themes of New Labour in governance. Thus, the premise of the aforementioned SEU was to engage particular groups whose excluded status was characterised by their behaviour, namely: school truants and concerns regarding how certain groups were over-represented in school exclusions (Ball, 2008); as well as teenage lone mothers; young offenders and rough sleepers (Bochel, Bochel, Page, & Sykes, 2005). Each area was tackled through a 'strategy' with examples such as the Youth Inclusion Projects which targeted young people living in high crime areas; the Connexions strategy which offered personal advisers who could guide young people aged 13–19 on a range of issues like education, housing and finance as well as 'careers' in its strictest sense (Conradie & Golding, 2013); and the *Teenage Pregnancy Strategy* which sought to engage young lone parents into education or training (Tabberer, 2000). In short, a collectivist responsibility to risk was replaced with an individualist one.

'Every Child Matters'

Arguably the best known example of New Labour's wider vision was *Every Child Matters* (ECM); an ambitious policy agenda set out in a Green Paper and eventually formalised in the Children Act 2004. Underpinned by the twin goals of ending child poverty and enabling every child to reach their potential, it prescribed a holistic approach whereby a child's well-being was considered in addition to their learning (Cheminais, 2009). ECM was 'activated' on the identification of five 'outcomes': *Be Healthy, Stay Safe, Enjoy and Achieve, Make a Positive Contribution and Achieve Economic Well Being* which were to guide practitioner interventions in statutory, private, and voluntary settings from the Early Years through to Youth Work provisions. In theory, the five outcomes were premised on a notion of universality rather than targeted protection alone. The ECM agenda represented the most comprehensive reform of child welfare services for 30 years (Hendrick, 2003), and more broadly an investment in *childhood* not witnessed since the introduction of the Welfare State in the post-war years. For example, Lisa Payne, principal policy officer for the National Children's Bureau, said of ECM: 'The ambitions were amazing, the investment was unprecedented, and the prioritisation of children unmatched in my memory' (cited in Gentleman, 2009). It also brought into view those children who had previously remained hidden and marginalised such as children of prisoners, looked-after children and unaccompanied children entering the UK (Williams, 2004).

As with the language of 'joined-up thinking' that had initially framed the establishment of the SEU, ECM also represented a sea change to the organisation of those professionals involved with children's lives in its requirement for a new multidisciplinary approach and a breaking down of professional 'silos'. For example, the Green Paper set out its intention to create 'joined-up' services for children, who were currently the responsibility of Social Services, Health, Education, the Police, Youth Services, and the Voluntary Sector (Department for Education and Skills, 2003b). This cultural change to working practices was to be realised through the establishment of Children's Centres, some starting life as a result of the *Sure Start* programme which initially had a presence in 250 disadvantaged areas with a budget of £450 million per annum (Powell, 2002, p. 89). Their purpose was to equip pre-school children for starting school and work intensively with families experiencing social exclusion (Powell, 1999). *Sure Start* Children's Centres were envisioned as a community hub which would house a number of professionals through the phenomenon of 'hot-desking'. This would ensure that services could be accessed locally and was seen as a radical departure from the aforementioned 'silo' working; a development that one seasoned Social Work professional turned Professor of Child Welfare did not think he would see in his working life time (Frost, 2014).

Despite the apparent universalism of ECM, some of its policies had a 'tougher' side such as enforcing parental responsibilities in ensuring children's school attendance and appropriate behaviour/engagement once there. For those who could not or would not conform to this 'outcomes' agenda a number of parenting orders and rehabilitations programmes were offered, which if not sufficiently engaged in led to benefit sanctions, fines, evictions (Thomas, 2007) and, in a handful of cases, custodial sentences (Garner, 2013). As illustrated in the extract below, New Labour in government were unapologetic about their proposed 'early interventions' directed at what they perceived as 'failing families':

> I am saying that where it is clear, as it very often is, at a young age, that children are at risk of being brought up in a dysfunctional home where there are multiple problems, say of drug abuse or offending, then instead of waiting until the child goes off the rails, we should act early enough, with the right help, support and

disciplined framework for the family, to prevent it. This is not stig-
matizing the child of the family. It may be the only way to save
them and the wider community from the consequences of inac-
tion. (Blair, 2006 cited in Ball, 2008, p. 154)

Labour also promoted what they termed 'protective factors' that would foster
children's resilience against disadvantage. These were identified as:

- Strong relationships with parents, family and other significant adults.
- Parental interest and involvement in education with clear and high expectations.
- Positive role models.
- Individual characteristics such as an outgoing nature, self-motivation,
  intelligence.
- Active involvement in family, school and community life.
- Recognition, praise and feeling valued (Department for Education and Skills,
  2003b, paragraph 1.13).

Here it is possible to see, once again, the contractual and conditional nature of
policy with the increased emphasis on parental agency in taking an active 'interest
and involvement' in their children's education.

ECM also led to new appointments; a new 'Ministry for Children, Young
People and Families' located within the DfES and Directors of Children's Services at a local level – developments which arguably represented a new seri-
ousness towards children as policy subjects in their own right. However, the
difficulty in striking a balance between strategies that on the one hand sought to
enhance opportunities and minimise risk at a *general level*; and those that sought
to minimise the specific risks faced by *particular* children should be acknowledged. From the early legislative stages of ECM, there was a lack of clarity in
identifying how these general and specific strategies might work in tandem and
more importantly, what values might drive them (Williams, 2004). For example,
a strong theme running through policies examined so far was the responsibili-
sation of parents, particularly around their children's engagement in education
and ability to desist from engaging in criminal behaviour. Such a culture has to
be counterbalanced by one of entitlement to parental support 'if services are
to be destigmatized and if trust is to be engendered' (Williams, 2004, p. 419).
In highlighting these tensions between entitlement and responsibility/protection
and punishment, early critiques skilfully summarised the 'poly-glot' nature of
the New Labour policy agenda:

So how do we understand Every Child Matters? Is it further evidence of the creeping social investment state? Is it recognition of
children's rights and a more child-centered society? Is it universalism and thin egalitarianism slipping stealthily in through the
back door? Does it herald a new, holistic and multidisciplinary
approach to the professional care of children? Or does it carry a
Foucauldian twist in its tail, inculcating parental responsibilities

in collaborating with the state to construct their children as educated, disciplined and self-responsible subjects? In true New Labour style the [ECM] Green Paper is a hodge-podge mixture which appeals to all these interpretations. (Williams, 2004, p. 408)

In sum, ECM was not based on any fundamental redistribution of wealth which could have had the potential to reverse increasing social and economic inequalities; rather a 'redistribution of opportunity' through its educational initiatives (Ball, 2017, p. 210). As Dorling (2011) observes 'While New Labour achieved so much … they had little notion of where they were falling down elsewhere' (p. 129) a comment related to his critique of how children became racially segregated in tower blocks under their period of governance. A situation which became possible because not only were prejudice, poverty and locality closely linked, but also that the richest tenth of the population became 271 times better off than the poorest tenth under New Labour rule (Dorling, 2011).

The 'Centrality of Work'

Earlier, I referred to a social integrationist discourse (Levitas, 2005) which envisaged that social inclusion was to be achieved primarily through participation in the labour market. In addition to the policy initiatives outlined thus far, a key facet of New Labour's approach to tackling social exclusion was reducing dependence on the welfare state in shifting people from 'welfare to work' and in doing so, reducing entitlements to benefits that were formerly universal rather than means tested and selective (Bochel et al., 2005). Alongside the care of pre-school children, the role of Children's Centres was to support and encourage unemployed parents to get back into work. Examples provided in the literature emphasise how relationships that were enacted between Sure Start workers and such parents led to a greater take-up of further education which in itself acted as a catalyst to enter the labour market. In some cases, parents went full circle, initially recruited as an adult learner, moving to Sure Start volunteer and then paid community worker (Power & Willmott, 2007). This in itself gave greater credibility to such initiatives in that they recruited local people who then acted as acceptable if not aspirational role models to their peers, who were being 'encouraged' in their own transitioning from 'welfare to work'.

The 'centrality of work' (Ball, 2008) was also illustrated through the establishment of a new Children's Workforce Development Council (hereafter CWDC). This is a large part of the 'story' of learning mentors and other educational paraprofessionals whose numbers, as indicated in Chapter 1, increased significantly during this era. In underlining the new multidisciplinary nature of working practices, paraprofessionals like learning mentors were seen as members of both the Schools *and* Children's workforce respectively (Department for Education and Skills, 2005). Attempts to not only formalise but give a greater sense of permanence to these new roles were brought about in the form of a newly established Sector Skills Council for Children and Young People's Services. This body oversaw yet another unprecedented development – a qualifications framework for educational support staff which encompassed an initial three-day mandatory course (Marshall, 2006), a nationally accredited training programme linked to National Vocational Qualifications (NVQs) and a new suite of foundation degrees written to reflect the different areas of work undertaken in both the Schools and Children's workforce. Like those enlisted by Sure Start above, this enabled people who were employed in support roles but had limited or no qualifications, to 'earn and learn', that is, gain qualifications whilst in paid work. What this meant in practice was that many working-class women were able to enter employment in (for instance) primary schools on the basis of their pre-existing links with schools as (for example) class room volunteers. Whilst for those already employed in this sector such as TAs or lunchtime cover staff, new roles like that of the learning mentor, afforded genuine opportunities for career progression in terms of not only earning a higher salary but also being in a position to offer a different, more nurturing type of support to children and young people. These developments in the workplace were viewed positively by many, as illustrated in the words of this paraprofessional:

> In 2001 when the first learning mentors were introduced to [—] I knew that it was the role I had been waiting for. I had been [employed] in school five years as an SNA [special needs assistant] and seen so many children with social, emotional and behavioural problems and yearned to help them. (cited in Bishop, 2007)

One example in a 'high-implementation school', meaning a school that had embraced the ECM policy agenda, shows how the changes which this *and* the aforementioned remodelling agenda enabled the Headteacher to 'redesign and re-shape the support staff' (Harris & Allen, 2009, p. 344). A member of support staff from the same study, illustrates how such policy initiatives were then implemented through the work undertaken by paraprofessionals:

> We see ourselves as part of the teaching team, offering support and 'just in time' interventions with certain young people. This often prevents exclusions or accelerated behaviour .... (cited in Harris & Allen, 2009, p. 344)

Amongst paraprofessionals there was a palpable sense of enthusiasm regarding the contribution that their work would make to the school experience, seeing it as premised on a holistic view of children and young people and providing an anti-dote to the increasing drive for attainment and achievement (Ball, 2008; O'Grady, 2006; Stephenson, 2006). However, other accounts regarding the increase in paraprofessionals were more cautious, voicing concerns over the cultural and organisational ramifications of having new groups of workers in schools with quasi-professional identities substantially different to those of teachers (Calvert, 2009). More overtly critical accounts questioned the status and pay of these new workers given that they would most likely be working with the 'neediest and most problematic children in schools' (Edmund & Price, 2009, p. 301).

A Closer Examination of the Learning Mentor Role

How the New Role Was Conceived ...

Learning mentors were envisioned as providing a complementary service to teachers and other support staff who would further contribute to raising standards and play a part in reducing truancy and school exclusion (Department for Education and Skills, 2005). A new emphasis on joined-up working (set out above) meant that they were also tasked with cultivating and maintaining links with agencies outside of the school setting such as local authority youth services and other relevant statutory and third sector agencies (Marshall, 2006).

Between 2001 and 2003, a Functional Map of the 'Provision of Learning Mentor Services' was drawn up and finalised in line with the National Occupational Standards for *Learning Development and Support Services*. This defined learning mentor practice as:

> [providing] support and guidance to children, young people and those engaged with them, by *removing barriers to learning* in order to promote effective participation, enhance individual learning, raise aspirations and achieve full potential. (Sauve Bell, 2003 in Cruddas, 2005, p. 74, my emphasis)

Whilst the government described the role as:

> [Helping] young people to *overcome barriers to learning* through one-to-one mentoring, [having] regular contact with families/carers and encouraging positive family involvement. (cited in Constable & Roberts, 2003, p. 4, my emphasis)

Once the role had been implemented the Government commissioned and published further advisory or 'Good Practice' guidelines which they saw as critical to the success of the role. These included the necessity for a whole-school understanding and appreciation of the role; a dedicated space for learning mentors to work in and from; and a clear system of line-management (Department for Education and Skills, 2001b).

As can be seen in the formal descriptions above, a phrase which became synonymous in describing the work of learning mentors was that of assisting pupils in 'overcoming' or 'removing' 'barriers to learning'. From a government perspective possible barriers to learning were cited as behavioural problems, persistent absenteeism, problems with transition from primary to secondary school, bereavement, difficulties at home, lacking focus and poor study or organisational skills (Department for Education and Skills, 2001b). Arguably such deficit constructions of children and young people demonstrate how the notion of 'duty' discussed earlier, is extended to children and young people in that they approach the education afforded to them by right; along with advice about what habits/characteristics they should already have or be appropriating. At the same time the absence of structural barriers such as poverty, racism and other forms of discrimination is interesting. Indeed, it could be further argued that the limited and prescriptive nature of the National Curriculum could be identified as a significant barrier in and of itself. Nevertheless, from the perspective of those pupils experiencing such barriers however defined, the learning mentor was to be viewed as a new resource who would provide a more individualised approach to their learning. The 'Good Practice' guidelines cited above stated that the learning mentor should be understood as a 'role model', an 'active listener', a 'professional friend' and a 'challenger of assumptions'. Equally emphatically they were *not* to be viewed as a 'counsellor', a 'disciplinarian' or a classroom assistant (Department for Education and Skills, 2001b, p. 8). With regards to the latter this can be understood as a conscious attempt to distinguish them from the more established paraprofessional role of the TA (Cruddas, 2005).

And received ...

However, these formal depictions of the learning mentor role were not always reflected in the understandings of more established professionals. The following examples illustrate varying views following this question posted by a teacher in an online discussion forum:

> I would like some advice regarding Learning Mentors and their role. I would like to utilise our mentor more but her role appears limited. What are they really supposed to do?. ('Olesammie', Times Educational Supplement, n.d.)

This post received several and markedly different responses from one which described the learning mentors in *their* school as:

> 'just a couple of (nice enough) middle-aged relatively uneducated people' who 'engaged in social chit-chat' with children and young people but had 'no experience or understanding of SEN/socieconomic [sic.] issues/barriers to learning' (Betamale, cited in Times Educational Supplement, n.d.)

To more positive perceptions like this:

> With the students I teach who get this support they [the mentors] seem to break down the barriers to the students learning ... taking away some of the pressures that they [pupils] may have that could hinder their school work and progress. (Helen123abc, cited in Times Educational Supplement, n.d.)

News Media and Academic Constructions of Learning Mentors

Earlier I stated that the learning mentor role was noted in the educational news media as the most successful strand of the *Excellence in Cities* programme.

One characteristic of the learning mentor role identified in both news media articles and academic texts was their positioning. Media accounts noted how learning mentors often lived in close proximity to the school in which they worked (in contrast to teachers who perhaps did not) and therefore had a more immediate and greater understanding of the locality, which apparently enabled them to 'act as a go-between if problems arose with parents' (Allison, 2008, p. 2). This can be understood as a type of 'bridging' social capital, that is, a form of social capital which is inclusive and outward looking, with the potential to generate reciprocity and broader identities (Putnam, 2000). The starkest example of this 'bridging' characterisation of the role is illustrated in this comment made by Russell Hobby, the then President of the National Association of Head Teachers:

> [Learning mentors] are valued members of *their* communities who can translate things to *their* communities that [the] middle-class teacher can't. (cited in Garner, 2013, p. 3, my emphasis).

In part the reason why learning mentors were characterised as having the ability to connect with 'hard to reach' families and communities in a way that had hitherto proved challenging for teachers, was because they were frequently identified as individuals who had themselves overcome challenging life experiences, such as growing up in 'tough areas' and under-achieving at school (Jones et al., 2009). Hence, recruitment to this work was often premised on assumptions regarding mentors' own biographies of 'coming good' despite a life history often marked by disaffection (see e.g., Jewell, 2010). Such experiences were then viewed as 'qualifications' for the role which once again cast learning mentors as school personnel who would appear 'less daunting' to parents whose memories of their [own] schooldays were 'less than fond' (Morrison, 2008, p. 3). Concomitant policy agendas at this time also indicate the increased recruitment of individuals previously viewed as members of 'outlier' groups in formal education settings. For example, the 1998 SEU report on the over-representation of Black boys in school exclusions and truancy (Ball, 2008) gave direct rise to the deliberate recruitment of men from BAME communities to act as 'credible' role models who were then given the not insignificant task of turning the tide of pupil disaffection (Odih, 2002).

Academic analyses of the learning mentor role offer are mostly premised on more agentic accounts of mentors' work with a tendency to downplay the social, economic, and political context in which they operate. One key contributor (Cruddas, 2005, p. 83) described learning mentors as a 'fledgling profession in a changing children's workforce ...' with the capacity (power) to question and disrupt institutional culture. In an attempt to conceptualise the learning mentor role, Cruddas draws on the 'theoretical anchors of established professional groups in other countries' (Cruddas, 2005, p. 92) referring explicitly to 'social pedagogy' – a concept originating predominantly in Europe (Smith, 2009) and having close links with the youth work profession in the UK; and 'child and youth care work' in North America (Brendtro & Ness, 1983). Other studies have examined the role from the perspective of learning mentors themselves (Bishop, 2011; Jones et al.,

2009; Rhodes, 2006). As with other mentoring literatures, a common starting point is a consideration of how the activity should be defined given the confusion in terminology which can often surround professional supportive roles such as 'coaching', 'mentoring', 'tutoring' and 'counselling'. Although Jones et al. (2009) recognise that there may be an inevitable overlapping between the activities of these activities, they, like Cruddas (2005) argue that the role of the mentor is person-centred and '… focused upon developing a relationship with an individual founded upon mutual trust and respect' (p. 43).

The issue of how some learning mentors became embroiled in the dual challenges of creating their own professional identity whilst securing recognition from the teaching profession is also taken up in the literature with accounts observing how a lack of clarity in the role (as seen in the online discussions presented above) has characterised the development of learning mentoring in schools (Rhodes, 2006). The rationale for research conducted by Jones et al. (2009) was specifically to provide a more detailed analysis of the role based on a consideration of the motivations that drove mentors in their work. They found that although the learning mentors recognised that their role was invariably shaped by school policies with a focus on learning outcomes, they also felt that it afforded them a unique position to meet an individual child's emotional and social needs. The learning mentors participating in this study contrasted their work with that of teachers whose respective changes to *their* professional roles and responsibilities via the remodelling agenda had meant that they could no longer offer the levels of support to pupils that mentors could. The mentors also reported experiencing a tension between meeting the expectations of fellow professionals (teachers, year managers, etc.) to operate *within* school policy, practice and culture, *whilst* supporting a child who might challenge some or all of these. When reflecting on this issue the mentors saw their primary motivator as building relationships with young people as seen in this particular respondent's comment:

> […] we are not the authority figure. We are the one in the school who won't have a go at them. (Jones et al., 2009, p. 48)

The authors claimed that neither money nor job security appear to motivate learning mentors; rather it was concern for the well-being of young people. This (apparently) took precedence over concern for an uncertain future in terms of the permanence of their employment:

> There was a clear sense of a shared vocation [in their responses] engendered by working with challenging young people in challenging circumstances [And] This was not a nine to four job but one charged with a real sense of vocation and energy. (Jones et al., 2009, p. 48)

However, they further warned that this may prove to be a 'double-edged sword' as such levels of commitment could also lead to the 'exploitation of these colleagues and a limiting of their impact as a result of low status' (Jones et al., 2009, p. 50).

This study also echoes the bridging function identified in news media accounts above where the onus is on learning mentors to build relationships *beyond* the school gate, described as working at the interface between family and school. Drawing on their observations and findings, the authors proposed a 'threefold categorisation model' termed 'the three realms of learning mentoring' to set out what effective mentoring within a school context looks like. The first realm relates specifically to the child or young person and is described as a 'highly personalised component of the model'. As such this realm considers the 'temperament, motivators, perspectives and challenges that characterise the young person's needs and aspirations' (Jones et al., 2009, p. 45). The second realm is the child/young person's wider context, taking into account the family and community within which they are located which according to the authors will have a strong influence upon the young person being mentored. The school environment constitutes the third realm and as the most formal this is understood as the place where the mentee has been identified by other professionals with whom s/he comes into contact as representing a cause for concern. This clearly shifts the direction of impetus for the relationship – a point which is explored from the mentee's point of view in corresponding research (Rose & Doveston, 2008). A key strength of the learning mentors function is their ability to interface with each of these realms in order to optimise opportunities for the development of effective, highly personalised relationships. They suggest that:

> [...] a mentor maybe *more embedded within the local community realm* than other school staff will be able or willing to be. This ability to be close to the mentee's preferred or family context can, on occasions, open more opportunities for meaningful interaction away from the perceived 'baggage' or bias of more formal or statutory environments. (Jones et al., 2009, p. 46, emphasis added)

A desire to help and a sense of the mentor having shared experiences with disaffected young people in terms of place and school experiences are common features of both media accounts and academic analyses above. What tends to be omitted however are more structural issues like poverty and social inequality that characterised earlier critiques of youth mentoring in post-16 contexts (Piper & Piper, 2000). One of these is termed engagement mentoring (Colley, 2003a). This valuable critique theorised how an individualistic discourse was utilised to explain young people's school-to-work transitions. But crucially, Colley's analysis also includes an examination of the personal impacts of the mentoring relationship on the mentor (e.g., the mentor's mental health and well-being) whilst s/he is putting into practice the 'demands of policy makers and employers', demands which have been premised on an altogether different stance than that of merely wanting to provide help and support to another human being. Using a case study approach framed within feminist readings of Marx and Bourdieu, Colley relocates mentoring within the socio-economic context from which it has been disembedded. Engagement mentoring can be understood as a game or 'field' which structures the ways in which players act through the relations of power which exist between them. Within this analysis, the gendered nature of mentoring, is utilised via Hochschild's notion of 'emotional labour' (cited in Colley, 2003a, p. 153). The demands placed on mentors to 'transform the dispositions' of their mentees (in attempting to re-engage them with the labour market) are then aptly demonstrated through qualitative data generated through the study. Such work calls for dispositions of 'devotion' and 'self-sacrifice' within the mentors themselves:

> We could replace the word 'disposition' with 'habitus' here. Habitus … is both structured and structuring, because it incorporates aspects of our predispositions created by factors such as social class and gender, as well as more individual aspects of disposition. (Colley, 2003b, p. 537)

Thus, the 'field' of engagement mentoring aims to transform the habitus of those on both sides of the mentoring dyad. Its goal is to produce and reproduce habitus as an ideal of employability which is determined by the needs of employers and other dominant groupings, rather than by those participating directly in the mentor dyad itself. Colley (2003b) describes this process as a 'brutal commodification of the self' but one that is cloaked in the guise of human relations 'commonly assumed to be based on warmth and compassion' and it is this which is one of the greatest contradictions of Engagement mentoring. The parallels between the act of mentoring high school pupils in preparation *for* the labour market with the mentoring of young people absent *from* it are easily identifiable, but unfortunately wholly absent from policy constructions of the learning mentor. Instead, mentoring is presented as an assumed positive intervention in a young person's life, without any rigorous analysis of the nature of mentoring relationships in and of themselves. This is despite the fact that such texts have existed for some time: take, for example, Levinson's seminal work on the notion that the mentoring relationship synthesises the characteristics of the parent–child relationship and peer support, as 'both [but] not purely either one' (Levinson, Darrow, Klein, & Levinson, 1978, p. 99). Furthermore, the contested question of whether the successful elements of an 'organic' mentor relationship, that is, that which typically emerges from *within* a young person's social support network, can actually be 'captured' and replicated in planned interventions (Rhodes, 1994). Finally, the failure to consider multiple manifestations of mentoring that exist alongside the assumed mono-construction of 'classic' mentoring, that is, the older, wiser knowledgeable guide (Philip & Hendry, 1996). All of these critiques of youth mentoring raise important issues, many of which made their presence felt in the ethnography and are duly discussed in the coming chapters.

In conclusion, policies that were enacted in the New Labour era to address social exclusion through early intervention did lead to an increased presence of paraprofessionals in the school workforce. Supported by a framework of in-work benefits and tax credits there was a genuine attempt to ensure that this type of work did indeed pay. These new employees were often consciously and purposefully drawn from communities whose engagement and achievement within schools represented a cause for concern – not only in the immediate sense, but in terms of the risky 'conditions' (school exclusion, teenage pregnancy, long-term unemployment and welfare dependency) that they might lead to. Paired with the heightened levels of optimism and, some might argue 'blind faith', that was invested in mentoring as a vehicle to engage young people at this time (Colley, 2003b), it is possible to see how the conditions arose for a significantly greater number of working-class people to take up occupational roles in schools other than those they had traditionally been assigned to, that is, as cleaners, caterers, and administrative assistants.

An important question for consideration is whether other Western industrial societies have responded to and dealt with the consequences of protracted and/ or rising social inequalities in a comparable way? I was interested to establish if similar attempts had been made to draw working-class people into areas of public service traditionally dominated by the middle classes and if so, on what basis and with what impact on those involved? The following chapter takes our focus to the USA in the 1960s to answer these questions.

Chapter 3

Historical and Comparative Accounts of Paraprofessional Experiences

As noted in Chapter 1, existing contemporary literature pertaining to all types of educational paraprofessionals is scarce. However, a number of rich historical accounts provide a credible basis on which to build a meaningful understanding of paraprofessionals that are more akin to the learning mentor role. Thus, this chapter takes an abrupt turn away from the discussion of the English situation in order to delve into an incredibly useful literature; one which provides a salutary tale of another geo-political context which envisioned and implemented a new type of paraprofessional across education and other human service organisations. This particular paraprofessional 'story' starts in the 1960s and focusses on the USA. The more familiar parts of this story relate to how the Johnson administration (1963–1969) transformed federal involvement in education and social action in 1964 and 1965 under the slogans of a 'War on Poverty' and the Great Society (Silver & Silver, 1991). The key strands in these developments had been visible from the late 1950s encompassing multiple issues such as migration, slums and cities; civil rights and the issues of race and desegregation as well as the interests of psychologists in early childhood and the effects of the environment:

> By the early 1960s all of these were converging into a set of policy definitions given impetus and focus by the 'discovery of poverty'.
> (Silver & Silver, 1991, p. 13)

Dunning (2018) further argues that a shortage of professionals in the human service sector alongside a number of unemployed and unskilled poor arising from de-industrialisation was an important but hitherto neglected strand of Great Society legislation.

Having set out a brief socio-political backdrop of the era under discussion, I turn the reader's attention to the level of policy enactment in an attempt to build up a picture of who took up paraprofessional work and what the work entailed. I start with a study by Stewart (1971, n.p.) who sought to establish 'knowledge not previously available' of the school paraprofessional. From this source it is

Propping up the Performative School: A Critical Examination of the English Educational Paraprofessional, 29–44
Copyright © 2022 by Jo Bishop
Published under exclusive licence by Emerald Publishing Limited
doi:10.1108/978-1-83982-242-120221003

possible to establish two key points: first, the date of this study which confirms that educational paraprofessionals existed in other western contexts at least two decades before being present in English schools. Second, the author's stated intent to gather knowledge about the role suggests that there lacked a coherent understanding about what these individuals did in their day-to-day work, a phenomenon also observed regarding learning mentors in the previous chapter. Stewart's study identified no less than seven major categories of secondary school paraprofessional with the two most relevant to this book being 'instructional aides' and 'student supervision aides'. The former are close 'relations' to the English TA and continue to have a presence in the USA with over half a million people employed in such roles (Mansaray, 2006). The latter, 'student supervision aides', bear the closest resemblance to learning mentors in terms of who occupied the role, what their work entailed and the nature of the supportive relationships with students that arose. At the time of the study (early 1970s), student supervision aides were the fastest growing type of paraprofessional.

The rationale for the introduction of such workers in US schools during this period reflects some of the issues that the English teaching profession were to grapple with in the 1990s as part of the remodelling agenda (discussed in Chapter 2). Some student supervision aides were also designated as 'community agents' (Stewart, 1971, n.p.). When looking at the descriptions of individuals undertaking this work (set out below) clear parallels begin to emerge with the modern day English learning mentor. So who were these paraprofessionals dubbed 'community agents' and what did their work entail? Stewart provides four detailed pen-pictures, the summaries of which will now be presented as they appeared in the original text:

1. The first, describes a 'male Negro [*sic.*]' aged 23, who had completed two years of college and continued to attend on a part time basis to pursue a teaching qualification. The school he was situated in had a significant percentage of Black students but no Black teachers. Based on observations of his work the researcher judged his impact on, and rapport with, students as 'outstanding' describing him as a 'communicator between the Black students and the faculty' who 'tried not to function as a disciplinarian' but instead counselled the students and reasoned with them. (Stewart, 1971, p. 28)

2. The second community agent, a woman, aged 59 [also described as 'Negro'] was observed as a 'bright, alert, dedicated person'. Her background involved a great deal of church work with special emphasis on high school and college-age students. She checked all the floors, halls, and girls' rest rooms of the [school] buildings on a regular basis. When she found students breaking the rules she took them to the dean. She knew who belonged in the building and took outsiders to the office. She watched for hall disturbances and tried to solve the problems on the scene. (Stewart, 1971)

The accounts given here suggests quite different roles with the male being depicted as a mentor, advocate and intermediary between student and 'school' (representing those in authority) whilst the woman's work activities presenting a more reactive and possibly punitive approach. This suggests that the designation of these two paraprofessionals as 'community agents' would not appear to be based on their work activities but rather their potential links with communities outside of the school. The woman's association with community organisations and her identification of actual pupils and potential outsiders highlights that she possesses local knowledge. Further comments about the first community agent note his ability to serve as 'a liaison between the school and family and between the school and community'. It goes on to state:

> All community agents visited homes, day or night, to foster mutual understanding. They accompanied sick students home and saw that they were taken care of. They accompanied suspended students home and explained the school's actions to the parents. They sat in on conferences between parents and school officials. (Stewart, 1971, p. 28)

The third pen-picture set out below, indicates that this particular paraprofessional's work involved a wide range of activities encompassing tasks which would currently be understood as both pastoral and inclusion work in English schools today and suggests a considerable degree of partnership working with his teaching colleagues:

> 3.   [...] a 56 year old Negro [*sic*.] who had three years of experience as a community agent and who had helped to develop the role for other agents. This community agent worked with both white and Black students. He maintained files on his students during their four years; he handled the attendance ... and took referrals from teachers on tardy [late] students; he assisted impoverished students with medical and clothing needs through a special fund; he counselled students on subjects ranging from academics to drugs; he sat in on all suspension conferences and helped decide the action to be taken; he handled part of the discipline load for the center .... (Stewart, 1971, p. 28)

The final pen-picture provides a further element to the work of paraprofessionals which is not seen in the accounts set out above:

> 4.   An 'Oriental [*sic*.] woman, aged 22 years ... this young woman had previously been employed in the Portland Model Cities Program and Head Start. She had an almost free hand in determining her role as community agent within the new high school. Her prime responsibility was outside the school where

she tried to get a community evening school functioning. She worked on community involvement, parent advisory groups and parent forums. Much of her time was spent working with agencies outside the school and attending inter-agency meetings'. (Stewart, 1971, p. 29)

The employment experiences of this particular community agent were very much bound up in significant policy initiatives originating from this era. *Head Start* was a programme that aimed to improve the health status, learning and social skills of poor children so that they could begin schooling on an equal footing with their more advantaged peers (Currie, 2001). The programme was initiated as part of the aforementioned Government's 'War on Poverty', legislated through the Economic Opportunity Act of 1964 (Pearl & Reissman, 1965). This connection with a policy of such magnitude seemed to generate a certain amount of status for this particular paraprofessional with references to the 'almost free hand' she was given in determining her role as a community agent. Again, parallels can be drawn here with the English learning mentor – a role which came about as one element of wider social and educational policy initiatives like *Every Child Matters* and *Excellence in Cities*. The degree of relative autonomy given to the community agent above was also envisaged for learning mentors in the earliest days of their role but, as shall be seen in due course, is not characteristic of the role where it still exists today.

This seminal account of US paraprofessionals work in the early 1970s provides a detailed account of what community agents *did*; but much of it was written from the perspective of an assumed knowledge about what a 'community agent' actually *was*. As no further definitions or explanations are provided within Stewart's account it is important to gain a retrospective understanding about the origins and impetus for such a role. To achieve this the discussion turns to a North American literature spanning the early 1960s to the late 1980s which sheds light on the wider economic and social context that led to the creation of the US educational paraprofessional, and specifically the designation of 'community agent'.

'New Careers for the Poor'

New Careers for the Poor: the Nonprofessional in Human Service (Pearl & Reissman, 1965) was a thesis proposing that the employment of 'non', 'sub' or 'para' professionals in Human Service Organisations (HSOs) should be vastly expanded in order to achieve two interrelated objectives. The first – 'to eradicate poverty by providing employment to the poor', provides the context in which the authors' work is situated and helps explain why the idea gained currency leading to implementation over a relatively short period of time. As referred to in the introduction, there was a growing awareness of an 'other America' in the 1960s that was characterised by severe poverty, chronic unemployment and social neglect. The election of Kennedy and the burgeoning struggle of the Civil Rights movement reflected that significant parts of the American people were not indifferent to the plight of many but had to take action. The aforementioned policy response by the Johnson Administration of *War on Poverty* was characterised in part by a desire to implement new ideas and alternative programmes. Particularly when these deviated from conventional HSOs and the professionals who staffed them, both of which were criticised for their increasing disengagement from, and insensitivity to the poor (Katan & Etgar, 1998).

The second objective – 'to promote changes in the structure and activities of HSOs *and* the interrelationships within them' – reveals the rationale for Pearl and Reissman's call for 'New Careers for the Poor' in their assertion that the employment of the 'indigenous nonprofessional' in economically disadvantaged communities could fill an important vacuum. Expanding on this they state:

> In this sense, the term 'non-professional' is limited because it does not specify the nature of the tasks to be performed; the usefulness of the term, however, lies in calling attention to certain distinctions between a professional orientation and the performance of various tasks by people whose training is less inclusive than that of professionals, *but who may have specific contributions to make* in the performance of tasks related to the helping professions. (Pearl & Reissman, 1965, p. viii, my emphasis)

The term 'indigenous nonprofessional' is used frequently and with very little clarity apart from one contributor who relates it to 'workless Americans' referring specifically to:

> [The] Negro, the Mexican-Americans, the Puerto Ricans, the rural whites of poor educational backgrounds [and] the Indians [*sic.*]. (Saltzman, 1965, p. 39)

That aside, it is clear that the 'specific contribution' of the indigenous HSO professional was their capacity to serve as a 'bridge' between the middle-class institution and the low-income population as exemplified by the school community agent above when being described as a 'communicator between the Black students and the faculty'. The bridge concept is credited to Herbert Gans (1962) who argued that 'nonprofessionals' should be people who in coming from a 'lower class culture' have 'successfully moved into a more stable way of life without rejecting their past' and therefore had '... a considerable amount of empathy towards both old and new culture' (cited in Pearl & Reissman, 1965, p. 186). Here, its function is explained within the context of a community mental health programme:

> Indigenous staff are [...] able to *interpret community life and values to* professionals ... as well as serve as *interpreters of* the professionals, and role models for lower-income persons. (Brager cited in Pearl & Reissman, 1965, p. 77, my emphasis)

Saltzman (1965, p. 48) gives similar designations within the field of education which shed light on the notion of the 'community agent' making reference to reference to 'school-community' agents or 'coordinates' who:

[...] [S]huttle effectively between the school and the community *helping each know more about the other*. (Saltzman, 1965, p. 48, my emphasis)

Another description of paraprofessionals as 'Bridge agents' further illustrates this premise on which the role was based (Field & Gatewood, 1976, p. 185). More recent accounts (Lewis, 2004) indicate that this characterisation of paraprofessionals has endured noting how teaching aides (the US equivalent to English TAs) are often called upon to be 'bridges' and 'cultural brokers' to the school community. This being based on the assumption that because they are similar in race, ethnicity, or class with pupils and their families, they can bridge a cultural gap between home and school.

Essentially, the 'New Careers' project argued for an original and new look at the status and functions of the nonprofessional worker. This would lead to a different perception of his/her potential contribution to the functioning of HSOs, a belief which was premised on their apparent ability to provide 'qualitative and meaningful services to their clients' (Katan & Etgar, 1998, p. 128). Varied arguments were presented to support this assertion: their '(peer) status attributes' meant that they had similar if not the same life experiences as the clients of HSOs so consequently had far less need to validate themselves to those they worked amongst, thereby allowing 'considerable advantage over the professional from the outset' (Pearl & Reissman, 1965, p. 85). Non-professional workers were credited with knowing how to deal with problems from the 'inside' not from above and their style was also noted to be considerably less formal:

They will hug clients, accept – and repay – their hospitality, and share first-name designations .... (Pearl & Reissman, 1965)

Aside from this informality, nonprofessionals were noted as more 'directive', 'active' and 'partisan' in comparison to their professional counterparts and more likely to provide active direction to their clients. Taking all of the factors together, the nonprofessional was viewed as having the means to develop comparably more 'rounded, everyday type of relationships' with their clients (Pearl & Reissman, 1965, p. 86). This seemingly 'unique' approach, along with the bridging notion set out above represents further parallels with how the learning mentor role was characterised, particularly in news media accounts.

By the early 1970s the ideas expounded by Pearl and Reissman could be seen in education, healthcare, social work and what would be understood in a UK context as 'youth and community development'. In the case of the latter, references are made to projects such as *Harlem Youth Opportunities Unlimited* – a social activism organisation which utilised the indigenous paraprofessional. The following extract, taken from a report examining a need for professional and paraprofessional social work personnel, provides a further meta-commentary by which it is possible to gauge the taking up of the New Careers idea:

The human sectors of health, education and welfare have recently expanded to include *new faces, old allies and in some cases former consumers*, the working and the non-working poor. The largest number of new faces is found in the work force of *paraprofessionals*. The paraprofessionals are those persons who tend to live in the areas of our cities needing the greatest improvement in human services, whether in the hospitals, schools or social agencies. Some of the paraprofessionals have high school diplomas, some do not. Many are members of the Black Community, some are not. However, all of them have had personal experiences with poverty and the majority have come to recognize *their extensive knowledge of their neighbourhood or community* (Austin, 1972, p. 59, my emphasis).

By this stage, it is noticeable that the term 'nonprofessional' is being replaced more and more by 'paraprofessional'. Although it is not possible to establish the reason(s) for this with any certainty, it could be that as the visibility and contribution of such workers increased, their designation as a 'nonprofessional' may have sat uncomfortably with all parties concerned, that is, amongst professional colleagues and/or in their interactions with their nonprofessional counterparts. There may have also been a need to disrupt, rebrand and ultimately change the narrative in order to attract more so-called indigenous workers to such roles.

Applying 'New Careers' to Education and Schooling: *'... Nothing About the System Belongs to the Poor'*

Given the parallels that are starting to emerge between 1960s paraprofessionals and the learning mentor role, I turn now to a more in-depth critique of how the 'New Careers' idea was applied to education. I start by examining the ideological beliefs that underpinned the desire to see nonprofessionals employed in HSOs then turn to a consideration of the issues and potential pitfalls identified by those pursuing this project.

Proponents of the 'New Careers' project noted how educators had joined the 'general orgy of consumption' that was gripping many services in post-war America which led to schools in affluent areas enjoying new buildings, new technologies and increased salaries for teachers. In his comment that '[The] slum school and neighbourhood were lost sight of in an actual and metaphorical rush to *Suburbia*', Saltzman (1965, p. 40) notes that in this expansion of the 'educational plant' there was little discussion of the poor and the deprived. This view is reinforced by others who argued a rationale for changing what was clearly a very segregated schooling system on both class and racial lines:

> Schools constitute a colonial imposition because *nothing about the system belongs to the poor*. [Thus] Introducing the indigenous poor into meaningful teaching roles could be an important initial step

> toward producing a fundamental change in the character of the
> school .... (Pearl & Reissman, 1965, p. 73, my emphasis)

However, this 'initial step' should be motivated by a genuine desire for change and not mere 'window dressing' meaning that the poor had to become 'truly a part of the teaching organization' in terms of helping to determine educational policy and programmes and crucially being given opportunity for 'meaningful advancement' (Pearl & Reissman, 1965). But how was this to be achieved? Arguments for utilising education as a model for bringing about 'new' careers were put forward on more than one front but anything that could be construed as pragmatism was quickly re-aligned with the aforementioned twin goals of eradicating poverty by employing indigenous workers in a way that would benefit *all* parties. For example, it was one way of solving the predicted teaching shortage but *only if* the teaching role was re-examined and effectively re-imagined, as illustrated in this extract and the discussion which follows:

> Currently in the classroom there is but one designated role –
> teacher. Incorporated in that role are a great number of diverse
> functions – the teacher is an educator, but he [*sic.*] is also a clerk,
> a custodian, an operator of audio-visual equipment ... *In many*
> *slum schools the impression gained is that the teacher is part lion*
> *tamer and part warehouseman.* The latter roles must be eliminated
> and many of the others can be assumed by less qualified personnel
> (Pearl & Reissman, 1965, pp. 56–57, my emphasis).

Nonprofessionals were already carrying out this work in some instances but such an approach was argued to be piece meal and insufficient; it was only the *re*definition of the teaching role that would usher in the formal structural change needed to enable the functions carried out by new personnel to be integrated into the 'fabric of the system'. This should involve the abstraction of no less than five different roles from the 'one omnifarious duty now performed' thus 'teacher aide'; 'teacher assistant'; 'teacher associate'; 'teacher' and 'supervising teacher' would exist along a continuum in which advancement from entry position ('teacher aide') to fully fledged professional ('teacher') could be negotiable on the basis of talent and motivation 'rather than economic means' (Pearl & Reissman, 1965). It would seem that this vision was realised at least in part, as 'teacher aide' was one of the school paraprofessionals highlighted by Stewart (1971) some years later. The all-important career advancement of the teacher aide to teacher assistant (or beyond) was to be achieved through a system of credit for on-the-job activity alongside college courses. Advancement to the level of associate teacher would follow a similar course of two years' work and academic training. Once operational, the teacher would '...no longer be burdened with menial tasks' but 'liberated to act as a true professional' (Pearl & Reissman, 1965, p. 61).

The authors are careful to acknowledge that there were already people working as 'non-certified' (i.e., unqualified) teachers but point out that they were not provided with special supervision nor was their role legitimated by tenure or official status; the more formalised role of 'associate teacher' would, they argue, deliver this. Persuasive cases were made for the adoption of the 'New Careers' concept which were also predicated on dominant constructions of youth as vulnerable and/or a threat:

> [...] a poor youth who had not completed a high school education could *revitalize an entire existence* and in less than ten years emerge as a fully-certified professional [...]. *During this entire period he would be socially useful.* (Pearl & Reissman, 1965, pp. 60–61, my emphasis)

The final role in the continuum – 'supervising teacher' – was seen as 'cardinal in this new career sequence', envisaged as individuals who would be drawn from teachers with 'outstanding histories of achievement' who were therefore equipped to provide 'constant and imaginative' supervision, counselling and training (Pearl & Reissman, 1965, p. 62). It was crucial that this position also became an affiliate of the higher education process who would in turn validate this new career structure. The role of 'supervising teacher' was also intended to provide an alternative avenue of advancement to the more usual paths of administration or management which would sustain incentives for those who wished to 'devote their lives to education' (Pearl & Reissman, 1965).

This attempt to redefine the teaching role provides some interesting parallels with the UK 'remodelling' policy agenda of the early 2000s. As discussed in the previous chapter, this was part of a group of policies which gave rise to the learning mentor role and other subsequent paraprofessionals such as behaviour support workers who were offered their own career advancement through the Children's Workforce Development Council, reflecting the optimism felt at the time about the expansion of education as a public service.

Critiquing 'New Careers'

One response to the optimistic accounts conveyed within the 'New Careers' thesis could understandably be cynicism and an interpretation of the project as mid-twentieth century middle-class 'do-gooding' premised on a deficit model of the poor. But whilst 'New Careers' is undeniably written from a 'them and us' perspective and the language used often stark – 'slum child', 'slum community', etc.– the analysis is one that understands poverty as a structural rather than cultural issue, in defining the experiences and 'choices' of the poor. In this regard its proponents do not follow traditional sociological traditions of placing structure and human agency as opposing explanations for human behaviour but view them rather as imbricated. Pearl and Reissman challenged the view (held by some of their contemporaries) that the poor were directly responsible for their own educational *under*achievement. They also questioned dominant constructions of young people which framed middle-class young people as 'reality-oriented' and willing to make the day-to-day sacrifices demanded by schooling in the interest of some future pay-off, in contrast with the low income (working class) young people, who were supposedly governed by the 'pleasure principle' and living only for the delights of the present:

> As enticing as this 'ant versus grasshopper' distinction might be, it fails to recognize a signal fact. There *is* a future in schooling for middle-class youth; this just isn't true for the great majority of the poor. Schooling is, by and large, a rewarding experience for the affluent; for the poor it is largely a misery to be borne. (Pearl & Reissman, 1965, p. 71)

This, they argued, was because middle-class students had a virtual monopoly on the rewards of the system through getting good grades, which led to positive pupil–teacher and home–school relations and represented a school experience which afforded dignity and enhanced self-esteem:

> In attaining success, the affluent youngster is required to make very few sacrifices and he attains one of life's most precious gratifications – he is allowed to have a feeling of competence .... and is given the greatest measure of self-determination that the system allows. (Pearl & Reissman, 1965)

In contrast, the poor, disadvantaged young person received few rewards because 'he has none of the attributes to attain rewards'. At points, the authors come close to looking through the lens of a deficit model as they cite a home-based 'language style and behaviour pattern that do not fit easily into the standard classroom situation'. But crucially, these observations are presented as part of a *wider* picture which identifies an educational experience that serves to stigmatise the poor whilst schools are portrayed as 'but another agency in the anatomy of the establishment overwhelming the poor' (Pearl & Reissman, 1965, p. 72).

Saltzman (1965) adopts a similar position in arguing how Compensatory Education (CE) could continue to play a part in the realisation of the 'New Careers' project. Noting the migration of the poor to central cities (and the middle-class response of flight to more affluent neighbourhoods noted earlier) astute mayors and school superintendents began recognising this new bloc of voters on the scene who had the capacity 'if not yet the organization, to veto their plans for urban and educational renewal' (Saltzman, 1965, p. 40). As a result, many federal school systems initiated programmes under the banner of 'compensatory education' which were guided by a number of principles that once again, illustrate understandings of this complex interrelationship between structure and agency. The first of these was a belief in the human potential for learning but recognition that this could be sharply curtailed by poverty. Exponents of CE challenged schools to no longer passively accept that a slum environment placed limits on a child's potential but instead to show no compromise 'in any effort to determine the limits of the slum child's potential ...' (Saltzman, 1965, p. 42). This could be viewed as an earlier version of New Labour's resolve to 'eliminate but never excuse' underachievement in areas of social deprivation discussed in Chapter 2.

But supporters of the CE movement were also insistent that whilst there were specific, identifiable factors in the social, physical and cultural environments of the poor which did 'retard' intellectual development, these factors existed because of *poverty*.[1] As such the response of the poor should not be 'causally related to inherent inferiority, inherent anti-intellectualism, or inherent insensitivity'; rather a more pro-active political and educational response should compensate 'for the deficits imposed upon by the child by the slum environment' (Saltzman, 1965, p. 42). The key argument was that the American school which served a poor community had to be different from that in a more affluent area and it is here that arguments for the New Careers thesis really take centre stage:

> For, while members of the slum community may lack much formal education, they may have wisdom dearly bought from the experience of surviving the rigors of their environment; while they may lack an understanding of the organization of the school, they may know intimately the organization of the community; while they may be unschooled in the nuances of middle-class mores and customs, they may know full well what will or will not 'go' in the slum community; while they may lack a grasp of educational philosophy and theory, they may be fully conversant with what is or is not perceived as important, honest and useful by the school's constituency. (Saltzman, 1965, p. 48)

In presenting this rather lengthy but nevertheless uncensored extract, readers may relate to the initial uncomfortableness with both the language and sentiment that I experienced on my own first reading. However, within the twin frameworks of 'compensation' and 'New Careers' it is important to understand how the employment of the poor was viewed and conceptualised as 'appropriate, logical and important, perhaps crucial' (Saltzman, 1965, p. 48).

More recent critiques are more dubious about whether the New Careers project was genuinely concerned to move away from deficit constructions of the poor. Dunning (2018, p. 675) argues that whilst its proponents 'outpaced many of their colleagues in social science' by linking macroeconomic trends to poverty, the theoretical underpinnings of New Careers still relied on notions of cultural difference which were popular in liberal academic and policy-making circles:

> In this way, they replicated some of the most pernicious aspects of existing manpower and antipoverty programs. Even as Pearl and Riessman turned from the deficit-oriented theories of cultural deprivation to their asset-oriented one of cultural difference that celebrated the contributions of poor people, they still reinforced this difference with language of the 'indigenous nonprofessional'

---

[1] A word that was applied only to children's situations in New Labour discourse, preferring instead to adopt the term 'social exclusion' when making reference to the situation of adults.

that naturalized class differences as inherent, permanent and inferior. (Dunning, 2018, p. 675)

Professionalising Tasks, *Not* People – the 'Pitfalls of Assimilation'

But this is not the complete story. Accounts by supporters of the 'New Careers' project also provide real time *and* retrospective analyses of the issues and pitfalls that can arise in such a venture and before looking at what the actual impacts were it is necessary to examine what its proponents wished to avoid hypotheti-cally. The most significant issue identified is the 'pitfalls of assimilation' (Gold-berg, n.d. cited in Pearl & Reissman, 1965, p. 196). This can be understood as a belief in the absolute necessity to maintain professional and non-professional distinctions; which I have duly summarised here to enable direct comparisons to be made (Table 1).

Table 1.   Distinctions between Professional and Non-professional Working Experiences and Practices.

Professionals	Non-professionals
Distinct career line	Talent comes from non-professionalised status – the task of the nonprofessional *precludes* a professional relationship (However) 'This view does not prevent us from teaching various professional skills to indigenous personnel; nor does it prevent us from "disciplining their practice", codifying their skills. We may want to professionalize their tasks, but not to professionalize *them*'.
Professionalisation includes, but implies more than task rationalisation. It encompasses a variety of norms and attitudes and a perspective that covers a broad spectrum, that is, looking at the broader implications of behaviour and practice	Very much task centred and 'now' centred
Professional socialisation constrains towards much more role-segmentation in relation to the client	Indigenous personnel have the capacity for a much more (w)holistic client relationship – that is their strength *and* limitation (Pearl & Reissman, 1965, pp. 196–197)

The most illuminating phrase from the comparison set out above is regarding the apparent 'danger' of professionalising the 'non' and paraprofessionals: 'We may want to professionalize their tasks, but [we don't want] to professionalize them' (seen in the top right of the table). Here the underpinning belief was that workers are more effective in their jobs when strains between the two groups are present as that means paraprofessionals are challenging professional observations and actions that might not be good for their clients. Thus, the typical strains between professional and paraprofessional were functional for maintaining the integrity and skill of the indigenous worker and 'professional contamination', that is, the way in which paraprofessionals may acquire professional attitudes, would interfere with their 'indigenous strength', and was therefore to be prevented at all costs. This adds further validation to Dunning's critique above that such projects only served to make class differences 'natural' and permanent.

In Practice – What *Actually* Happened to 'New Careers' Paraprofessionals?

The reality of such projects was rather different to the lofty ideals on which they were balanced. 'New Careers' had a significantly negative impact on 'non' and paraprofessionals with outcomes like rapid turnover of personnel, 'burning out' and watered down training. For example, a key finding by Stewart (1971) was that the role of student supervision aide was highly stressful and considerably more complex than the title suggested. The pen-picture of community agent #3 (above) serving three years in post would appear to be atypical as most individuals occupying this role either transferred to another position in the school or resigned within the first year. This suggests that the systematic and directed training that had been seen as a crucial element of the 'New Careers' project did not materialise and links to a further issue identified, that of the paraprofessional being 'Locked out' – a term used to describe the '... ever-present danger that the new nonprofessional positions [would] provide jobs but not careers' (Pearl & Reissman, 1965, p. 203). This fear was realised as early as the mid-1970s as social, political and ideological changes signalled a more limited role for the state in the welfare arena. With project funds disappearing, paraprofessionals started to experience the 'last in, first out' rule of hiring and firing, meaning that '... while they were hired as their brother's keeper, they soon found that the realities of organizational life that required them to look out for themselves' (Austin, 1972, p. 60). This was coupled with an erosion in public awareness of the problem of poverty *and* its readiness to cope with it (Katan & Etgar, 1998).

'Psychic Stretch' or Emotional Labour?

By the mid-1970s one of the original proponents of the New Careers project argued that paraprofessionals were being used in a number of exploitative and demeaning ways. First as 'cosmetics' – in terms of supplying ethnic authenticity to programmes that remained dominated by traditional thinking; as 'pacifiers' – of the communities they were assumed to represent and finally as 'cheap labour' (Pearl, 1974, p. 266). One of the ways in which paraprofes-sionals were particularly affected was termed 'Psychic Stretch' and occurred when people were selected and recruited for new roles on questionable and spurious bases:

> They [paraprofessionals] were recruited and hurriedly trained, if at all, and told to help both the agencies and their clients unscram-ble the web of human needs and misery. They were selected on the basis of their low income, if they had any at all, the color of their skin, their political connections, and their *presumed knowledge of the low-income community* and the related agencies serving the community. (Austin, 1972, p. 60, my emphasis)

This representation stands in stark contrast to those earlier images of the paraprofessional characterised as moving smoothly between the domains of work and community 'helping each know more about the other' (Saltzman, 1965, p. 48). Within Austin's account, it is apparent that the paraprofessional is being pulled in two directions – by the demands of the agency and the demands of the community – so that 'returning to their neighbourhoods as salaried members of the establishment actually produced immense personal strain' (Austin, 1972, p. 59).

When considering the experiences of US 1960s educational paraprofessionals the theory of 'emotional labour' (Hochschild, 2012) has the potential to offer something perhaps more tangible and enduring than that of 'Psychic Stretch'. This concept is critical of how labour processes are traditionally presented as a simple dualism of manual or mental labour, and emphasises the relational rather than the task-based aspects of work. Emotional labour is a process which requires individuals in certain roles to 'induce or suppress feeling in order to sustain the outward countenance that produces the proper state of mind in others' (Hochschild, 2012, p. 7). The existence and impact of emotional labour has been researched in the service sector and helping professions (Steinberg & Figart, 1999) with some providing an alternative and arguably depoliticised concept of 'emotional management' in organisations (Bolton & Boyd, 2003). Other authors robustly defend Marx's theory of alienation on which the concept was built (Brook, 2009; Colley, 2003a) and it is this latter interpretation of emo-tional labour which I argue offers a more relevant application to Psychic Stretch. Here, researchers have considered issues regarding the impact of providing emotional labour on an employee's well-being, finding that there are negative consequences such as burnout, fatigue and emotional inauthenticity:

> To perform emotional labor, and in contrast with mental and phys-ical work, employees must give something of themselves to oth-ers with whom they have no ongoing personal, noninstrumental relationship. Although sometimes they may form what would be considered authentic, caring relationships with clients or co-work-ers, this is not necessarily a requirement of the job. (Steinberg & Figart, 1999, p. 12)

There is a gendered element to this discussion as emotional labour is found to be extensive within many female-dominated professions and in occupations involving considerable work in helping and caring for others. For example, Hochschild provides statistical data of 'Kindred' and Service Workers from the same period – 1970 – when Pearl and Reissman were espousing their 'New Careers' thesis. These data indicate that out of just over 131,000 teacher aides, 1,180,000 were women; statistics for 'Welfare Service aides' showed similar disproportionality (Hochschild, 2012, p. 249). However, it is Dunning (2018) who arguably provides the most eloquent critique of this era:

> The top-down funding strategy of the Great Society might have created new jobs in the human service fields, but the content and quality of those jobs depended on the bottom-up efforts of the people hired into them. (Dunning, 2018, p. 671)

Although not designed as such, she notes how New Careers programmes and jobs became opportunities filled predominantly by African American and Latina women who having experienced poverty as a product of sexism and discrimination in the workforce welcomed the 'respectable, community-oriented jobs created with federal funding'. Not surprisingly, they applied for positions in overwhelming numbers but, as with the findings of Stewart (1971) and Austin (1972) above, quickly discovered that:

> [O]nce employed ... [the paraprofessionals] encountered the disappointing reality that their experimental roles did not necessarily lead into upwardly mobile tracts, and recognized the hypocrisy of a strategy that proclaimed a commitment to poverty reduction and instead reinforced longstanding hierarchies of race, gender, and credentials. (Dunning, 2018, p. 671)

This chapter has demonstrated that the New Labour Government were not the first to introduce new groups of workers into public services as a means to resolve entrenched social issues of poverty and disaffection. Historical policy agendas which underpinned the 'New Careers' project have clear parallels with those more recent initiatives. That said, it is also important to underline significant differences as well; the 1960s was a period of economic expansion, along with the start or rejuvenation of emancipatory ideals (women's liberation, Black and civil rights, the anti-war movement, etc.); thus the introduction of the American paraprofessional must be seen in this light. By the 1990s both the USA and the UK were dealing with radically different economic landscapes: neo-liberal agendas of reduced state intervention; a rapid de-industrialisation of areas that had previously 'worked'; widening disparities in income and extended, more precarious youth transitions.

Nevertheless, a previous attempt to employ poor and working class people *purely on the basis of their designation as such* provides much to reflect on. At the time of writing there is no sign of a renewal of the 'New Careers' project but the issues that have been raised in this analysis are particularly pertinent as we move towards ever-increasing social inequalities in twenty-first century Britain (Dorling, 2010).

Chapter 4

Introducing Institutional Ethnography as a Means to Research Marginalised Work

> [L]earning institutional ethnography commits researchers to a particular way of looking. There is something distinctive not only about *how* the institutional ethnographer looks at the world but what she *looks for* … She asks and sets out to discover: 'How does this happen as it does? How are these relations organized?' Institutional ethnographers cannot step out of their bodies and histories to know 'in general'. They explore the everyday world. (Campbell & Gregor, 2004, p. 7)

The above quote encapsulates the influence of Institutional Ethnography (IE) (Smith, 2005) as a means to research marginalised work. As such, the primary task in this chapter is to set out my own experiences in 'learning' IE; namely how I went about explicating the social relations of a school setting in which learning mentoring is conceptualised and practiced. Described as both a form and critique of sociology (Walby, 2005), IE informed and guided many aspects of this project so it is fitting that I start by presenting some terms and concepts that characterise IE, these being:

- Standpoint.
- The 'relations of ruling' and the notion of the problematic.
- Texts.

The discussion will then move on to offer a commentary on the research design, methods employed and ethical considerations. Here I pay particular attention to how IE conceptualises the interview as a tool to investigate organisational and institutional processes that have generalising effects. To illustrate this idea, I include data generated during the study on some of the paraprofessionals' paths to employment at the school and pupil's experiences of their education. Strategies of data analysis and writing up are also presented including how composite accounts were built and the use of quotes in analysis.

Propping up the Performative School: A Critical Examination of the English Educational Paraprofessional, 45–65
Copyright © 2022 by Jo Bishop
Published under exclusive licence by Emerald Publishing Limited
doi:10.1108/978-1-83982-242-120221004

Standpoint

Qualitative field research often begins in a particular *experience* and the conditions under which that experience arises and is lived by *someone* (Campbell & Gregor, 2004). As such, this project began with a desire to learn about the experiences and everyday practices of learning mentors in English state secondary education. The concept of standpoint is integral to a project premised on IE, understood as both 'starting point' – meaning that the investigation is initiated via the experience of a person or group; and 'process' in terms of how this leads on to an understanding of how local and translocal institutional processes have shaped that experience. In essence, the standpoint of individuals (such as learning mentors offering support to pupils) located as they are in the everyday world, is the point of leverage for an explication of the relations in which our everyday lives are embedded.

Once I had achieved the standpoint of the learning mentors, it was necessary to do the same with other staff groups across the school hierarchy from those in other roles designated as 'support' (behaviour support workers and HLTAs/TAs) to teachers, middle managers and senior leaders. Pupils were also considered as key participants. All of the above groups, positioned and participating differently in the social relations of the setting provided their own standpoint which then afforded a broader picture that revealed the multiple activities required to sustain the day-to-day business of the school.

The 'Relations of Ruling' and the Notion of the Problematic

IE may start with both a description and an expression of people's lived experiences within the local (in this case, a school), but IE is not about producing an account of relations as a system in and of themselves. Nor is it about resorting to simplistic macro/micro distinctions such as seeking an ethnographic understanding of learning mentoring as it happens in the field, and directly comparing this with the more sanitised guidance provided in government-produced or commissioned literature. Such an approach would miss the point that social relations exist as *extended* sequences of action which link together individuals' experiences and institutional processes. They do not exist, nor can they be discovered, as self-sufficient phenomena or self-enclosed spheres of organisation (Grahame, 1998). As Dorothy Smith, the founder of IE argues:

> The everyday/everynight of our contemporary living is organised by and coordinated with what people, mostly unknown and never to be known by us, are doing elsewhere and at different times. IE proposes to address this as its problematic. (Smith, 2002, pp. 18, 19)

Two points require further explanation here: firstly, the trans-local mode of organisation and coordination implied in the quote above are what Smith (1990a) refers to as the 'relations of ruling'. This is more than just the notion of government as political organisation; it is the total complex of activities, differentiated into many spheres, by which Western industrial societies are ruled, managed and administered:

> It includes what the business world calls management, ... the pro-
> fessions ... government and the activities of those who are select-
> ing, training and indoctrinating those who will be its governors ...
> These are the institutions through which we are ruled and through
> which we, and I emphasize this *we*, participate in ruling. (Smith,
> 1990a, p. 14)

An understanding of the relations of ruling further enables one to see how the notion of 'institution' is developed within IE. Somewhat counter-intuitively, the term does not designate a bounded organisational space as might be suggested when undertaking (for instance) a school ethnography; rather it is the multiple activities of individuals, organisations, professional associations, agencies and crucially the discourses they produce and circulate, organised around a particular function. Essentially, the 'institutional' in IE, concerns the ways in which discourses and practices become institutionalised across many different localities. In relation to my study this could be understood as the pastoral care element of state education and how it is positioned alongside the other school activities of teaching and learning.

Turning now to the notion of the problematic. Through an IE lens this is not meant in the sense of everyday life being troublesome, perplexing or difficult; or as something which can be used to refer to a set of theoretical questions and related concepts which are there prior to the researcher accessing the field. Rather, it is best understood as a research tool which enables investigators to treat everyday life as sociology's problematic, that is, the complex of concerns, issues and questions which 'generate a horizon of possible investigations' (Grahame, 1998, p. 348). It identifies how the researcher will take up the inquiry to achieve a standpoint, directing attention to a set of possible questions, some of which may not have yet been formulated but are implicit in the way the everyday world is organised. Smith (1987, p. 91) refers to these as 'puzzles' which are '"latent" in the actualities of the experienced world. As will be shown in the coming chapters, it was through achieving the standpoint of the learning mentors initially, that the problematic became apparent: that although warmly received by pupils, learning mentor practices were marginalised, misunderstood and relatively unseen; casting doubt on the role's level of influence suggested by formal prescriptions. Furthermore, despite the support systems in which they worked being formally presented as coherent and straightforward entities, they were in fact found to be 'messy' and contested spaces which were inhabited by different groups of practitioners, whose differing identities (both prescribed and self-defined) informed and underpinned their own respective practices.

Texts

The question of *how* institutions succeed in generalising across multiple local settings and coordinating our activities with the 'mostly unknown and never to be known others' (Smith, 2002, p. 19) brings the discussion onto a further characteristic of IE – that of 'texts'. First, we will look at how they are defined and activated within an IE approach, then the focus will switch to how texts were 'listened for', asked about and explicated in a more practical sense.

Defining Texts

In institutional settings, texts are integral and ubiquitous in how people's work is organised. The form of text can be many and varied encompassing the written, spoken, visual, digital and numeric. It is the proliferation of these texts and the extent to which they are embedded in social relations which enables an understanding of how social life is organised *across* geographical sites (Campbell & Gregor, 2004). Texts are explicated through a combination of approaches: harvesting pre-existing knowledge prior to entering the site of research, then once in the field being identified by the participants themselves or observed or explicated by the researcher. My primary task as an Institutional Ethnographer was to gain an understanding of these texts and the forms of knowledge that they gave rise to, *in operation*. But, asks Smith (2005), how is this achieved given the apparent inertia of texts? I now briefly outline two approaches:

Texts in Operation

The first approach is described as a 'text-reader conversation' (Smith, 2005) where a person activates the text by responding to it and taking it up in some way. This can differ according to who is taking the text up and furthermore, whether they apply a set of informal rules about how they take it up (Walby, 2005). For example, during the ethnography I noted a marked difference in the approaches of learning mentors with other staff in applying school rules about (for example) permissible school uniform or what was deemed appropriate behaviour. These differing approaches arose from the different types of interactions between staff and those pupils who did not conform. Thus, the text, in this case the school rule, was successfully imposed but that imposition was experienced differently depending on the approach of the particular member of staff. The text-reader conversation can also be explored as a process that translates the *actual* into the *institutional* and conversely, the distinctive ways in which institutional discourse subsumes and renders 'institutional' the particularities of everyday experience. A clear example of this was how staff articulated their varied understandings of the term 'Barriers to Learning'. Initially, I was interested to see if an overall or dominant consensus existed regarding what such barriers might be; this would then suggest a greater likelihood in a 'whole school approach' to tackling them. What emerged in actuality was that a myriad of divergent issues were bundled together under this label, many of which had been informed from government discourses (as extra-local texts) which tended to emphasise the deficit individual, family or community rather than consider that issues of school organisation, curriculum content or modes of delivery and assessment as significant barriers to learning for many.

The second approach involves focussing on texts as they enter into and coordinate people's actions or 'doings', thereby bringing an external regulation into the immediacy of the everyday/everynight world. Smith (2002, p. 45) describes this as having the 'extraordinary capacity of double presence'. Thus, it is precisely this ability to replicate themselves in multiple different settings that enables people's work and other activities to become standardised:

> It is, I suggest, texts that produce, in and out of the ephemerality of people's everyday activities, the stability and replicability of organisation or institution. (Smith, 2002, p. 45)

Put more simply, if people handle and process the same texts, they find their actions coordinated by the requirements of working with that text. At an early stage in the data generation period, I had written up some field notes into a vignette named 'Eddie and the missing mobile phone' which appears in the 'guided tour of the school' in Chapter 5. Interested to see how someone who worked in a different school would respond to the critical incidents outlined in the vignette, I sought out a personal contact – an experienced secondary school teacher and pastoral leader – who was based in an academy on the opposite side of the country. Their immediate reaction on reading 'Eddie and the missing mobile phone' was 'That's spooky; you have just described a typical morning in *my* school!' Thus, in returning to Smith's words above regarding the 'double presence', 'replicability' and external presence of texts, the onus that schools place on dealing with issues like problematic behaviour, clearly has a commonality across geographical sites. As this account illustrates: what takes place in one state school is seen as highly familiar and relatable to what takes place in another. This demonstrates how it is not only the activities of those people who produce texts but how these conceptual frameworks are then taken up and circulated (DeVault & McCoy, 2002).

Within IE, the materiality of texts is emphasised because it is this which enables us to see how they create a 'crucial join between the everyday actualities of people's activities and the social relations they coordinate' (Smith, 1990b, p. 45). Specific to *Priory Park High*, the pseudonym given to the school featured in the ethnography, texts were many and varied and are summarised in Table 2. The point at which texts were identified and who identified them is also shown.

Planning an Ethnography and Accessing the Site

Having given a flavour of the key tenets of IE, the discussion now outlines how ethnographic tools were employed. A consideration of ethical issues and power relations present in the research is included along with the reflexive practice that was required to address these. Of particular significance in this chapter is an explanation of how the interview was utilised in a way that was very much informed by previous IE researchers, such as the importance of distinguishing between institutional and experiential accounts of work. This is important because it is here that the discussion departs from a mere description of research tools employed to how I started the process of transforming the data, drawing on IE as method of inquiry.

Time to Do Ethnography?

Traditional ethnographies entail a commitment on the part of the researcher to full immersion in the field for a considerable period of time (Van Maanen, 2011). For reasons of practicality namely, combining an undertaking of the study

Table 2.   Overview of Texts Identified at Priory Park High.

Texts Identified Prior to Entering the Field (by the Researcher)	Texts Identified by Participants	Texts Observed/explicated Once in the Field (by the Researcher)
Excellence in Cities (EiC) *Local Education Authority, EiC – Draft* *Learning Mentor Policy* *Good Practice Guidelines of Learning Mentors (DfES)* *Resources for Learning Mentors:* *Practical Activities for Group Sessions* *Every Child Matters* *Excellence in Learning* *Supporting the new agenda for children's services and schools: the role of learning mentors and coordinators (DfES)* *Learning Mentor National Training* *CWDC Induction Training Programme for level 3/4 children's workforce practitioners* *Local Authority 5-year plan* *School Ofsted reports* *School website/prospectus*	*Passport curriculum* *Standards Fund* *Gaining Ground* *Building Schools for the Future* ASDAN foundation curriculum (cited by the Headteacher) *Excellence in Cities* (cited by the Headteacher, the learning mentors and the HLTAs) *Every Child Matters* (cited by numerous staff across the school) *Restorative Practice* (cited by the Head of Behaviour Support) *Safer Schools Initiative* (cited by the school's attached Police Officer) *Kidscape - A Behaviour Support intervention* 'Aims' work – a previous mentor intervention undertaken with young male pupils around appropriate/inappropriate sexual behaviours (cited by the Director of Pastoral Care)	*National:* *Time for Standards: Transforming the School Workforce* document (and the *'touching tomorrow'* by the national remodelling team) *Local:* Local Education Authority mentoring initiative forms used with mentees *School-based:* Institutionally generated learning strategies such as the 'Priory Park Learner' Staff briefings – weekly and one-offs Institutionally generated notice boards for staff (and the presentations which activate them, e.g., Bankers/RAPs – See Chapter 5) Institutionally generated notice boards for pupils (attendance, punctuality, attainment) Subject-specific posters to 'sell' to pupils and signpost classrooms Posters generated by mentors and pupils Communications from VIP's displayed in public domains, for example, letter from Education Minister in visitor reception

alongside full-time work and caring/domestic commitments, I adopted a 'selective intermittent time mode' (Jeffrey & Troman, 2004). This means that although not present on site continually, I was present regularly and consistently. Thus, the fieldwork component of the ethnography was conducted over an eighteen-month period with attendance of one day per week in the first year and then going in when participants were available for interviews or to attend significant events like governors and staff meetings in the last six months.

This mode of attendance afforded greater opportunities for the development and sustainment of research relationships and thus ensured a more collaborative investigation between the varying participants and myself as researcher. It also enabled time *between* visits to reflect on my field note observations and conversations that had taken place which meant I could identify issues that required further information or clarification on entering the site again. This continual need to look, learn and ask questions which would then lead to further looking and learning, was vital and is characteristic of IE.

Accessing the Site

It can be challenging to find and access a setting that is willing to accommodate an ethnographic study so it makes sense to approach an organisation with which the researcher may already have contacts and meets the sampling criteria for the study. Thus, I opted for a school with which I had professional links and which met the criterion of (a) being a Local Authority maintained school which (b) had continued with provisions that could be considered as legacies from the *Excellence in Cities* initiative (which as outlined in earlier chapters had introduced the learning mentor role). I made initial contact with one of the learning mentors to explain my intentions and seek advice on what my next steps should be. Given the proposed length of the project it was agreed that I should first informally consult the mentor team to gauge their views on accommodating my presence alongside their daily workloads before making a formal approach to the school. Once their broad support was confirmed, an outline of the study was presented to the Headteacher and Board of Governors, suggesting that in the spirit of reciprocity, I could join a voluntary mentoring scheme at the school and undertake some mentoring for one or two pupils over the academic year.

Considering Ethics, Power Relations and Reflexive Practice

Permission to enter the school and carry out the ethnography was eventually granted by the Headteacher with relative ease. However, I was aware that this access should not be seen as 'total' but more usefully viewed and approached as an incremental continuum moving from initial permission to developing and sustaining trusting relations with key participants (Walford, 2008, p. 17). It was imperative to apply the notion of situated ethics (Piper & Simons, 2005) in terms of seeking ongoing, informed consent from participants for all aspects of the data collection, from formal interviews to both lengthy *and* fleeting observations of staff–pupil interactions. Initially I worked on building relationships with the mentor team and then after a few weeks started to actively engage with other pastoral staff, teachers, middle and senior managers. The pupils of Priory Park High also formed a significant participant group within the study so it was of primary importance to consider how genuinely participatory and ethical research is designed and carried out with young people. This will be presented in the following section as it forms part of a broader discussion regarding how actual research methods were employed.

Employing Ethnographic Tools to Generate Data

Observations-and-Talk

Ethnographic data collection draws on 'a repertoire of methods' (Bright, 2012, p. 221) encapsulating recorded conversations, observations, imaginative memos, the study of institutionally driven texts and comparisons with other research (Smith, 2002, 2005). Although all of the above were utilised in this ethnography, I focus discussion here on the 'interview'; understood in its widest sense from the pre-arranged and formally conducted, to 'observations-and-talk', meaning participant observation leading to further questions in order to glean greater understandings. This latter approach was particularly useful in developing an understanding of how the mentors' work differed from other support roles (such as behaviour support) which despite being two quite different interventions were still conceptualised broadly as being 'pastoral' in approach. Thus, observations-and-talk took place with the mentors as I accompanied them in the running of Breakfast Club; the staffing of the Mentor Base at breaks and lunchtimes and (where appropriate) during their one-to-one interactions with pupils, both planned and ad hoc throughout the school day. Time spent with the behaviour support workers was mostly through 'on-call' activities which involved patrolling the corridors during lesson times and observing how they assisted teachers in resolving behavioural issues as they emerged in class sessions, often leading to the removal of pupils if deemed necessary. Shadowing one particular behaviour worker whilst she was carrying out her 'on-call' duties added up to several hours observations-and-talk and further enabled me to get on-the-spot clarification as she discussed her work 'in the moment'.

'Speaking in Social Relations' – Utilising IE in Planning and Executing the Interview

As stated in the introduction, IE conceptualises interviews as a tool to investigate organisational and institutional processes that have generalising effects. They are a vehicle to explicate the relations of ruling that shape local experiences rather than as a means to reveal the subjective states of individual participants (DeVault & McCoy, 2002; Smith, 1996). Smith (2006) contends that when anyone speaks in a sensible and coherent manner about their lives, they also speak in 'social relations'; thus the key when talking with participants is to listen for and probe towards institutional connections so that you can build, piece by piece, a view of the extended organisational process. It is useful therefore to think of the IE interview as a co-investigation in which both the interviewer and participant build a knowledge base around the actualities of their work. At this point, it is pertinent to note that 'work' as conceptualised within a traditional (and patriarchal) sociology, is constructed as a paid activity which takes place away from the home and has as its corollary, 'leisure time'. In contrast, an IE lens defines 'work' generously as:

> [...] anything done by people that takes time and effort, that they mean to do, that is done under definite conditions and with whatever means and tools, and that they may have to think about it. (Smith, 2002, pp. 151, 152)

In this sense then, 'work' is taken as a metaphor that focusses the examination of experience on what people do, rather than on the idea of work as competency-based activity. This notion has been further developed into broad categorisations which can be used as a framework to plan and guide interview talk (DeVault & McCoy, 2002). I utilised two components of this: firstly, 'organisational paid work' (which is then sub-divided into 'frontline workers' and the 'ruling work' of managers as discussed below) and secondly, 'everyday life work' of (for instance) caring for family members. I extended this latter definition in consciously and deliberately describing young people as 'pupils', engaged as they were in their 'everyday life work' of schooling. By this I mean navigating through formal learning situations, problem-solving to overcome barriers to their school experience (be these external to or originating from within school itself) and ultimately attempting to make what is deemed to be a 'successful' transition to adulthood. However, regardless of which of the above categories is being deployed, the primary focus of interest for the institutional ethnographer is the informant's activity, as it reveals and points towards the interconnected activities of others. This can be understood as 'a conception of the social as residing in the concerting of people's actual activities' (DeVault & McCoy, 2002, p. 758).

Organisational Paid Work: Frontline Workers

I now move on to discuss how I utilised the above framework starting with frontline workers which were first and foremost the learning mentors but also other support staff like behaviour workers and HLTAs/TAs. These groups are particularly significant because they make the linkages between 'clients' – in this case pupils – and ruling discourses. As frontline workers, the learning mentors could be understood as intermediary actors, positioned as they were between the actualities of pupil's everyday worlds and the school's decisions about what 'should' happen to them; decisions which are informed by state-imposed prescriptions of what schools are for. Thus, when focussing on the work situations of those on the frontline, I was looking at how their activities were organised, controlled and directed by managers whose actions might limit their capacity to act autonomously. I was interested in how the mentors' consciously or unconsciously modified their work in response to this perceived control in a way that coalesced with their own values (which in some cases were predicated on youth work values) or conclusions about what they felt the 'correct' course of action to be.

Organisational Paid Work: The 'Ruling' Work of Managers

Also within the categorisation of 'organisational paid work' is 'ruling work' explicated through interviews conducted with those who were implementing policy that had been formulated elsewhere at the translocal or extra local level. The generation of this data meant it was possible to 'see' beyond the interchanges of frontline settings and track those macro institutional policies and practices that organise local settings. For example, policy initiatives cited during interviews required a synthesising or piecing together of the institutional complex, in that I had to constantly move back and forth, tracing and investigating particular policies that participants had named and then going back to an interview recording and transcript done at both the ruling and frontline levels to listen again and understand how that text organised actual systems and actions at a local level.

'Everyday Life Work' – The Experiences of Support Staff

Apart from the pupils whom I have already made brief reference to, the categorisation of 'everyday life work' may not seem immediately obvious to participants who have hitherto been presented as organisational paid workers on the frontline. But IE's 'generous definition of work' (Smith, 2002) reminds us that what people's daily lives require them to do is in itself a significant data resource. Reflecting national data presented in Chapter 1, the overwhelming majority of support staff at the school were women and their paths to employment at Priory Park High were inextricably bound up with the care work of their 'everyday/everynight worlds' (Smith, 2002, p. 42). Therefore, as the following interview extracts illustrate, the 'everyday life work' of these participants as parents and carers, was central to the question of how they came to be employed at the school as frontline workers:

1. [My path to Priory Park High] … *was purely and simply, looking at being a better parent for my children. I was working full time and it got to a point where myself and my husband were separated and his part of looking after the children disintegrated. [The situation] wasn't working and I had to look at an alternative career – a job where I could look after the children and be part of their lives in holidays and make sure that they were safe and happy and had the interaction that they needed.* (Year Manager)

2. *I went to work in the NHS, just twenty hours a week, at (–) hospital, in the pharmacy department, just doing clerical work. But as the kids got older, as they got to ten or eleven year olds,*

they didn't want to be uprooted and go to my mum's through the
holidays, so that I could work. So I decided to look for some-
where that I could work term-time. [Priory Park High] were
advertising for teaching assistants and I had helped out a little
bit at primary school with my own kids with reading .... So I
applied for that and got it ... I've been here for seven years. (Pat,
an HLTA running the ASDAN foundation curriculum)

This next excerpt is particularly illuminating in evidencing how care work as
both paid work *and* 'everyday life work' is carried out across different spheres
of production, rendering conventional conceptualisations of 'work' and 'leisure
time' at best inadequate if not entirely redundant:

3. *I left school, trained as a nursery nurse and worked in a hospital*
    for about four years in an intensive care unit for babies that were
    having operations. Then I left there to have my own children and
    then I became a child minder because that fitted in with the role
    of, you know, being able to stay at home and work and sort of
    used my qualification that I had. I did that for fifteen years, was
    successful at it, and employed two other people to work with
    me, so it was like a small business. But then I was just, you
    know, being at home, working all the time, the children were
    getting older, I had four children. So I went to work in a nursery
    and also did homecare for the elderly. Then, what did I do then
    ...? Then I became quite ill, I had cancer, so [after recovery]
    decided to change direction and went to work in a high school
    as a teaching assistant at (–) and worked there for a couple of
    years, and then I came here. (Marie, former learning mentor,
    year manager and currently working as a TA)

These excerpts demonstrate how work processes are typically reconstructed as
social or psychological. The respondents describe and present their decisions as
related entirely to their individual situations, and/or as responses or adjustments
they have had to make in relation to 'what life threw at them' be that marital
breakdown, juggling paid work with parenting or long-term illness. But this has
the effect of omitting their 'necessary anchorage in an economy of material conditions, time and effort' (Smith, 1987, p. 163). Thus, this type of data keeps the
social and its interconnectedness in view which is an important facet of IE as a
method of inquiry.

'Everyday Life Work' – The Experiences of Children and Young People as 'Pupils'

Earlier, I argued that pupil work could also be viewed as a type of everyday life
work. In the research conducted with young people, my aim was to draw on their
experiences or 'work knowledge[s]' (Smith, 2005, p. 151) within the school system.

This term is used to denote a person's experience of and in their own work, meaning what they do, how they do it and what they think and feel. It also refers to the implicit or explicit coordination of their work with that of others (Smith, 2005). At the same time, I remained mindful of conducting ethical research so in the planning stages drew on literature which provided practical guides for achieving this with children and young people (Clark, 2004; Lewis, Kellet, Robinson, Fraser, & Ding, 2004) adopting strategies such as posing questions in the third person so that participants were not under pressure to draw directly from their own experiences; giving the option of paired or small group interviews in addition to one-to-one, and providing paper and pens so that participants could doodle whilst talking or express their answers pictorially so that emphasis on (just) the spoken word was redirected (Shaw, Brady, & Davey, 2011). My approach to the pupil research was also influenced by Youth Work National Occupational Standards such as facilitating 'young people's exploration of their values and beliefs' (nya.org.uk). I had a strong desire that the research should enable young people to speak about issues which had a clear impact on their lives, in this case, their school experience but to do so in an ethical manner. Thus, in considering and putting into practice the above issues the opening question for the pupil interviews (set out below) provides one example of how their thoughts and insights were generated:

> You are walking down the street one day and you bump into an alien who has just landed from another planet. The alien tells you that it has to go to school but doesn't know *anything* about it. They want to know what it is like and what they should expect. What do you tell them?

Although some pupils were initially a little taken aback at this question, most seemed to relish the idea of talking about school from this 'fresh' perspective and in a way that afforded them the opportunity to draw on their own experiences, albeit indirectly and should *they* wish to do so. Their responses generated much discussion around the varying factors that can shape experiences of formal education, such as the physical and social environment of the school; and (for some participants) the relentless pressure to do well. The open-endedness of this question further enabled the pupils to make observations, which *they* identified as relevant, shown in the response given here by two Year 11 girls – 'Serena' and 'Louise':

Serena: This alien … is it a boy or a girl?

Jo: It's just an alien … [pauses] … would that make a difference?

Serena: I think it would make a *big*_difference
[Louise nods vigorously in agreement].

Jo: Okay, let's just pretend for now it's a female alien.

Louise:　　　I think you get a lot of different expectations, simply because teachers feel we [girls] should be on top of things, more organized … which is not always the case.

Serena:　　　First of all we're teenagers, second of all – girls, … there's a lot to say about high school girls [pauses] like expectations to look perfect; then there's all the high school drama … that people get over eventually.

The need for a 'gender lens' in order to describe an educational experience was clearly important for these two young people. For other pupils the 'alien' question did not lead to such an immediate response but helped to convey that I welcomed a 'warts-and-all' pupil take on their schooling. 'Eliza' was a case in point. She had initially volunteered to take part in the research when it was first publicised at a Year 11 assembly. Her Year Progress Leader had described her as an exemplary pupil in terms of her academic performance and her contribution to the school community, remarking that 'she could have been the school Head Girl, if we had such a position'. Eliza's initial response to the alien question offered a 'common sense' description of school which was very much in contrast to Serena above:

A place where you learn stuff … I don't know … you'll get up, you'll spend most of your day there, you'll have different lessons and learn about different things … meet up with friends, come home, do some homework and basically you'll learn and get educated.

But as the interview progressed, her presentation altered dramatically from the conforming model pupil she had (knowingly) been presented as, to an agitated young person who ultimately delivered a damning critique of the school system. The more cynical researcher could interpret this as a case of 'tales told to tourists' – that is, you have entered a young person's space as an outsider and invited them to tell you what they think of that space, potentially leading to sensationalised accounts. But I offer a counter argument in drawing on the aforementioned youth work ethics and principles which believe a young person to be a competent witness of their experience, *alongside* the notion of 'work knowledges' as defined above. Many of the observations that Eliza made further into the interview, mirrored those in the wider literature such as the 'overlooked middle' (Hodgson & Spours, 2013). Eliza verbalised this issue as those pupils who 'didn't get noticed by teachers' because of the 'top pupils' (which, pragmatically and without vanity she understood to be her own position in the school) and the 'bottom pupils' – that is those deemed as troublesome and disruptive. In Eliza's view, each group received a disproportionate amount of attention from school staff, albeit in different ways. Towards the end of the interview, she disclosed that despite the regard with which she was held by teaching staff she had in fact lost motivation and was not currently doing any homework or revision:

> They [teachers] say: 'your homework is to learn this part of the
> spec because we haven't got time to teach it' so I know I need to
> do this for my exam but you just ... get to a certain point where
> you can't be bothered .... I say I'm busy but I literally just sit in my
> bedroom or at the kitchen table and do nothing all night. I'm not
> tired but I'm just at that stage where ... I've had enough.

This incident illustrates my belief that the approach I undertook generated
authentic, rather than sanitised or, conversely, sensationalised accounts of schooling. But this then gave rise to another ethical issue: did my invitation to young
people to speak honestly about their experiences of education, open up (for some
at least) a 'Pandora's Box' of stress and difficult emotions? Although support
mechanisms had been put into place in the event of a pupil becoming distressed,
I was concerned at how much Eliza's emotional state altered during the course of
the interview and wondered if these avenues of support amounted to little more
than a disingenuous tick-box approach that researchers are required to put in
place in order to generate data.

Further issues were explored in the pupil interviews by again posing questions
framed in the third person. For example, the following question was intended to
identify which staff roles pupils associated with accessing help and support:

> Who could a pupil go to if they were experiencing difficulties in
> the school day or having a tough time generally?

And then later:

> How might someone explain what learning mentors do, to people
> who didn't know about the role?

Interestingly, the same question was posed regarding behaviour support workers but it was only pupils who had had direct contact with them who were able to
give an accurate account of what they did whereas the learning mentor role was
more widely understood amongst the pupil body. A more detailed account of
the data that were generated with the pupils' is presented in Chapter 7 but what I
wish to emphasise at this stage is that their viewpoints and experiences provided
important descriptions of and insights into their 'everyday life work' of being a
high school pupil which was invaluable for me as someone very much removed
by age from this experience. It also added a greater degree of authenticity and
validity to the mentors' perceptions of pupil experiences as their accounts cor-
responded with many of the issues identified and raised by the pupils themselves.

Distinguishing Between Institutional and Experiential
Accounts of Work

So far I have set out how the interview enables an explication of 'work knowledges' which to remind the reader describes a person's experience of and in their

own work, meaning what they do, how they do it and what they think and feel, as well as referring to the implicit or explicit coordination of their work with that of others (Smith, 2005). The data that are generated by this type of knowledge is a major resource for IE, but they are not always accessible to the researcher if it is not possible to differentiate between institutional and experiential accounts. To explain further, it is common (and understandable) that people in an institutional setting describe their work using the language of that institution, or describe a work process as if it were performed by a position or category rather than by the person the researcher is talking to. Such accounts are viewed as problematic from the perspective of IE as they subsume or displace descriptions based in experience, containing little usable data beyond the expression of institutional ideology-in-action, described helpfully as 'institutional capture' by Smith (2005, p. 156). This was a situation that arose not infrequently in the study, the most apposite example occurring during an interview with a Year Manager who we meet in Chapter 9. This person drew heavily on the 'outcomes' speak established by the *Every Child Matters* agenda – to describe her everyday work.

Thus, in contrast to institutional accounts, are experiential accounts or 'work knowledges' as defined above. One strategy to encourage experiential accounts (and thereby prevent institutional accounts from dominating interviews) was to utilise questions such as the examples given below which enabled participants to recognise this distinction for themselves:

> Can you tell me your job title and something of what this *actually* entails?
>
> (And/or)
>
> Does your job title and job description reflect what you actually do?

Having a grasp of institutional and experiential accounts also made it possible for me, as researcher, to reflect during and immediately after the interview on what type of data have been generated, and decide whether any follow-up was necessary to get beyond an institutional account that may have been presented. For example, in a formal, pre-arranged interview conducted at a relatively early stage in the project, Paul, one of the learning mentors, appeared quite nervous, disclosing that he had been worried about whether he would be able to answer one of the questions in the pre-seen interview schedule (which was attempting to establish if, and to what degree, the work of mentors was evaluated by the school). As the interview progressed it became increasingly apparent that he, as interviewee, saw his task as giving a good account of Priory Park High to me, the outsider. The resulting transcript was one where institutional accounts dominated as Paul attempted to present more official or 'glossy' explanations of his work, an issue which I return to in Chapter 10. As the fieldwork progressed, I came to realise that formal interviews were often not the appropriate choice for those who I was going to be spending a significant amount of time with. Eventually through more informal discussions with Paul, both one-to-one and alongside the other mentors, he opened up and gave increasingly more experiential accounts deriving from his work knowledge. One such example was when I asked Paul about the frenetic nature of the mentor's day as he was gulping down a hastily microwaved meal. I had just observed him carrying out a series of one-to-one interventions with pupils, interspersed with his facilitation of a particularly lively break time in the mentor base, and now as the midday bell was sounding, the further facilitation of a lunchtime football club. Commenting on this he shrugged saying:

> I love football and besides I never go to the staff room at lunchtime. I did once years ago but I was so disgusted at some of the things staff were saying about the kids, I've never been back since.

I asked him whether he felt it [discussions held in the staffroom] might be better now, to which he frowned, reflecting for a few seconds before saying:

> This is a good school, we just need a break [then smiling] ... we're all working together and we're all knackered. The signs are good.

This extract from an experiential account, demonstrates what I would have missed if I had not gone beyond the formal interview with Paul. It reveals that there were certain parts of the school that he, as a learning mentor, did not feel entirely comfortable in and the reasons why. It also acknowledges that although the school had been through challenging times this experience had, in some ways, brought staff closer together.

It has been suggested by Institutional Ethnographers that the 'test' of whether you are getting an institutional account as opposed to an experiential account is if you, the listener, can't see every step without having to imagine or insert missing pieces. Researchers are advised to ask questions at every point in the story, especially where 'steps are skipped or discourse words substitute[d] for "what actually happens"' (Campbell & Gregor, 2004, p. 78). As I became more adept in the process outlined above, fieldwork interactions coming later in the study felt much more akin to those of other institutional ethnographers who describe the interview as an 'analytic rehearsal' where they are checking their understanding as it develops and offering it up to the informant for confirmation or correction (Mykhalovskiy, 1999 in DeVault & McCoy, 2002).

As set out above, experiential accounts as a form of work knowledge also enable an explication of the implicit or explicit coordination of a participant's work with the work of others. This refers to the ubiquitous 'they', familiar to us all when referring to aspects of our working and wider lives and described by Smith (2005, p. 151) as 'the nebulous other'. Thus, the mentors' verbalisation of 'they', was often accompanied by a vague wave of their hands in the direction of the door to 'somewhere' beyond the immediate vicinity of the Mentor Base. In this example, the 'they' was clarified (through the 'analytic rehearsal' described above) as being the middle managers in the school hierarchy whose own prescriptions of the mentoring role were often influenced by objectives which had in turn been handed down to them from senior management and of which a full account is given in Chapter 9. In concluding this part of the discussion, fieldwork conversations which are informed by an IE approach, can be seen as both potentially problematic but also a rich resource. The objective for the researcher is two-fold: firstly, to obtain a description of the actuality rather than descriptions which are couched in institutional language; and secondly, to explicate how such terms, and the discourses they carry, operate in the setting.

Transforming the Data

So far I have outlined how IE is a method of inquiry which generates and uses data to discover the connections between peoples' activities; what triggers these activities; and how they are coordinated. The final part of this chapter sets out some of the issues I needed to consider when analysing and writing up an ethnography which is based on this premise. If in IE, the task of the researcher is to reveal these material connections and make explicit and understandable the implications they carry, then a different kind of analysis is required to the more commonly used thematic approaches found in qualitative studies which interpret and then formally codes people's talk into topics or variables. Within an IE approach, data are utilised to map out complex institutional chains of action; where the mechanics of text-based forms of knowledge are described and the conceptual schemata of ruling discourses are elaborated (DeVault & McCoy, 2002). Once the task of describing and understanding the everyday work of the learning mentors from their standpoint had been completed, I had to undertake a back-and-forth method of exploration which traced the connections between what they did, what other staff did and the texts and other processes that governed that 'work'. Analysis in this sense is described by Campbell and Gregor (2004) as a matter of moving back and forth between generated speech and the context that produced it. The final stage is the examination of the 'ideological character' of the institutional process: for example, IE analysts look at those stories provided by informants through both interview data and observation-and-talk in a way that makes visible the juxtaposition of primary narratives and ideologically oriented accounts. As one IE researcher says:

> [...] I'm on the lookout for segments of the interviews where 'fault lines' can be detected, as the two modes of telling – the narrative and ideological – rub up against each other. (McKendy, cited in DeVault & McCoy, 2002, p. 769)

This thorough and painstaking process is intended to guard against long-standing and common critiques of qualitative data analysis which argue that methods associated with this approach are not well formulated, resulting in the analyst having very few guidelines for protection against 'self-delusion ... let alone the presentation of unreliable or invalid conclusions to scientific or policy-making audiences' (Miles, 1979, p. 591). I will now set out the process I went through regarding how I worked to transform the data (Wolcott, 1994) encompassing issues like the reduction, display and organisation of data (Miles & Huberman,

1994), associated decisions made regarding the transcribing of interviews and writing strategies adopted.

Reduction, Display and Organisation of Data

It is important that the activities of data reduction and display are not viewed as a linear process but as concurrent streams or activities throughout the analysis. My first task was to organise the data by type, the first being the data generated by the formal interviews that had been pre-arranged and recorded ($n=20$). These were then grouped by role, for example, learning mentors, paraprofessionals other than mentors, pupils, teachers, senior leaders and so on. Transcription is an obvious example of data display but the value of a full transcription of interview data in qualitative research remains a contested area. In ethnographic circles it is a viewed as a fundamental criterion of what qualifies data analysis as authentic (http://www.ethnographyandeducation.org) but in other forums views range from an acknowledgement of the 'tremendous if unspoken influence of the researcher as author' (Fontana & Frey, 2005, p. 713) to this more strongly worded take on this issue:

> The transcript is a bastard, a hybrid between an oral discourse unfolding over time, face to face, in a lived situation – where what is said is addressed to a specific listener present – and a written text created for a general, distant public. (Kvale & Brinkman, 2009, p. 192)

Within the existing community of IE researchers, there is no fixed view on the issues of whether or not to fully transcribe and what the resulting transcription actually represents. On the one hand, transcripts are seen as important texts in themselves and not only in the obvious sense of facilitating analysis but also as a means for research participants to 'speak' in published accounts. This alone is an important point given that IE studies are often seeking to promote the experiences of oppressed or hitherto neglected groups. There is some concern however about privileging the textual representation over the embodied actuality of the research conversation. For example, the view of one IE researcher appears to be more in line with Kvale and Brinkman above, but not so much in terms of what the transcript comes to represent, more on the premise that Dorothy Smith's concept of the 'everyday' begins with the fundamental fact that we are always in our bodies:

> In insisting on bodies being there [Institutional Ethnography] sensitizes us to bodies as part of the data … it's not just about words but how the words live in embodied experience. (cited as T. Diamond, personal communication, in DeVault & McCoy, 2002, p. 758)

I made the decision to fully transcribe all of my formal interviews with staff. Once completed it was essential to continue the work of listening to the interviews (usually on numerous occasions) *alongside* the completed transcript, initially to check for errors but also to annotate the transcript with those attitudes, emotions or gestures that went along with the spoken word. Diamond's words above chimed especially in relation to two lengthy recorded interviews I conducted with one of the learning mentors who spoke in an intricate and rich narrative and without warning would often move from recounting an incident in the third person to actually entering the incident and 'role-playing' interactions she had had with pupils and staff, adopting an array of voices, facial expressions and physical gestures when doing so (examples of which are given in the chapters presenting the ethnography).

The second category of data to be grouped were all of the varying ways in which research had been directly generated by the participants and myself which are common to ethnography. This included informal conversations, researcher observations and observations-and-talk recorded through field notes, photographs taken by myself and researcher reflections. The third category of data were the more contextual, drawing on information which had derived from the setting such as staff briefings, statistical information regarding the pupil demographic, Ofsted reports, promotional literature generated by the school such as the prospectus and learning resources displayed around the school. Finally, news media reports retrieved by myself were also included in this category.

Because qualitative data are often large and extensive as well as bulky and dispersed, data displays help at all stages in the analysis as they organise, compress and assemble information. The earliest data displays in my study were a series of spider grams where data from interview transcriptions were arranged according to issues raised by participants through their respective work knowledges. In one example, the Progress Leader and Year Manager as participants with middle management responsibilities were placed side by side which enabled a direct comparison of their work activities *and* their understandings of commonly used terms like 'barriers to learning'. The spider grams provide an example of both data reduction and data display. Data displays should be repeated and iterative as this shows how analysis is progressing. Thus, Table 3 shows how the data relating to 'barriers to Learning' was developed from spider grams into corresponding tables. Each participant's response is summarised and links to transcriptions given where necessary.

Writing Strategies

Building Composite Accounts. When analysing data in IE, the researcher works towards the goal of keeping the institutional in view. There are a number of ways in which this can be achieved and those outlined here all played a part in the analysis of this ethnography. Firstly, data from interviews (understood in their widest sense) and observations were used to produce a description of the institutional processes under examination. Although penned in the writer's voice, an account of this nature is a composite built up from those multiple sources listed earlier when discussing different categories of data. In this study I also drew on realist and impressionist writing styles as a means to enable others to

Table 3.   Data Displays.

	Year 10 Progress Leader (Interview 3)	**Year 7 Year Manager (Interview 10)**
Barriers to learning	Cites: Illness – specific to her year as many conditions present linked to unease about MMR vaccination some years before. Medical conditions/unstable home life in the short and long term/lack of organisation amongst students with dyslexia/lateness to school cos students come from 'disparate areas of the city' and changing bus times when university students return/Pupils' own feelings about the school, its size is daunting, etc.	Uses an example of an intervention undertaken with one of the LM's with a boy who was being bullied to answer this. Good example here of 'institutional capture' as uses ECM language (see underlined p. 4) Parents not working in partnership with schools *see red section on p. 5, 6 where she sees her role as much about supporting families as pupils through CAF's, etc. notes some parents want to relinquish their responsibilities once child is in school but she pushes the need for partnership working and sees mentor role as particularly useful here in accompanying on home visits (see 'we're not all bad guys' quote on p. 6) This links to mentors represented in the news media as forming a type of credible 'go-between' function

see the actualities of the everyday (Van Maanen, 2011). This was particularly useful when writing about complex incidences involving a number of people or when analysing the detailed observations I had made of interactions between both mentors and pupils and other staff and pupils (as it would of course have been ethically inappropriate to record them as they happened). The building of data through composite accounts is best illustrated through the example given at the start of the next chapter entitled: 'A guided tour of Priory Park High on a typical Monday morning', thus acting as a device to familiarise the reader with the school as research site, in all its layered complexity.

The Use of Quotes in Analysis.   The final two issues under focus are in relation to the use of quotes in the analysis. The first is whether and how biographical details should be included in the analysis. Some IE researchers regard the 'tagging' of quotes, that is, including the participant's gender, ethnicity or class, as problematic because this type of identification may invite an individualising line of analysis in which class and ethnicity are treated as inherent in individuals rather than produced through coordinative social processes (DeVault & McCoy, 2002). Thus, writers subscribing to this view suppress personal information about informants in their analyses and identify quoted speakers only by their location in the institutional work process of which they speak (e.g., mentor, behaviour worker, pupil, etc.). This was an approach I broadly adopted – seeing the learning mentors first and foremost as learning mentors; the teachers as teachers and so on. However, there were other times where I deemed it essential to not only use life stories in explicating a particular experience but also reveal the gender or ethnicity of the participant. This was demonstrated in the earlier examples given in this chapter of participants whose paths to employment at the school had involved a negotiation of other aspects of their 'everyday life work'. This decision was also extended to the example of the pupils who raised the importance of gender as a lens through which schooling is experienced and whose gender was thus identified through their given pseudonyms.

The second issue considers how quoted excerpts from interviews are used in the analysis of data. As is a common feature of qualitative enquiry, I utilised quotes to carry forward the description and analysis in the final text but in doing so drew on a useful notion of the 'exhibit' (Smith, 1998). This specifies a distinctive use of interview excerpts as creating a window within the text, bringing into view the social organisation of the participants' lives for the reader to examine. Although what is brought into view emerges out of the dialogic relations of the interview, Smith warns that excerpts must not be read simply as extensions of descriptions penned by the researcher. Rather they bring the actual social organisation of the institutional into the text of the analysis, dialogically, rather than illustratively. I used participants' descriptions in this way when the matter was their actual work and the experience of doing it but then used my own composite accounts when describing generalised relations or chains of action that transcended the local experience of any one person.

Having explained the strategies in the writing and presenting of the data, my final point is intended as a clear instruction to how the reader should approach the data. Here I draw on the words of another institutional ethnographer who calls for 'respectful attention' to be paid to the life experiences of those whose work does not gain as much exposure as others or which is trivialised as a role that 'anyone could do' (DeVault, 1991). In reading the data which inform my analysis, I too am calling on the reader to pay respectful attention to the descriptions and experiences of those doing work in schools other than teaching. Like DeVault, my goal is also that such attention might enable a deeper understanding of the nature and significance of such work; a new and better vocabulary with which to discuss it; and a clear and honest assessment of both the value of such (care) work whilst also recognising '... its darker side [and] the ways it can diminish the one who does it' (DeVault, 1991, p. 4).

Chapter 5

Introducing Priory Park High School

Significant Developments and Policy Milestones

Priory Park High[1] is a state-funded and local authority maintained secondary school situated in the suburbs of a northern English city. Established in the 1930s by the merging of two, single sex grammar schools, it evolved into a co-educational mixed ability school as part of the comprehensive reorganisation in the 1970s (Best, Jarvis, & Ribbins, 1980). At this time, it was hailed in the local press as 'the last word in secondary schools' and maintained this reputation for the following three decades. At the time of the study (2013–2015) the school had just over 1,200 pupils on roll, a number which had been steadily decreasing since 2009 due to a change in its fortunes which will be set out in due course.

Up until the early 2000s, the pupil population of Priory Park High had been drawn from two contrasting catchment areas which epitomised its comprehensive status. To the north of the school there is an affluent area containing private housing fetching some of the highest prices in the city, whilst to the south there is a large post-war council estate. During the study many staff, including the Headteacher below, voiced a clear sense of pride that Priory Park High was a school where achievement 'happens' but was also keen to emphasise the inclusive nature of Priory Park High in order to make clear the challenges that he and his staff faced:

> I want this on record, this is a true comprehensive. When you look at the measure(s) … on race, we are a large school, we have a large EAL[2] population; we have a large transitional [population], you know, children who come in and go out, because of the nature of [–] as a city. We have more boys than girls, and we have a large

---

[1]The pseudonym given to the school in this study.
[2]Denotes 'English as an additional Language' and refers to pupils whose first language is not English.

Propping up the Performative School: A Critical Examination of the English Educational Paraprofessional, 67–76
Copyright © 2022 by Jo Bishop
Published under exclusive licence by Emerald Publishing Limited
doi:10.1108/978-1-83982-242-120221005

percentage of free schooling[3]. You couldn't be more comprehensive because we equally have affluence at this end [of the city]. We are absolutely on every level. So it's a tough management because you need varying strategies for all these varying groups and needs change every time.

In its current incarnation, the all-inclusive status of Priory Park High is celebrated with reference to its diverse ethnic make-up of the pupil population, noted to be 'well above the national average' by Ofsted in 2013, the year of its last full inspection at the time of the ethnography. The increasingly diverse makeup of the pupil body is explained by staff as a result of inner-city schools deemed to be 'failing' and parents then opting to send their children to 'leafy lane' suburban schools such as Priory Park High, meaning that some pupils are now making anywhere between one and three bus journeys across the city to Priory Park High. Longer-serving members of staff describe how this situation has caused a 'ripple effect' whereby some parents situated in the school's more traditional middle-class catchment area were in turn 'bussing-out' their children to schools in two neighbouring, mono-cultural towns or, opting for fee-paying schools within the city. The result is illustrated in one teacher's observation that:

> [...] the school is bang in the middle of an affluent area, but the kids don't come from this area!

These recent changes in the pupil population of Priory Park High illustrate the marketised nature of education which can cause a high degree of parental anxiety (Mortimore, 2013). Other commentators are more pointed in their critiques arguing that it is precisely these systems of 'choice' that create social spaces within which middle-class parents use their social and cultural capital at the expense of others thereby indirectly promoting inequality (Ball, 2008; Gewirtz, 2001). A further useful analogy offered is that of a modified version of 'musical chairs' where although there are enough chairs (school places) to go around, some are more desirable than others (Burgess, Briggs, McConnell, & Slater, 2006) and for reasons which will become clear, Priory Park High became one such casualty of this 'game' in recent times.

A further significant development in the school's history came about as a result of *Building Schools for the Future* (BSF) with Priory Park High becoming one of the first 'new builds' in the city during the early 2000s. BSF, alongside other policy initiatives such as PFI (Private Finance Initiative), was a scheme whereby the previous New Labour administration controversially reconfigured the relationship between the state and the private sector to enable an overhaul of school buildings and infrastructure, neglected for some time under the Conservative administrations of the 1980s and early 1990s (Ball, 2008). Another policy

---

[3]This refers to children in receipt of free school meals which is used to measure the socio-economic background of pupils in England.

development in this era which signalled a further disarticulation of the state system (Ball, 2008) was that by the mid-2000s, Priory Park High, along with many other state schools, had secured specialist status by attracting sponsorship from a well-known banking family. At this point, the future of the school looked bright, situated as it was in a new, apparently state-of-the-art building and reported to have the biggest increase of pupils achieving five A* to C GCSE[4] grades in Maths and English it was hailed as the most improved school in the city.

Challenging times were ahead however. Towards the end of the 2010s the school was one of the first in the country to be inspected under the then new Ofsted regime, and was found to be 'inadequate' on the basis of concerns regarding achievement; pupil behaviour; and a failure to improve attendance levels since the previous inspection. The after-shocks of this judgement reverberated across the city, earning 'how the mighty have fallen' type headlines in the local press like *'most improved school faces special measures bombshell'*. This Ofsted judgement proved to be a disastrous chapter in the school's history resulting in falling pupil numbers and, as a consequence, whole-school redundancies affecting both teaching and support staff. There was an abrupt change in leadership with the instalment of an interim head teacher and a further inspection two years later. This deemed the school to be making good progress in the key areas cited above and it was subsequently taken out of special measures. However, during this time it was also named as being in the bottom 50 schools in England in a national league table highlighting persistent pupil absenteeism. The Headteacher in post at the time of the study was one whose career path and reputation had been built whilst working within a number of policy initiatives of the last Labour Government (1997–2010) specifically *Gaining Ground* and *Building Schools for the Future*. Once these had ended, his stated desire for 'a new challenge' coincided with a national recruitment agency 'head-hunting' him as a school leader in possession of those skills deemed necessary to either improve 'coasting' schools or turn around failing ones.

The above discussion has set out how policy milestones and other regulatory mechanisms have impacted on the evolution of Priory Park High in its journey as an all-inclusive English state school in the twenty-first century and where staff are working extremely hard to regain past status as one of *the* state schools in the city. Now the scene has been set we embark on a 'guided tour' of the school. This pen picture is based on composite accounts (as explained in Chapter 4) and has the explicit purpose of familiarising the reader with provisions that exist outside of the 'mainstream' classroom as well as introduce the paraprofessionals who staff them. Three different types of paraprofessional roles feature in this account and the ensuing chapters namely, the learning mentor, the HLTA/TA and the behaviour support worker.[5]

---

[4]The GCSE (General Certificate in Education) is the academic qualification used to measure pupil attainment in all subjects in the final year of compulsory schooling. At the time of the study it used A–E grading.

[5]Descriptions of the activities associated with these roles are presented in Chapter 1.

Pen Picture: A Guided Tour of Priory Park High on a Typical Monday Morning

7.50 a.m.

It is just before 8.00 am on a Monday morning and we are entering the staff and visitor reception area which is a vast open, light and airy space. Huge banners hung from the ceiling, display photographic images of pupils posing with objects that illustrate different areas of the curriculum whilst simultaneously challenging gender stereotypes and celebrating the ethnic diversity of the pupil body. These visuals were produced and installed as part of a 'make-over' at the behest of the Headteacher who on his appointment at the school, had described the entrance and reception area as 'sterile' and failing to convey anything about the school's mission, values or purpose to parents or visitors. Now, from the comfortable seating (complete with cushions made from up-cycled school ties), visitors can view a range of pupil art work adorning the walls, as well as the ubiquitous glass cabinet displaying a collection of sports trophies and accolades. At the reception counter a copy of the school's glossy prospectus is displayed on a stand next to a framed letter from the Minister of State for Schools in which he comments enthusiastically about his recent visit to Priory Park High.

The pupil entrance, about two minutes' walk away, is notably less grand in scope. The space is organised around two parallel glass automatic doorways which open fully at the start and end of the school day to allow for the high volume of human traffic entering and leaving the building. At other times, these doorways constitute a 'holding area' in which pupils arriving or leaving outside of the formal registration hours sign in and then wait to be 'bleeped' through the doors, or are collected and delivered to the appropriate classroom by 'on-call' staff. The Headteacher spoke of the refurbishment of this particular entrance as his 'number one job' on arriving at Priory Park High, expressing his concern that the high, steel-barred gate previously *in situ*, gave the impression of a prison rather than the entrance to a school:

> It didn't say 'welcome', 'this is for you' [or] 'you are part of this community' … We didn't even have a ruddy first aid room, for crying out loud!

Like the staff and visitor entrance, the pupil 'holding area' described above has also undergone a transformation, albeit lower budget, with colourful bunting made out of the flags of different countries representing the pupils' varied countries of origin. The impetus for this particular make-over was undertaken by a Textiles teacher who shared the Head's concerns regarding the design and aesthetics of the pupil entrance.

8.00 a.m.

Back in the staff and visitor entrance, people are arriving and queuing to sign-in at the reception counter, before 'bleeping' their way through the double doors that lead through to the rest of the school. Like all schools in this era dominated by safe-guarding concerns, access is highly restricted and dependent on electronic pendants which are essential to move around different parts of the school. Once through the double doors we enter a long, dark corridor which displays more pupil artwork. A right turn leads to facilities which house the central nervous system of the school's operations: administration, reprographics and the Head's office which was relocated to this part of the school on his arrival remarking that in its previous situation at 'the butt end of a corridor [in a room] that nobody could ever see' did nothing to help his 'visibility' or 'approachability'.

The staff room is also on this corridor and entering it this morning at around 8.10 a.m. there is standing room only because the usual Monday morning staff briefing is taking place. Delivered verbally by the senior leadership team (SLT) and backed up by the dissemination of the weekly paper bulletin it is intended to outline and reinforce key objectives that staff must work towards. As the Headteacher explains:

> [...] It's about setting the stall out ... and then driving that and just not relinquishing it. So for example on Monday morning, welcome back, hope you had a nice break, these are the priorities for this term. Bang, bang, bang, that's how it should be ... Communication is a key in any organisation and you can't best guess that people have assumed what's our priorities.

This morning the Year 11 Progress Leader leads the briefing, drawing staff attention to a new display on a large notice board just inside the staff room entrance. This is organised into three columns, the first two of which are headed respectively as 'BANKERS' and 'RAPs', standing for 'Raising Achievement Programme'. A small passport photograph of every Year 11 pupil has been organised into one of the three columns and some of these photographs are further bordered in red which denotes that they draw down 'Pupil Premium' funding, the policy initiative spearheaded by the Liberal Democratic component of the Coalition Government (2010–2015). The Progress Leader explains that the 'BANKERS' are those pupils estimated to get 5 (or more) A* to C grades in their GCSE's including English and Maths. The second column – the 'RAPs', are all those pupils who are likely to get *either* Maths *or* English but on current estimations not both and will therefore need targeted support. The final group are referred to only briefly in this presentation because they are undertaking foundation qualifications and are therefore not significant in terms of the measures which will decide the school's place in national league tables, i.e. its GCSE results. The language being used in this briefing is highly illuminative: the 'BANKERS' are those pupils whose results ensure the school's continued post-inspection recovery; but, staff are told, it is the 'RAP' pupils that will make the difference between a 65% GCSE A*–C achievement rate rather than the 44% currently being projected. Thus, all staff are urged to study the board in their break and lunchtimes and sign up an individual 'RAP' pupil for intensive coaching and support over the coming months.

8.20 a.m.

After a note of thanks from the Head to the staff, the briefing is over and we retrace our steps back down the corridor, eventually passing a classroom which houses the school's ASDAN[6] provision. This is run by Pat, a recently qualified Higher Level Teaching Assistant (HLTA) who tells me that she was approached shortly after the Head teacher's arrival and asked if she would consider heading up this provision within Key Stage 4[7] on the condition that she undertook the HLTA qualification at the same time. Another intervention that runs outside of mainstream classes is the Pupil Nurture Centre[8] (PNC), staffed by Cath, also an HLTA. Originating from an intervention commonly used in primary schools, this provision is accessed by pupils who are unable to participate in an ordinary classroom situation for a range of reasons such as experiencing a bereavement, being identified as a 'school refuser' and therefore having problematic attendance or as a means to induct new pupils joining the school mid-way through the term. The PNC also accommodates those who have come to the school via a 'managed move', a process whereby pupils are given the potential for a fresh start in a new school or maybe just a few weeks away from their original school thus also providing some respite

---

[6]ASDAN is the Award Scheme Development and Accreditation Network which emerged out of a project to develop alternative education provision in both mainstream and alternative settings.
[7]The last 2 years of High School for pupils usually aged 15–16 years.
[8]The name of this provision has been changed to protect the anonymity of the school.

for teachers and support staff who may have worked intensively with that young person. As HLTAs, Pat and Cath oversee provisions very much removed from the experiences of 'BANKER' pupils, thus are key informants in terms of helping us understand a paraprofessional experience which pre-dates that of the learning mentors. We will meet up with them again in Chapter 11.

Moving on down the corridor we pass through some double doors coming to the entrance of the Key Stage 3[9] Diner. Directly opposite are large institutionally generated notice boards displaying competitive year group statistics on homework completion targets, attendance and punctuality suggesting that the hidden curriculum is alive and well! A lack of both indoor and outdoor permitted social spaces is another issue of concern raised by some staff and pupils regarding this new-build school; the oblong buildings of the school we are currently touring are designed and built around an internal space referred to as 'the quad' which is an uncovered outdoor area that pupils access at break and lunchtimes. Continuing on from the Key Stage 3 Diner we come across classrooms designed for Textiles and Food Technology. One of these is used as a Breakfast Club and if we look through the glass section of the door we can see the three learning mentors, Angie, Paul and Cheryl setting out cereal, juice and toast whilst chatting to seated pupils and greeting those newly arrived. This is just one aspect of the mentors' work with which we will soon become thoroughly acquainted.

Continuing around the next corner we enter a long corridor where the pupil toilets are situated. These remain locked during lesson times— a measure brought in as a means to prevent internal truancy. One of the consequences of this is that it is not uncommon to come across lone pupils walking the corridors in lesson times searching for a member of the on-call team who are able to unlock one of the accessible toilets situated around the school. Now passing two Design and Technology classrooms, the corridor takes a slight dog-leg and we find ourselves outside the Mentor Base. Previously a large walk-in storage cupboard with a small adjoining office, it was then converted to serve as a small social space for pupils during break times and a forum for the learning mentors to carry out their one-to-one interventions during lesson times. Like Breakfast Club, we will be returning to this provision very soon.

Towards the end of this corridor is one of two newer Key Stage 4 Diners, created out of existing classrooms after the realisation that the original Diner was too small to practically cater for the school over a thirty minute lunch break when it was at full capacity. Beyond the Diners is a small office inhabited by the School's

---

[9]The first three years of High School for pupils usually aged 11–14 years.

attached Police Officer whenever he is on site. This peripatetic role came about due to the *Safer Schools Partnership* (The Police Foundation, 2011), a policy initiative which was intended to signal a new approach in school-police relations, leading to a greater police presence within many English state schools.

Close to the Police Officer's base is a much larger room which houses the school's own internal pupil referral unit (IPRU), run by Marie, a Teaching Assistant (TA) who, previous to this study, has also worked in the roles of learning mentor and Year Manager at the school. The IPRU is where pupils are given a final chance to engage before the imposition of permanent exclusion. It should not be confused with another provision, 'Internal exclusion', which is run by behaviour support workers and is tucked away at the end of a second-floor corridor. 'Inclusion' as it is simply referred to by staff and pupils alike has been rebranded nationally from its more traditional name of 'Isolation' (DCFS, 2009) which is perhaps a more familiar term to some older readers. It serves as a means to isolate pupils from their peers on a temporary basis and is a planned sanction for poor behaviour and/or repeatedly not adhering to school rules such as not wearing correct uniform.

We now climb some stairs to the first floor of the school. During the ethnography, anonymous concerns were expressed that a footfall analysis of subject areas had not taken place as part of the design process of the new build with the result that the darkest and narrowest stairwell led up to the busiest classes of Maths, Science and English. Along this corridor, photographic images of pupils have been utilised with the dual purpose of signposting subjects whilst 'advertising' each one in an appealing and marketable way. Taking into account the colourful bunting in the student reception along with the imaginative subject-promotion seen here, one gets the impression that staff are 'making the best of a bad job' with this particular new build.

10.00 a.m.

By now lessons are in full swing and as we pass each classroom, we hear snatches of sound: teachers in full pedagogical flow, the blare of audio-visual resources or the chatter of pupils in small group discussions. At this moment the corridor is empty apart from Kim, a behaviour support worker who is carrying out her 'on-call' duties. The walkie-talkie she is holding crackles into life as someone from Student Reception requests for 'on-call' to go to the assistance of a Science teacher who has activated this intervention via their classroom laptop. Such requests come about if a pupil's behaviour in class is disrupting learning in some way or the teacher needs a pupil to be escorted elsewhere. Confirming that she is on her way, Kim breaks into a brisk pace and on arriving knocks loudly on the open classroom door, greets the teacher and asks how she can help. Breaking off from her delivery, the teacher beckons to a pupil, Eddie, to come to the front and all three steps into the corridor just out of the view of the class who, from their seats, are watching keenly to see what happens next. The teacher briefs Kim as behaviour support worker, that she witnessed Eddie using his mobile phone to photograph another pupil's GCSE coursework; they had then instructed him to hand the phone over, a request he had refused, several times. Thanking the teacher for this information, Kim now turns to Eddie who is somehow managing to combine a wide smile with an outward show of being highly offended at the allegation, suggesting in turn to Kim that the teacher has 'lost it' and is 'proper "rajed"'.[10] Ignoring this depiction of her colleague, Kim calmly informs Eddie that if he hands his phone over now, he can go back into class and get on with his work. Eddie continues to deny the accusation and the teacher, perhaps sensing that this situation is not going to be resolved quickly, leaves them in the corridor and returns to her class closing the door firmly. Kim then tries a number of strategies to get Eddie to 'fess up'. First, she appeals to Eddie by pointing out how much more focused and engaged he has been in class recently compared to previous episodes of anger and poor behaviour which had resulted in numerous visits to Inclusion. Eddie however is not receptive and now clearly agitated, challenges Kim to 'search me if you don't believe me!' The behaviour support worker shakes her head sadly implying that she cannot believe it has come to this, then uses the aerial of her walkie-talkie to prod the pockets of Eddie's blazer. Her search of both Eddie and his bag (which has been retrieved from the classroom) fails to reveal a phone so Kim threatens to call the member of senior management who is also on-call, in effect ramping up the potential consequences. Eddie merely continues to protest his innocence and folding his arms and leaning against the corridor wall, refuses to cooperate with any further requests or instructions. Kim then tells Eddie that she will have to contact home because of his non-compliance and it is at this point that he explodes, marching off down the corridor shouting 'Oh my days! I don't believe this place!' As Kim alerts Student Reception that Eddie has gone 'AWOL', three loud beeps blare out, signalling the start of morning break. Within seconds, doors open and the corridor erupts with the sound of several hundred pupils emerging from their classrooms.

---

[10]'rajed' is slang to describe someone who is very annoyed or something which is seen as strange or weird.

Summary

This tour of a 'typical Monday morning' at Priory Park High offers a snap-shot of the school at the time of the study. The situations and observations recounted in this opening pen picture along with the discussion regarding significant developments that preceded it, are probably not that unique or remarkable, likely mirroring the fortunes and experiences of many other all-inclusive state schools as they deal with Ofsted inspections, league tables and the changing demographics of pupil populations. Of central importance in this account however is the prominence given to provisions and activities *away* from the classroom, carried out by those who are presented and understood generically as 'support' or pastoral staff. We met TAs and HLTAs, Pat, Cath and Marie who were tasked with running different provisions for students who struggle with or have been temporarily prevented from the mainstream classroom; behaviour support workers like Kim carrying out on-call duties and reacting to conflict situations as and when they arise. Finally, we briefly observed the learning mentors: Angie, Paul and Cheryl engaged in their first task of the day – Breakfast Club. It is this latter group who we turn to in the next chapter to begin a critical examination of the 'everyday work' (Smith, 2006) of this paraprofessional group.

Chapter 6

The Official and 'Seen' Work of the Learning Mentors

The purpose of this chapter is to convey the formal or what I have termed 'seen' aspects of the learning mentor role, namely Breakfast Club, the Mentor base and the one-to-one official interventions they are tasked with carrying out. Following the example of the 'guided tour' in the previous chapter the accounts given here are presented in blue type and gleaned from composite observations and 'interviews' with Angie, Paul and to a lesser extent Cheryl. The learning mentors are all of African-Caribbean background and have worked at Priory Park High for a number of years. Their paths to this work came about in part as a result of the New Labour policy agenda of *Excellent in Cities* and an increased emphasis on mentoring as a tool to work with young people perceived as 'disaffected' and/or having barriers to learning (as discussed in Chapter 2). The varying approaches adopted by the mentors were often consciously (and unconsciously) informed by a number of theoretical models. Their desire for genuine interaction with and an unconditional positive regard for pupils, illustrated elements of person-centred practice (Rogers, 1961; Rogers & Freiberg, 1994); They drew on the notion of the 'skilled helper' (Egan, 2005) in relation to pupils' problem management and opportunity development and one mentor in particular expressed a desire to implement the 'voluntary principle' when working with pupils which underpins British youth work practice (Batsleer & Davies, 2010). In combining these approaches, it became apparent that the mentors often navigated a 'tightrope' in supporting and occasionally advocating for pupils whilst simultaneously keeping teaching staff 'on-side'.

Breakfast Club

It is about ten to eight on a cold and damp Monday morning and the learning mentors are setting up Breakfast Club in the Food

Propping up the Performative School: A Critical Examination
of the English Educational Paraprofessional, 77–92
Copyright © 2022 by Jo Bishop
Published under exclusive licence by Emerald Publishing Limited
doi:10.1108/978-1-83982-242-120221006

Technology classroom; not the corporate-sponsored 'Greggs'[1]
version seen in some schools, but a home-grown provision initiated and run solely by the mentors themselves. Paul and Cheryl,
are setting out mini cereal boxes and jugs of milk whilst Angie
is methodically feeding bread into two toasters, adding to the
not insubstantial pile of golden brown toast already plated up.
Diamonds by Rihanna blares out from the radio as the pupils
of Priory Park High start to drift into the quad from the student entrance, some making their way over to Breakfast Club.
On arrival, one or two of them hand over a *Metro*[2] newspaper to
the mentors picked up from their bus journey and look exceed-
ingly happy when they are thanked profusely for this act. This
is just one of several daily rituals observed frequently at Breakfast Club, another being the warm welcome that pupils receive,
regardless of whether they are first-timers or regular attendees.
The rules of Breakfast Club are simple, pupils must sign in, eat
the food which is provided whilst sitting socially and then clear
up after themselves before leaving.

During the physical process of distributing the food, each of
the mentors takes the opportunity to interact more directly with
individual pupils. Their actions suggest that they know each one
well, such as the Year 11 girl who always gets the crust of the
bread saved back and toasted, this being her personal preference.
This morning, Taylor, a Year 7 pupil is excited to show Angie
a print-out of her family tree that she and her mum did at the
weekend and which seems to indicate that she is a very distant
cousin of Justin Bieber. Some of the older pupils seated at the
same table overhear Taylor's excited explanation and pause in
their own chat glancing over amusedly. One of them starts to say
something in a sneering tone but stops abruptly when Angie, who
has been engrossed in Taylor's print-out shoots them a warning
look. Joe, another Year 7 pupil who is usually very upbeat, displays a different demeanour today, opting to sit on his own at
another table. Paul joins him there asking how his recent rugby
league trials have gone.

Shaun, a Year 10 pupil, stands tentatively at the doorway and
asks if it is possible to see Angie in private. Breaking off from Taylor with an apology, the mentor beckons him into a small kitchen
which leads off from the main classroom. Sean wants to apolo-
gise for 'losing it' in the mentor base at lunchtime the previous

---

[1]Greggs is a national bakery chain in the UK. The 'Greggs Foundation' sponsors a
number of school breakfast clubs directly and indirectly.
[2]*A free daily national newspaper which is distributed to commuters on buses and trains.*

Friday. They spend a few moments discussing this incident and Angie warns him that if it happens again, he will forfeit the right to come into the base at break times. Shaun agrees looking relieved and Angie invites him to get some toast whilst Cheryl calls back another pupil who has just left, telling him in no uncertain terms to 'clear up your mess!' All three mentors 'tut-tut' and shake their heads in mock disapproval whilst the boy in question returns sheepishly to the table and gathers up the remains of his breakfast, the rest of the group looking on laughing. By now it is 8.15 a.m. and a few latecomers are admonished but never-the-less 'clucked around' by being handed hastily buttered toast wrapped in paper napkins which they are instructed to eat en route to registration because, the mentors tell them, 'It's important to have something in your tummies at the start of the day!' As the last pupil leaves, Paul and Cheryl clear away the toasters, radio and any unused items whilst sharing their observations of the pupils. Angie has left early in order to attend the weekly briefing taking place in the staff room.

During the ethnography I became a regular participant and active observer at Breakfast Club and was continually struck by how this one, relatively brief intervention met an array of young people's needs; from the more obvious supply of physical nutrition offered to the pupils (which they might not otherwise be getting), to the social and emotional dimension of this provision which was revealed in varying ways. Breakfast Club, as the first activity of the mentor's working day, encapsulated their approach in terms of how they viewed the pupils and worked with them, seeing them first and foremost as young people. The distinctiveness of the pupil/mentor relationship was clear to see: for example, the mentors were the only staff in school who pupils could address using their first names (although some still stuck with 'Miss' and 'Sir') and this seemed to afford a different relationship to other adults in the school. Furthermore, the way in which the mentors' modelled certain types of behaviour was also striking – sitting down to eat socially, actively listening to and interacting with others in a genuine and respectful manner, remonstrating with or challenging pupils when needed, but always in a way which focussed on the behaviour, rather than the person, thereby maintaining the approaches congruent with person-centred practice outlined above.

Breakfast Club provided a forum for pupils to spend 'downtime' with one another which, as could be seen in the guided tour, was a facility that was lacking at the school. Pupils attending this provision could rely on a consistently warm welcome and a positive affirmation of themselves as unique individuals be that through an acknowledgement of their food preference, a new hair style being commented upon or the recognition of an out-of-school achievement. It afforded pupils the opportunity to share problems, seek advice and in the case of Shaun, reflect on and then put right a previous incident before embarking on a new school day. Breakfast Club was also a tool for the mentors to constantly observe the presentations and demeanours of pupils, looking out for how these might change from day-to-day and week-to-week. Interactions with pupils enabled the mentors to gather, and where necessary, share with other staff what they had learned about any significant events that pupils might be experiencing both inside and outside of school. Thus, the wider benefits of Breakfast Club to the school seemed self-evident from the outset of the fieldwork period – a nourished and attended to pupil who was potentially more focussed and happier at the start of the school day.

Puzzling then that on arriving for my first day at the school and asking to be directed to this provision, the school receptionist and the three teachers who were also present at reception were unable to tell me of its actual location. Moreover, it received very little mention in the interview data subsequently generated apart from the Deputy Headteacher, who cited the provision directly when giving an example of how the mentors had carved out an identity around supporting 'vulnerable pupils'. As if to confirm this lack of presence in the school's organisational schema, there was no mention of Breakfast Club in the school prospectus, further suggesting that its place (and thereby those who ran it) was marginalised within the school. Drawing on a concept recognised in Institutional Ethnography, this situation illustrates a 'disjuncture' (Smith, 2005, p. 199) – on the one hand Breakfast Club exists, it is a social reality where, day in day out, a significant part of the mentors' work of establishing and building positive relationships with pupils takes place; but at the same time, in relation to both its (seemingly unknown) physical location and its textual absence in the school's promotional literature, it has an element of invisibility. Perhaps it is the comment made by the Deputy Headteacher above that helps us understand how this situation has come about, specifically her identification of those 'vulnerable' pupils who are more likely to use Breakfast Club, casting this as a provision for 'the other'. I had a brief glimpse of what happened when Breakfast Club was brought in from the margins and actively promoted to the majority which was during the period of GCSE examinations. At this time, both senior and middle managers encouraged pupils to leave home early and have breakfast at school in order to prevent lateness and optimise their performance in their exams. This led to a much busier Breakfast Club for a short period in which pupils attending for the first time sometimes appeared slightly uneasy in being at what they had previously perceived as something which 'wasn't for them'. For example, I observed how one pupil as part of a larger vocal and confident friendship group was looking around the room tentatively whilst queuing for toast and then asking of his peers: 'why are we here again?', to which the group's 'leader' rolled his eyes and replied 'Cos it's cool!'. Accepting this explanation, he overcame his unease and dived into the toast with no further need of encouragement. Thus, when linked with the core business of the school, in this case, exam preparation, Breakfast Club came in from the margins. At all other times, it remained peripheral and to some staff and pupils, entirely invisible.

Time Spent with Pupils – Building Relationships to Affect Change

Back to Monday morning and the bell for Period 1 has just sounded. As I accompany the three learning mentors from Breakfast Club to the Mentor Base I observe how their work of interacting and building relationships with pupils continues as they greet and are greeted by many pupils moving about the school. For example, one girl calls out to Cheryl: 'Are you around at lunchtime today? Can I pop in to see you?', whilst the other two mentors are conveying a sense of urgency to late-comers saying: 'Hurry to your class!' and 'Get to where you need to be', reinforcing this instruction to some with a mock 'kick up the bum'. The mentors also use their presence in the corridors to enforce school rules regarding correct uniform such as the boy wearing a prohibited baseball cap who Angie is now walking right up to exclaiming:

That's a nice hat; can I have it? It would look much better on me!

Their approach in these matters is noticeably less authoritarian in comparison to other staff and the boy half-smiles in response, sheepishly removing his cap before stuffing it into his bag. Acknowledging his compliance Angie smiles and shouts a 'Thank you!' over her shoulder and as we turn the corner, Paul laughs at this exchange informing me that 'We keep them on their toes!'

We arrive at the Mentor Base which, as observed in the guided tour, had formerly been a walk-in storage cupboard but has since been reconfigured as two rooms, the larger of which acts as a social area, open to pupils during most breaks and lunchtimes for chess, card games (UNO seems to be a particular favourite), and general socialising. The smaller room is set up as an office and overlooks the quad. Mind maps which are currently being promoted across the school as study aids are displayed on the walls of the Mentor Base. There are also posters advertising the learning mentor role which have been produced by pupils with experience of this intervention. One of them takes the form of an acrostic poem as a means to explain what the learning mentors do:

M ega helpful
E ncourgaing
N Nonsense
T alented
O ptimistic
R espectful
S urprising

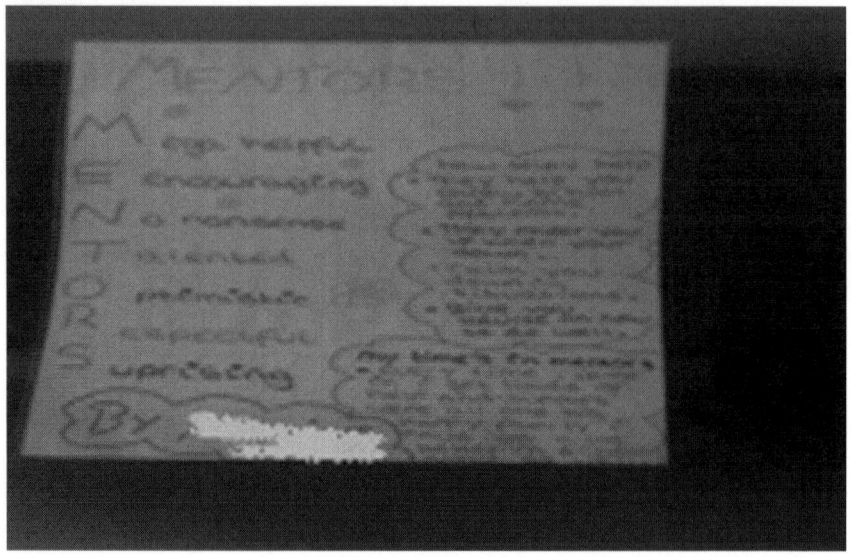

Other posters give pupil perspectives of what learning mentor support entails with statements like:

They help you threw [*sic.*] school and home problems.

They calm you down in situations.

They give you advice on how to do well.

Unlike the institutionally-generated notice boards hanging outside the Diner which focus on homework, attendance and punctuality, it is 'alternative' examples of learning and achievement that are celebrated here in the Mentor Base. One sign on the outside of the door to the base announces:

Aqeel only learned to play chess 5 weeks ago and now he smashes the opposition!!!

One-to-One Interventions: The 'Officials'

The way in which pupils access time with a mentor happens in a number of ways which can be understood as coming under two broad categories, the first being the 'officials' of which we will learn more about here. As the name suggests these are pupils whose need for a mentor is initially decided and then instigated by a member of school staff who is at middle-management level, usually a Year Manager (a non-teacher with pastoral responsibilities) or Progress Leader (a teacher who is responsible for the academic attainment of each year group). An official intervention lasts for a period of six to eight weeks and is intended to assist a pupil in overcoming their 'barriers to learning', which as discussed in Chapter 2 can have varying interpretations. However, sometimes official referrals take place for more pressing reasons such as the one outlined here:

An Official Referral to Engage Pupils with the School's Core Objectives

> We are well into Period 1 with lessons in full swing. During this part of the school day, the base is a fairly quiet yet industrious space as one-to-one interventions are carried out with pupils.
>
> This morning Cheryl is supporting a Year 11 pupil who has been sent by her Year Manager to complete a letter as part of an application to study at a local College of Further Education. A draft of this should have been completed some time ago and the pupil appears unenthusiastic about the task in hand saying:
>
> *Oh Cheryl, I don't what to do this, I can't write letters!*
>
> In an attempt to combine kindness and humour with a clear sense of purpose Cheryl responds:
>
> *Aw, don't you Honey? Oh well, welcome to the real world.*
>
> With much coaxing and encouragement the letter is eventually completed despite the pupil's reticence. Once the pupil has left I ask Cheryl about her approach and she maintains:
>
> *Well I'm not going to do it for them; that's not the real world and they've got to learn. She's had three months to do this!*
>
> Cheryl goes on to explain that sometimes it is more productive to focus on what pupils are actually doing rather than what they are saying. Angie, who is also present agrees, voicing that other

staff can sometimes get too hung up on what is coming out of pupils' mouths rather than whether or not they are actually getting on with a particular task. She recounts a recent example which typified this. A pupil had been sent to her by a Progress Leader to complete a piece of coursework but whilst getting on with it hadn't stopped talking or (as Angie described) 'complaining, you know, "effing" and "jeffing"[3], being really rude about a particular teacher who apparently (mimics pupil) 'hates me and really picks on me'. Angie had listened to the girl without being drawn into any of the comments about the teacher and spoke only in relation to the written piece as it was taking shape. Angie concluded:

She returned to the teacher with her course work completed which as it turned out was apparently to a good standard so … job done as far as I'm concerned.

'Welcome to the real world' along with '*Now* you're getting [understanding] it!' were phrases heard frequently in mentor–pupil interactions and used not just to introduce humour into a situation but also as a means to encourage pupils, particularly those in Key Stage 4, to acknowledge that the adult world is beckoning. The two one-to-ones set out above (one directly observed and the other recalled) offer further illustrations of the mentor–pupil relationship but also convey how the nature of such interactions lead to the achievement of wider school objectives. Obviously, the ratio of time to pupil numbers is clearly in the learning mentors' favour compared to teachers' situations but to see this simply as a matter of constraints on teacher time and numbers neglects the question of the *type* of approach underpinning this support. Specifically, the pupil–mentor relationship begins on first name terms and takes place outside of a formal classroom-setting in a space (the Mentor Base) where hostile outbursts expressed by the young person are tolerated and/or overlooked by the mentor in order to 'get the job done'. This produces positive outcomes for the school, which in the cases above are a college application and a completed piece of coursework – both tangible items of 'paperwork' which ultimately contribute to official school data regarding pupil destinations and academic attainment.

So far we have seen how official one-to-one mentor interventions are used to engage pupils with the core objectives of the school. We will now examine three further examples which illustrate the different reasons why one-to-one interventions were instigated by third parties. The first focusses on how the mentor interventions are used to complement other initiatives whilst the second has come about due to a pupil's changed demeanour in class. The third and final account titled 'Michael from Year 8', illustrates the concerns sometimes raised by mentors in relation to this aspect of their work.

---

[3]A colloquial term referring to someone who swears a lot.

An Official Referral Designed to Complement Other Interventions

Paul is also in the mentor base this morning working with a Year 7 boy (aged 11–12 years) who originally from Russia is now residing in the UK, which is the fourth country he has lived in to date. This intervention has again been set up by a third party but this time to complement another school provision as the boy is being supported predominantly by the EAL (English as an Additional Language) Department. The boy's Year Manager who requested the referral, is concerned that he is struggling to get to grips with this latest culture and language, notwithstanding the idea of forming lasting relationships with both teachers and pupils alike. Thus, the sessions with Paul focus on the pupil's social and emotional needs with the intention of building his self-confidence and resilience. Their interactions centre on the construction of a visual time-line which whilst drawing on his previous memories of significant events and people, also ties in with his hopes and fears for the future. In today's session I observe how through stilted conversation, numerous gesturing, written words, doodles and pictures, the time-line is starting to take shape. This one-to-one is more traditionally 'pastoral' in nature and the boy appears to very much enjoy this time spent with Paul.

An Official Referral Responding to a Changed Demeanour/ Behaviour of a Pupil

As we move into Period 2 Cheryl leaves the Mentor base to go out on a home visit and Paul's next one-to-one has arrived. Antony, who is a regular attender of the base at break times, has been referred to the mentor team due to concerns about his recent conduct in class. Not having raised any previous worries and being known as the youngest of three male siblings who have already been through the school, Antony's demeanour has changed since the start of Key Stage 4 and in class he is reported as being either completely unengaged or exhibiting low-level disruptive behaviour. The Progress Leader has expressed that Anthony might benefit from time with Paul as an 'older and wiser' male whom Antony already knows. In contrast with the last one-to-one, Pauls approach is noticeably different as he is much more direct from the outset, taking Antony to task regarding some 'silly behaviour' that had taken place in a lesson the week before. Antony agrees with Paul's assessment and appears initially embarrassed but then agrees to Paul's invitation to 'get to the bottom of this'. Later on when I ask Paul about his more direct approach with Antony the mentor explains that because Antony has been coming into the base at break times for so long he is considered to be 'family'. Elaborating further Paul says '... and what happens in families? They tell you when you've messed up!'

An Official Referral Over Which Mentors Have Reservations: Michael from Year 8

This morning Angie also has a one-to-one, scheduled with Michael from Year 8. While we wait for him to arrive, she tells me a little of the background to this intervention. Michael has been through most of the support systems in school with no apparent success and is now one step away from a 'managed move'. The time he is going to be spending with Angie is, in her view, a last ditch attempt by her managers 'who are scratching their heads about what to do next'. Michael's behaviour is deemed problematic in that he is described as attention-seeking and disruptive in class but not in a particularly hostile or aggressive way, quite the opposite in fact. Without disclosing any details, Angie tells me that his family are known to agencies external to school such as the Local Authority Social Services.

On seeing Michael approaching the base through the quad, Angie invites me to observe the session from another table and breaks off from our discussion to welcome him at the door. Far from showing any sign of fatigue at yet another intervention, Michael is clearly upbeat about being here and having his first meeting with Angie whom he knows from Breakfast Club. Angie explains my presence asking him if it is okay for me to remain. Knowing me a little also from Breakfast Club (he asked me about cycling as he saw me puffing up the hill one morning), Michael smiles at me and confirms that this is fine. Seated at a table in the social area of the base, Angie starts the session by handing Michael a piece of paper and a pen saying:

I want you to write down all the people who help you inside and outside of school.

To which Michael immediately responds:

I already told Miss – [Year Manager] all this. Can't you just ask her?

Angie smiles and says:

The thing you'll learn about me Michael is that I have a <u>very</u> bad memory so I need <u>everything</u> spelt out to me and written down.

Michael sets about his task and in less than a couple of minutes he flourishes the piece of paper at Angie asking:

Can we play cards now?

Ignoring his request she studies the piece of paper and exclaims:

This looks like a crime scene! Let's start again.

Getting out a fresh sheet she divides it into three columns. In the first column she instructs him to write down all the people that help him, both in and out of school. In the second column he is to write down what each person does and in the last, how he would describe his relationship with each of them. Angie finishes these instructions by saying:

I know you have already told Miss this but now I want you to write it down for me. I want to know your take on everyone and what they do.

She then joins me at my table and purposefully busies herself with some paperwork. Perhaps sensing that the game of cards is not going to materialise soon, if at all, Michael picks up his pen and starts to write calling over to Angie:

Does that kettle work?

Angie responds that *if* he works hard she *might* make him a cup of tea. Twenty minutes pass and Michael, who is now busily filling up the columns, hasn't spoken at all. Angie wanders back over to him and peering over his shoulder says 'Much better!' before asking 'how many sugars?'

Afterwards I ask Angie how she felt the session had gone. As often happens in our discussions she smiles ruefully and shrugs her shoulders saying:

If they [the school] want to tick a box because they want to exclude them, they are going to ask: 'have they had a learning mentor?' and if they have, they can get rid of them.

Expanding on this remark, she explains that as a team, the mentors feel that their work of building relationships in order to effect change is often used to meet other, less transparent objectives. She is concerned that this hidden agenda can undermine what her and her colleagues are attempting to do in their work of assisting pupils in removing their barriers to learning, in order that their participation in their schooling is either supported or resumed.

The question regarding the 'real' purpose behind this particular intervention with Michael is of course impossible to verify. Priory Park High, along with many schools at the time of this study, are under pressure to reduce exclusion figures (as noted in Chapter 2) and thus a variety of strategies are implemented, often underpinned by little more than a fervent desire that one of them 'might just work' for the pupil in question. However, an observation that the needs of the institution determine the agenda and goals of mentor relationships is useful to note here reflecting Colley's identification within Engagement Mentoring of the mentor becoming the 'vehicle for external interests' (Colley, 2003a, p. 37) rather than a facilitator for the mentee. In cases such as these, Colley argues, it would be more accurate to see the mentoring relationship as *triadic*, rather than in its traditional construction of a dyad. The extent to which the mentors resist the imposition of this third party was an issue I picked up with Angie who for her own reasons consciously set out to disrupt the orchestration of official referrals. To explain further, the vast majority of pupils referred officially, accepted a mentor intervention and appeared happy to receive their support and guidance. In spite of this, Angie felt it important that the referral was presented as an option, rather than something that the pupil was compelled to attend having been initiated by a third party:

> I'll say to that young person 'Miss — [the Year Manager] has come to me because she thinks you could do with some help. Do you know who I am? What my role is?' And I'll go through the reasons … what the Year Manager thinks and I'll say 'do you feel this is right what they are saying? Do you think you might benefit from talking and looking at different ways of coping and dealing with that situation? Does that sound alright? Are you interested? You can say 'no' …. I won't cry, I'm a big girl' then they'll laugh and go 'yeah, ok then'. I say 'I just have to make it clear that nobody is forcing you to have a meeting' …. I make it voluntary, because you can't force someone to come and see you. That just wouldn't happen, it wouldn't work. It might be the perception of others of how it should work but [stated emphatically] no!

In an earlier study (Bishop, 2011) I raised the issue of whether it is possible to see the learning mentor role as a youth worker operating in a school setting as opposed to their 'natural' territory of an informal education setting. Angie, who possessed a youth work qualification practises a key professional principle here by emphasising the voluntary relationship. Within the Youth Work profession, this is viewed not only as an abstract principle but also as a practical justification in that young people involved by choice are much more likely 'to *own* whatever gains they take away from that […] experience' (Batsleer and Davies, 2010, p. 2). In the extract above, Angie is keen to distinguish her approach from that of other staff, based on her belief that an intervention which is imposed on pupils or on which they are not consulted is not only undesirable, but would not achieve what it was intended to: 'you can't force someone to come and see you … it wouldn't work'. Her comments further imply that other staff, essentially those doing the referring, either do not agree with or more notably do not *understand* the need for this premise of voluntary participation: 'It might be the perception of others of how it should work but no'. At a number of points during the study, the mentors expressed that because pupils had so few opportunities to exercise choice within a formal education setting, they felt it important that conversations such as the one above characterised their approach. We return now to the mentor's day.

Morning Break – Mentor Base Becomes 'Youth Club'

The bell sounds again signalling the end of Period 2 and the start of Break time. In less than a minute, the base transforms from quiet work space to rowdy youth club. A lot of banter and the occasional swear word can be heard but in this part of the school the pupils generally police themselves with offenders hastily being told to 'shut up' in the knowledge that the mentors will close the base temporarily if the rules of its use are not respected. Paul joins in with a round of *UNO* which is played at a furious pace and which he loses, much to the delight of the pupils. Angie and Cheryl are in the office chatting with Becky, one of the peripatetic careers advisors. A Year 8 pupil hovers at the open door waiting to be invited in. He is eager to show Angie, seated at the desk, the new X-box which came out 'literally at midnight just gone!' Searching for an image of it on her laptop, she invites him to pull up a chair and as with Taylor's family tree at Breakfast Club, listens carefully whilst he tells her all about it. Later, using her position overlooking the quad she waves and calls out to some of the pupils there, addressing one boy in Jamaican patois to 'pull up your trousers 'bwoy' – we don't want to see your backside!' Beckoning two other pupils to the window, she asks one about their recent birthday celebration and the other how they have got on with some course work she had supported them with at homework club the week before.

Spontaneous Ad Hoc Interventions – The Angry Year 11 Girls

Break time now over, pupils are hurried off to lessons and the base is restored to its former quiet and calm space. Angie is in the office making her way through a list of telephone calls to parents whilst Paul is settling into another one-to-one in the social area of the mentor base. Twenty minutes later the relative peace of the base is shattered abruptly as two, highly agitated Year 11 pupils burst in demanding to see a mentor. Angie quickly ushers the girls into the office so as not to disrupt Paul and his mentee, asking them which lesson they have just walked out of. She gestures for them to sit quietly whilst she phones Student Reception requesting that they let the on-call person know that the girls are with her. Then, turning to face the girls Angie suggests that they try to calmly explain what has just happened. Speaking in quick and angry bursts, sometimes at the same time, they tell her that some boys in their class were being racist (the girls are Black African/ Caribbean heritage whilst the alleged perpetrators are of Somali and Pakistani heritage).

[…] Saying how we live in trees and stuff … but the teacher did nothing!

The girls say this is not the first time this has happened by which they mean both the boys' comments and the teacher's apparent lack of intervention. Once the girls have finished speaking, Angie pauses for a moment and then asks for and writes down the names of the boys, informing the two pupils that she will speak to both them and the teacher about the incident over the next few days. She gently puts it to the girls that in one day, teachers will see around 150 different pupils suggesting therefore that it must be difficult for them to remember every single event. Having set out this point she invites them to imagine what it must be like to manage a group of 30 people who, unlike them, do not all want to listen and engage. Angie then suggests a further possibility for what unfolded in the lesson saying:

Maybe this teacher lacks experience or confidence in dealing with this issue [of racism] – can you blame her for not being bold?

By this point the girls have visibly calmed down and the mentor asks them to think about more constructive ways they could have dealt with this situation rather than simply walking out of the lesson. Reflecting on this, one of the girls suggests 'wait until the end of the lesson and then speak to our Head of Year?' (meaning the Progress Leader) and, nodding vigorously in response, Angie affirms this to be a very good strategy adding that they could tell the Head of Year how the situation is 'affecting your learning', reminding the girls that as the Progress Leader's role is to oversee educational attainment 'this is the kind of language she will understand!' Angie then advises the girls to keep not only their English teacher but, 'all your teachers "on-side"', pointing out how important it is to maximise their working relations at this stage in their school career thereby giving them the best chance to 'achieve the results you want'. This entire interaction has lasted no longer than fifteen minutes but the girls, now appearing visibly placated, get up to leave. Abruptly switching to a noticeably more authoritarian tone, Angie instructs them to go straight back to class asking: 'Do you feel the situation has been dealt with for now?' to which they nod. She continues:

So there will be no need to walk out again. I don't want to hear that you've gone back in there and kicked off again.

Assuring her that this will not happen, the girls thank Angie and leave. Paul's session has just finished and he joins us in the office to get the 'low down' on what has just occurred. Angie discloses that in her view incidences of pupils racially abusing other pupils have not always been dealt with effectively by the school, to which Paul agrees, 'but' says Angie 'I make it my business to ensure that they are taken seriously'.

This incident is a key piece of data. At the micro level it gives a detailed and accurate picture of what learning mentors do in that an incident brought to the attention of the mentors by pupils, was utilised to encourage those young people to reflect on events from viewpoints other than their own and develop strategies to deal with conflict constructively. Within exchanges such as these, the mentor ensures that the onus is on what the pupils *themselves* can do to resolve the issue rather than looking to support staff to take it up on their behalf. In that sense it provides an apt example of Egan's 'problem-management, opportunity development' approach facilitated in this instance by Angie as the 'skilled helper'. It further illustrates how the mentors can walk a thin line in not colluding with pupils who are expressing negative views about other staff whilst also advocating *for* the pupil/s in the sense of giving them a platform to speak about their experiences, air their views and feel genuinely listened to. The mentors recognise that as the stakes are high for these pupils in the final year of High School, they are more likely to secure an intervention at middle-management level if it is framed around their learning and the results they could potentially achieve. This is evidence of how operating in a performative culture (a concept introduced in Chapter 2 and which I return to in Chapter 12) influences those everyday school-based micro interactions.

What is not known is how the teacher in question felt about pupils simply walking out of their lesson to seek out another member of staff. The incident also raises wider concerns: for instance, whether pupil-to-pupil racism is being brushed under the carpet in the school's haste to drive up its academic standards and regain its previous standing; an issue which has been noted elsewhere in the English educational landscape (Belgutay, 2016). In a separate discussion, the issue of racism was also identified by one of the other learning mentors, recalling how the school residential had been an effective way of working intensively with pupils on this issue. Unfortunately, this was no longer formed part of the school's offer. When I asked why, the mentor did not know, having not been informed of the reasons.

Formal, 'Seen' Provisions – A Partial Picture?

This chapter has set out the formal (official) or 'seen' activities of the mentors' work, illustrating the varying approaches used by the mentor team as they seek to support pupils who find it difficult to access formal learning and/or build positive relationships with their peers and teachers. It is clear how the mentors' work activities contribute to the school's pastoral endeavours be that in the bodily and emotional nourishment of pupils at Breakfast Club or the facilitation of more informal education 'youth work' type relationships in the Mentor Base during break times. It has also conveyed a series of one-to-one interventions which although instigated for different reasons, offer pupils qualitative and nurturing time away from the classroom, in which they are sometimes challenged and asked to account for their own actions/behaviour, albeit in a safe and supportive environment.

What is less apparent at first notice is how these interactions, both big and small, planned or ad hoc, also enable the school to continue in its path to 'recovery' in retaining its status as a 'Good' school. Thus, ensuring that a college application is completed; working intensively with a pupil by taking him away from a class because his behaviour is deemed as having a negative impact on others' learning and therefore potentially their results; and finally, keeping 'BANKER' pupils such as the Angry Year 11 girls, focussed on the 'prize' despite the mentors' own misgivings about the inadequacy of the school's response to issues like pupil-to-pupil racism.

But to look only at the activities that the mentors are *formally* tasked with – i.e., their 'seen', official work – gives only a partial picture. The next chapter starts by focussing on the less formal or 'unseen' domain of their work, predominantly those pupils who the mentors describe as their 'unofficials'. In examining the varying natures of these interactions the discussion highlights the peripheral nature of the mentors' work and role, raising questions about the mentors' relative *in*visibility and the liminal spaces they occupy. This aspect of their work becomes even more apparent through an examination of pupil perspectives/understandings of the mentor role and how this is situated within their wider school experience.

Chapter 7

The Unofficial and 'Unseen' Work of the Learning Mentors

In Chapter 2, it was noted that the phrase 'removing barriers to learning' had become synonymous with the work of learning mentors and that policy documents tended to locate such barriers as 'deficits' within the pupils' lives and circumstances, citing examples like behavioural problems, persistent absenteeism, difficulties at home and poor study or organisational skills (Department for Education and Skills, 2001b). No evidence was offered as to how these barriers had been arrived at and the voices of children and young people were, quite simply, absent at the level of policy conception and implementation. Furthermore, it was notable that barriers to learning were not seen to have arisen as a result of (for example) a prescribed curriculum in terms of both content or delivery, nor the emphasis on academic attainment as the measure of 'success'. This context is important when considering the previous chapter which offered an examination of the 'official' or 'seen' everyday work of the learning mentors; important because it shows how those approaches envisaged in government documentation were realised in practice. Thus, third party engineered one-to-ones that combined learning and pastoral care were regarded as both appropriate and adequate in terms of helping pupils navigate their way through secondary schooling.

In contrast, this chapter draws on data which reveal the 'behind the scenes' or what I have designated as the 'unseen' aspects of mentors work. Following the protocol set out in the previous two chapters, the accounts given here are presented in as indented text and gleaned from composite observations and 'interviews' with key participants following the typical day scenario used thus far. To ensure that children and young people's voices are captured and included in my analysis, this chapter also presents pupil data which evidence their understanding of the mentor role and crucially on whether/how they distinguish it from other staff roles. A key aspect under consideration is the focus on pupil agency in relation to how they navigate pastoral systems, deciding on when and how support is accessed. However, in order to provide a meaningful context to the pastoral provisions under discussion, I deemed it necessary to explore with pupils their more general experiences of and perspectives on their schooling. A reminder

Propping up the Performative School: A Critical Examination
of the English Educational Paraprofessional, 93–106
Copyright © 2022 by Jo Bishop
Published under exclusive licence by Emerald Publishing Limited
doi:10.1108/978-1-83982-242-120221007

to the reader that in the earlier discussion regarding methodological approach (Chapter 4) I argued that one aim of the research was to draw on children and young people's experiences of school as 'work knowledge[s]' and therefore refer consciously to them as 'pupils' in their undertaking of this 'everyday life work' (Smith, 2005).

Working in the Unseen Domain: Mentors and Their 'Unofficials'

The first identification of the way in which mentors worked unofficially with pupils was when a young person themselves would 'call in' short-term help from someone who they saw as a credible adult. Although contact was minimal, the example below can still be described as an unofficial mentor–pupil interaction.

Fleeting Encounters

> It is lunchtime and the Mentor Base, reverting to its youth club function, is starting to fill up again. Paul is gobbling down a microwaved meal prior to the football club which he runs twice a week. As he leaves, an older pupil, perhaps Year 10 or 11, appears at the entrance of the mentor base and looks furtively around in the corridor before ducking inside and making a bee-line for Cheryl. A whispered discussion ensues which lasts no more than twenty seconds during which Cheryl reaches for a directory of local health and welfare services, flicks through its pages and then scribbles something on a piece of paper which she passes to the pupil. Nodding her thanks, the young person shoves it in her blazer pocket and leaves in a similar manner to how she arrived.

Later I asked Cheryl whether (confidentiality permitting) she is able to explain what had happened in this interaction. Cheryl refers to this pupil as 'one of our "unofficials"' explaining that the girl had stopped her in the corridor last week to ask for some information that might help her deal with an issue that her older sibling was experiencing but that she did not want anyone, friends included, to know about. In this instance then an 'unofficial' is a pupil whose need for help is of a fleeting and/or practical nature and the role of the mentor is to act merely as a signposting service.

Long-term and Complex Unofficial Interventions

Pupils Self-referring

More common however were those pupils who referred themselves to a mentor for unofficial meetings. In contrast to the prescribed six- to eight-week period on which official referrals were premised, unofficial interventions could take place intermittently over periods of weeks, months and sometimes even years. The 'unofficials' in these instances were young people dealing with complex issues in their everyday lives. One example was a Year 11 pupil 'Josie', who had initially approached Angie some months earlier, independently of her Year Manager – the person that pupils were normally instructed to approach as their first 'port of call' pastorally speaking. In their first meeting Josie had disclosed to Angie that her home life was in turmoil due to her parents separating and her mother having left the family home then subsequently returning some months later. During the time of her mother's absence, Josie, as the oldest of three siblings had become more involved in caring for the family in terms of preparing meals and helping her father with other day-to-day domestic tasks. In later meetings, she expressed anger towards her father, disagreeing with his decision to accept her mother back into the family home feeling that she was not genuine in her motives for wanting to return.

Being present in the mentor base for at least one of these sessions, I was struck by the way in which the learning mentor supported Josie in what could be considered a very adult conversation. Through discussion and gentle questioning, Angie helped the pupil explore her immediate situation and then family relations in a wider sense. In time, she was encouraged to start to see her parents beyond *her* immediate relationship with them; that is, not only as parents but people who, like her, faced changes and challenges in their daily lives. This unofficial intervention illustrated a young person seeking support that was entirely 'off' the radar in terms of by-passing official pastoral systems.

Mentor-initiated Unofficial Interventions

A further type of 'unofficial' intervention observed were those initiated by the mentors themselves. Although not pupil-instigated I have classed these as 'unofficial' because the mentors, as a discrete staff team, had limited to no input in the formal referral process, a situation which will be examined in more depth in Chapter 10. To learn more about this particular aspect of the mentors' work we return to the Mentor Base at the end of a school day:

> The bell has just sounded signalling the end of the formal teaching day and Paul is gathering up the materials needed for Homework Club which he is facilitating today. Angie is waiting for Sally, one of her unofficials to arrive. The meeting has come about because some months ago Angie had noticed a change in this pupil's demeanour and decided to approach her. After one or two informal chats, Sally had then shared with Angie that she was worried about her mum who had started drinking at home during the day, making it hard for Sally to focus in lessons. Sally's overriding concern was for her mum, but also how this inability to concentrate during the school day was going to affect her performance in her GCSEs. As her disclosure suggested a potential safe-guarding issue, Angie duly alerted and informed the relevant Year Manager and also suggested to the Director of Pastoral

Care (part of the Senior Leadership Team) that Sally might benefit from a learning mentor intervention – in effect asking for the pupil to be referred to the mentoring team as part of their official caseload. This request was however denied with no reason given. A few weeks after her initial disclosure, Sally had come to the Mentor Base to speak with Angie, having just had a heated argument with a one of their peers. Unable to find Angie who was not in school at that time, Sally had ended up punching a wall, rather, she said, 'than the boy who was winding me up'. Having heard about this incident on her return to school, Angie had eventually caught up with Sally and arranged to meet briefly with her after school today.

On her arrival Sally receives the usual warm greeting characteristic of pupil–mentor interactions. Angie explains my presence by telling Sally about my research and in particular my interest in how the learning mentor role is perceived by pupils. Thinking about this for a few seconds Sally replies:

Like an older sister … [pauses] … or maybe mother …?

At this latter depiction, they each burst into spontaneous laughter joking that if that were the case then Angie should be getting Sally a Christmas present although Sally says she would be happy with just 'a period [session] with you and a cup of tea'. Angie agrees to this and jokingly asks what present she will be getting to which Sally replies humorously 'my company for an hour!' Angie then raises the 'punching the wall' incident asking Sally if she is happy for me to remain. Sally nods her consent and tells Angie that immediately after it had happened, other staff, including the school's attached police officer had intervened. As a sanction for her actions Sally was told she would have to attend the Anger Management programme (run by the behaviour support team). Not very happy about this outcome, Sally explained: 'I told them about my mum but I don't think they listened to me'. Angie advises Sally that she might have to just 'suck it up' and suggests that she might even find the sessions helpful. Sally shrugs then the discussion moves on as Sally starts to tell Angie about a part time job she has just secured which she is both excited and nervous about. After she leaves, I ask Angie about the decision to refer the pupil to a behaviour modification intervention. Smiling wryly, she expresses that it doesn't seem like an appropriate or adequate response given what Sally has disclosed about her home life but that it illustrates yet example of the 'tick-box' approach taken by the school, meaning, that a process has been duly followed in that the pupil in question had been referred for an intervention so the matter was dealt with.

What is striking about this incident is that the initial request for an official referral by the learning mentor was refused by her line manager whose response to the 'hitting the wall' incident was to immediately refer the matter to the school's police officer, followed up with a more mid-term intervention of the Anger Management programme. Had this pupil had a learning mentor intervention when her need was first identified, there is the possibility that things might not have escalated as they did or that Sally might have been empowered to develop skills that would enable her to deal with conflict more constructively. Sally's need for support was subordinated, until a point was reached where she was at risk of being blamed and potentially excluded (had she assaulted the boy instead of hitting the wall). Thus, it was her angry behaviour, rather than her need for emotional support which came to be seen as the primary issue. This situation further illustrates the contested nature of pastoral care as measures which can be both supportive and punitive. Some might well view a six-week course in Anger Management as being supportive but a counter argument is that the programme merely offers pupils the 'opportunity' to take responsibility for this aspect of their behaviour but with minimal support, summed up bluntly by another paraprofessional Marie (who at the time of the ethnography was working as a TA but had previously held posts of both learning mentor and Year Manager) as:

> We are telling children to be more in touch with their feelings and then when they are, it's like … well get on with it.

Pupil Perspectives of the Mentor Role

Notions of the Familial in Both Name and Presence

Sally's description above of the learning mentor as an 'older sister' or 'mother' was one of many 'familial' identifications which emerged from discussions with pupils as well as observations of pupil–mentor interactions. For example, Paul, being the 'elder' of the mentor team was often referred to as 'Gramps' by male pupils, particularly during periods of down time such as playing card games in the Mentor Base at lunch break. Another similar viewpoint which distinguished the mentors from other school staff, was how they were likened to a 'friend' as shown here by Eliza, a Year 11 pupil who was asked how she would explain the learning mentor role to people who were not familiar with it:

> I'm pretty sure they're just here to talk to people … I've been talking to Angie about her role … she says 'one of the main things I do is observe' and she observes everyone and even when you don't realise she's doing it she observes everyone, how they look, how they act, how they present themselves, because a lot of people aren't gonna tell you how they're feeling so it's kind of her job to observe how people are feeling. They run clubs and stuff like that, I know Paul goes out and plays football with everyone and I think [pauses] they are just … here. I'm pretty sure they've probably got

a deeper job than what they do behind all that but to the kids, their perception [is that] they are there like an older friend … like someone you can talk to, someone you can be close with.

Describing the mentor 'like an older friend', Eliza fuses notions of friendship with the seniority ascribed to some family members expressed prior to that by Sally. This is reminiscent of two conceptualisations which appeared as part of a typology of mentoring forms developed from research conducted with young people (Philip & Hendry, 1996). First, it is possible to see in the pupil's descriptions, the 'classic' style of mentoring where young people identified an older, more experienced person who is seen as a role model that gives recognition to the mentee through supporting and challenging them. However, the typology also referred to a more 'long-term' form of mentoring with 'risk taking' adults who although similar to 'classic' mentoring in many respects, were also perceived by the young person as adults who resisted (dominant) adult definitions of the social world and were therefore seen as more credible and accessible (in contrast to say the young person's own parent). Although the typology was generated through research undertaken in less formal contexts such as youth work provisions, it is possible to see how these formulations of the 'classic' and the 'risk-taking' can be applied to the learning mentors in school settings. From Eliza's comments it is possible to strip the learning mentor role down into its key functions: someone 'you can talk to', someone 'you can be close with' and someone who maintains a constant presence – 'they are just … here' – in their work of looking over, and 'looking out' for pupils. This constancy in the sense of being dependable and enduring, contrasts with how other avenues of support in the school were viewed, as although some of the pupils talked about having good relationships with teachers, these arose and were premised much more on support with their formal learning. Only one member of the teaching staff, a Drama teacher, was perceived in a similar way to the mentors and in this instance the pupil in question had spent a significant amount of time with this teacher through her involvement in school productions.

Similar themes are identified in this extract of a paired interview with two Year 11 pupils, Teisha and Lenny who were asked about the learning mentor role. Interestingly their answers incorporate both descriptive elements of the role as well as comments about the individual mentors themselves which again emphasises the importance of the relationship:

Teisha: Everyone in the school … [Lenny interjects] loves them [the learning mentors].

Teisha: Yeah, they're like trustworthy, they're easy to get on with straight away.

Lenny: They are friendly. To be respectful you can call them Miss ----- but when you get to know them you can call them Angie or Paul; you know like at a youth centre? They're like someone you'd see at a youth centre and they are friends with you instead of teachers.

Jo:	So is it a different kind of relationship to other adults in the school?
Both:	Yeah.
Teisha:	It is more like your friendship group than they are your learning base if you see what I mean. So I talk to Angie in the same way I talk to Lenny.
Jo:	And how would you describe the role to others who didn't know it?
Lenny:	They are always there – especially when you need them. When I needed Angie in Year 10 I would come down here [the mentor base] and I would just sit with her. When I first came here to Angie it was then, like hard times, yeah? But now I can just come in and say 'hi' and end up talking for about 20 minutes …. so it's just somewhere you can go to talk. It's like it doesn't feel like you're at school (Teisha and Lenny).

The first half of this account identifies the mentor as something different to other adults in the school – *'they are friends with you instead of teachers',* whilst in the latter half the theme of constancy is yet again clear to see: *'They are always there – especially when you need them'.* For Lenny, the relationship had come about due to difficulties she was experiencing, summed up above as *'hard times'.* But the longevity of the relationship was evident, cemented through her continuing to make ad hoc 'social visits' to see Angie once her difficulties had been resolved and she no longer needed that support. Also, of note here is how this account views the Mentor Base, being likened to a *'youth centre'* which suggests a space which is perceived to be something different to and separate from the school despite the fact that its actual physical location was positioned deep within the school estate.

Pupil Understandings of Different Forms of Support

The degree of young people's agency in their decisions to seek support was also something that pupils themselves identified during the study, specifically when asked a question about who pupils could go to for support *in* school regarding difficulties they were experiencing *outside* of school? One response given by Teisha and Lenny was that it depended very much on what the difficulty was with the pupils offering two hypothetical situations to explain their answer. In the first scenario they talked of a pupil who was in imminent danger due to a child protection matter which they deemed as 'serious' suggesting that in this case they would talk to either the Year Manager or Progress Leader, who they saw as authority figures and crucially people who had the power to intervene and 'contact social services'. For situations which were impacting on the pupil but in a less serious way, that is, something which did not necessarily require any outside intervention, they felt that pupils would go to the mentors because they 'just talk to you about it more'.

Mentors More 'Available' and More 'In-tune'

Pupils also voiced how accessible and available mentors were in comparison to teachers. Some pupil participants perceived the learning mentors as having a better understanding about the potential sensitivity of conflict within peer and friendship groups, seeing mentors as willing to take the pupil's lead in terms of deciding what type of action should be taken, or, whether any should be taken at all. Here a Year 11 pupil 'Alison' talks about one of the mentors:

> Angie … she'd just sit and listen … she'd never go directly to the person unless you asked her to, whereas the teachers, I think they just jump into it and think 'right we need to sort it now' [but] it doesn't get sorted, usually it makes it worse because you end up being seen [by your peers] as … [pauses and thinks] … a bit of a snitch somehow.

Shaun, a Year 11 pupil who we met earlier at Breakfast Club, also recognised this ability of the mentors to be closer to and therefore have a better grasp of pupil situations. He attributed this to how their work positioned them much more alongside pupils, perhaps based on his own observations from being a regular attender in the Mentor Base at break times:

> Well, their job is better than a teacher, because they get to understand more aspects about pupils and know things about them and they're a lot more social, like a big kid of their own.

As is apparent from the two examples just given, pupils identified and drew out a number of comparisons between the approaches of the mentors and teaching staff. Shaun's observations that the mentors *'understand more aspects about pupils'* linked with another issue of concern that some teachers did not appear to know how to 'do' emotional support or did not feel comfortable in this aspect of their role. Here Eliza explains:

> I've noticed how a lot of teachers don't know how to deal with like a crying child! It's difficult but if a person starts crying they're like [quietly] 'oh, do you want to go outside?' Or … 'cheer up!' and it's like [they] don't really seem to know what to do in situations like this. (Eliza)

To illustrate this observation, she described an occasion where having finished a controlled (timed) assessment she returned to a lesson and noticed one of her peers was crying. The teacher present had immediately approached Eliza and whispered an instruction that she should go and talk to the crying pupil. Feeling that this instruction was 'a bit strange given that he was the authority figure' she had found herself in the position of encouraging the teacher in his role, recalling this situation as: 'I told him "but you can talk to her, you are a teacher!"' to which he responded that as a girl of the same age she would deal with it better. Clearly this is only one example of a teacher not feeling comfortable or confident in tackling an issue they were being presented with and is certainly not intended to represent the profession as a whole. However, it is interesting that Eliza recalled this incident when asked a question about any changes that she as a pupil, would like to see in schools and/or the education system more widely, ending the account of the incident above with the words:

> So that's one of the things I would say; make sure people can deal with it [emotional upset]. (Eliza)

Clarifying that by 'people' she meant teachers in this instance but extending this point further still, she expressed the view that knowing how to deal appropriately with pupils' emotional upset and distress was 'surely a basic skill that any adult working in a school needed to be in possession of!', a comment that was particularly striking coming off the back of a discussion about how she considered the learning mentors to be very skilled in this respect.

Pupils' School Experiences

It became evident through data generated with pupils that the mentors were very much in tune with pupils' perceptions of, and feelings about their school experiences. It is important to note that the activities of other support staff also enabled this knowledge of pupil experiences. For example, during one of the 'on-call' (corridor patrol) sessions I undertook with a member of the behaviour support team, I could see how they too were able to quickly assess how pupils were feeling, particularly when exam deadlines were looming and the team noticed an increase in disruptive and challenging behaviour. The crucial difference between these two paraprofessional roles however was that the mentors' everyday work afforded them time to explore these incidents and work with pupils in both the short and long-term. In contrast, the behaviour support role had a more reactive, punitive function with limited opportunities to sit down with the pupil and discuss more constructive courses of action in the future, given that their conversations usually happened whilst walking down the corridor on the way to a removal room with a pupil who was often in a highly emotional state.

The 'Everyday Work' of Pupils: '… Expect To Be Disappointed Because Everything You Do Is Never Good Enough'

In the interests of establishing a broader context to the situation in which pupil–mentor interactions occurred, I turn now to a more in-depth discussion of pupil experiences of their formal education. Adhering to ethical practice whilst in the research field, these experiences were investigated and constructed indirectly through the aforementioned 'alien question' (set out in an earlier discussion of ethical research procedure in Chapter 4) along with a 'magic wand' question where pupils were asked what they would wish to change about schooling and education more generally. In answering these questions, some participants clearly chose to draw on their peers' experiences as well as their own and the issue most talked about by pupils who identified as cisgender female, was a feeling of being under relentless pressure to try and attain what were, in their view, unrealistic academic standards. For many, the locus of this pressure lay in target grades. Here, pupils expressed frustration that assessments they underwent at the age of ten or eleven years old, predicted what grade would be achieved five years later. This prediction was then ever-present and, if not being achieved, appeared quite literally as an amber or red area on a pupil's progress report, which in their words '[put] a downer on things' (Alison) or '[left] you no room for failure' (Eliza). Alongside this, pupils were extremely aware of what had at the time been a shifting of grade boundaries by examination bodies which in their view would lead to lower grades, as Lenny stated:

> [...] grade boundaries keep going up, so it looks like we are going down.

The conclusion that many pupils drew from this was illustrated by Teisha's apt advice to 'the alien' in its quest to know more about school:

> [...] expect to be disappointed because everything you do is never good enough

and expanded on this by explaining that pupils were required to do pieces of work again and again to make it 'better' although 'better' was not always explained sufficiently.

'Enrichment' – Attempts to Offer Something Beyond Academic Targets

In what might initially appear as contradictory to this perceived relentless pressure to achieve academically, the issue of enrichment was also identified by many pupils as a focus of their concern. In this particular context 'enrichment' meant pupils being encouraged to undertake activities other than those associated with formal learning. One pupil (Alison) said she was aware that teachers were required to fill out spread sheets 'on what we do outside of school' but feared that these were 'a bit thin'. During the period of time that the ethnography was conducted, the school launched a project named 'Recharge and Refuel' with two aligned purposes of increasing in-school enrichment for all pupils in the form of lunchtime and after-school clubs, and to involve older pupils in the leading, organising, and running of these activities so they might gain skills beyond those that were purely academic. The rationale for the project was explained by the Headteacher who felt strongly that within the current context, eleven years of education amounted only to 'targets which the school had to hit' and thus neglected other important preparations for the world 'out there':

> Children don't see and experience the skills that you learn and acquire across the piste that we apply to the workplace.

The Headteacher envisaged that the project would provide a balance between academic and non-academic activities within school and simultaneously enable some pupils to contribute whilst developing wider skills. However, both pupil and mentor accounts saw the actualities of the project in a different light with the former asking how this could realistically be accommodated alongside the expectations around their academic work. Eliza was encouraged to get involved in the project to develop her leadership skills through her involvement in a peer-mentoring programme and talked about the problems she had encountered:

> [...] they [teachers, senior leaders] don't realise that the 'freedom' (uses her fingers as connotation marks) given to the pupil leaders is hard to put into practice [For instance], getting messages to other pupils, [and] setting up meetings. They [teachers and senior leaders] expect a lot of the older children ... [and when things don't go to plan] ... people feel like they're just disappointing the teachers.

The introduction of 'Recharge and Refuel' had ironically ended up with herself and her peers actually feeling more pressured. This state of affairs was in turn recognised by the learning mentors who came to refer informally to the launch of the project as 'Weepy Week' due to the steady stream of older pupils dropping in to the mentor base, tearful and 'stressing' about how they were going to fulfil their new leadership roles *and* keep up with their work.

This tension between off-setting the desire (and need) for pupils to achieve certain grades with ensuring extra-curricular experiences were offered and taken up, was explored during the pupil interviews by discussing the varying levels of importance that the school applied to each (academic work or enrichment). All of the respondents saw the school's priority as being academic attainment and for some pupils like Mina this was not problematic referring to 'the push you get to get your grades' as one of the positive aspects of the school. Others, like Eliza, had a broader recognition of how academic attainment was tied more closely with the school's recent history and was therefore aware of what was riding on her Year's performance:

> I think at the moment it's grades because the school was in a bad place quite a while ago because of the whole Ofsted thing so they're very big on getting everyone's grades back up ... but they still put on the whole pressure of [mimics teachers] 'but you still need to build your CV up... you aren't going to get into university if you don't have all these certain things because a lot of people are getting all the grades now so you have to have the extra stuff' and we are just like 'oh [exasperated] okay then' [resigned].

Underpinning many of the comments and views expressed by the pupils was a feeling that the higher up Secondary School you went, the harder things became. For example, a viewpoint expressed by older pupils was that they did not enjoy coming to school anymore and when asked if they could pinpoint the time at which they stopped enjoying it, their response was usually from Year 9 (13–14 years) onwards:

> We didn't get prepared for how bad it was going to get. Teachers don't realise the pressure we're under [or that] the enjoyment's been taken out of it … when I think about school now I just think 'uhh' (upper body droops) [But] when I was younger I thought school was the best place in the world! (Louise)

And in the words of another pupil:

> Two weeks ago for about a week … I thought I was like seriously depressed because …. I don't even know what was going through my head but it was proper hard. I wasn't suicidal but just being in High School made me think like 'what's the point in living if we're just going to live to die' and stuff like that [laughs] but it's because of what High school does to you … I don't think High School should be fun but it shouldn't (pauses to think) make me think about my life that deep like I did for that week! (Teisha)

Mentor Responses to Pupil Experiences: '… They Tread So Carefully … Some of Them Don't Even Want to Tread At All!'

For their part, the mentors were keenly aware of the pressure voiced by the pupils above, particularly those who had been identified as 'Gifted and Talented'; a strand of *Excellence in Cities* that along with the learning mentor role had survived the policy's demise in 2008. The mentors however saw the source of the pressure as not just coming from within the school but also the home environment (parents, older peers) *and* the pupils themselves. As such, one mentor saw part of her approach as reassuring pupils that it was alright not to be good at everything, observing that:

> They [the pupils] become despondent and beat themselves up, and there's so many of them, even when they've gone on to the Sixth Form …. who struggle with failure and think it is better not to try than try and get it wrong.

In relation to this fear of failure, she saw it as her role to reassure pupils that it was acceptable, indeed necessary, to get things wrong:

> Giving them that reality check that it is okay to fail …. getting them used to making mistakes.

Here the mentor made specific reference to some pupils who spent a significant amount of time playing computer games where repeatedly making mistakes and starting again (and again!), was the order of the day. But this was in great contrast to their real lives because:

> [...] they don't want to try it [because] there's no restart button (chuckles) ... they tread so carefully ... some of them don't even want to tread at all! But they have to, they are being pushed and it overwhelms them.

These are extremely useful observations in enabling an understanding of the contemporary experience of youth. Particularly for those whose age means that they cannot draw on a parallel experience from *their* youth given that schools were previously not the explicitly performative institutions that they have become. But there is a clear tension here. On the one hand, learning mentor interventions which give the young person 'permission' to fail in order to encourage an understanding that it is in the making of mistakes that effective learning actually takes place, appear to be at odds with the wider core business of the school, viewed by some pupils as a relentless focus on getting better and better results and summed up earlier by Eliza as leaving a young person *'no room for failure'*.

To summarise, over the course of the ethnography, it became clear that the extent of learning mentor support that a pupil might experience was variable and specific to differing contexts. For many pupils the mentors were only ever known as a friendly face around the school corridors. In their official 'seen' work they were for others, the familiar adult who greeted them first thing at Breakfast Club or the 'youth worker' who played games with them and/or chatted and showed an interest in them during breaks and lunchtimes in the Mentor Base. In the previous chapter we saw how for pupils like Michael, they were the visible face of a formally engineered intervention initiated by a third party which, depending on a range of circumstances beyond the reach of both pupil and mentor, may or may not have a positive outcome. However, in this chapter which has focussed in part on the unofficial 'unseen' work of the mentors, it is clear that for a small but not insignificant number, the learning mentor role at Priory Park High provided the means to access a more inconspicuous and unofficial type of support for those pupils dealing with complex issues. It is worth noting that the existence of 'official' and 'unofficial' types of interventions are certainly not unique to Priory Park High as this phenomenon can be found in both news media reports (Wallace, 2001) and academic accounts of learning mentor work taking place elsewhere and illustrated here by a learning mentor describing their work in an earlier study:

> Emotional support is linked to each student who is *targeted* for support. [And] Pupils also *ask for this support* through [unofficial] drop-in sessions. (cited in Bishop, 2011, p. 34, my emphasis)

In this short quote, it is possible to identify many elements of learning mentor work which have appeared over this and the previous chapter: the identification of pupils in need of support by a third party, a blurring of the pastoral and academic approaches and the agentic pupils who self-refer. Having considered the pupil perspective of the learning mentor role, the next two chapters will examine how the work of learning mentors is viewed across the school hierarchy, starting with the senior leadership team and then moving onto middle managers. This data reveals the complex and often contradictory nature of how others understand the role and in doing so, starts to provide some of the answers to the frustrations often felt by the learning mentors in carrying out their work.

Chapter 8

View from the Top – A Coherent and Consistent Senior Leadership View of the Learning Mentor Role?

The previous two chapters set out the learning mentors' everyday work of supporting pupils, told directly from the standpoints of each. It was possible to see how through their interventions, both official and unofficial, the mentors were able to gain an authentic and accurate picture of pupils' lives and provide a qualitatively different input to that of teachers, middle managers and other support roles. It also became clear that whilst there were formal or 'seen' elements of their work such as Breakfast Club and one-to-ones conducted in the Mentor Base, there were also many 'unseen' activities such as pupils self-referring and meeting with the mentors both fleetingly or for significant lengths of time. The purpose of this chapter is to gain an understanding of how the learning mentor role and its activities was viewed and understood from the standpoint of the Senior Leadership Team (SLT). The ensuing discussion will focus on the Head Teacher, the Deputy Head Teacher and the Director of Pastoral Care (DPC). All three were asked to set out their understanding of the learning mentor role, both as it had been perceived in policy terms and how it was being enacted at Priory Park High. Different lines of enquiry were then followed for each participant, according to their respective roles and the issues that their 'work knowledge[s]' (Smith, 2005) gave rise to.

The Head Teacher – '… They Can Quietly Get in, without Suit and Tie'

As noted in the introduction to Priory Park High (Chapter 5), the Head Teacher had been recruited to turn the fortunes of the school around after a poor inspection outcome. Drawing on his experiences in both Priory Park High and previous schools which had benefitted from *Excellence in Cities* funding, he described the learning mentor role as one that required a 'tough skills set' in that it represented 'an amalgam of social work, health and wellbeing and education' if done well.

Propping up the Performative School: A Critical Examination
of the English Educational Paraprofessional, 107–117
Copyright © 2022 by Jo Bishop
Published under exclusive licence by Emerald Publishing Limited
doi:10.1108/978-1-83982-242-120221008

He also identified the value of a role which could access places, people and contexts *outside* of the school setting which perhaps other staff could not:

> [...] they can quietly get in, without suit and tie ... Because I look official I think that there is [a need for] a tier that needs to be not in the face, but getting in there, finding out what those core issues, underlying things are .... (Head Teacher)

The Head Teacher extended this notion of accessibility to other support roles present within the schools workforce remarking specifically on another paraprofessional role – Attendance Officers – who he argued could 'get through doors that any policeman or anybody else who was official couldn't'.

Switching his focus to the work of the learning mentors *within* a school, the Head Teacher conceptualised the role as someone who provided a package of support to identify and eradicate barriers so that learning could take place.

> That is what the child respects, 'you [the learning mentor] are sitting with me and talking to me'. Once you have got that, you can start drilling into the learning and supporting them and [get them] doing their bloody homework again.

Crucial to this was the time that the role afforded. Time, which he argued, teachers simply did not have, given that they were, 'paid to get results, as well as [doing] the pastoral side', suggesting that the latter had become a secondary issue for the then newly remodelled teaching profession. Here then is a clear acknowledgement of the importance of the mentor–pupil relationship in order to effect change. It also offers a contrast to the teacher relationship which is inextricably linked to the imperative of academic outcomes.

The Head Teacher felt that the learning mentors approach was one that differed to other staff, citing examples of pupils addressing them by their first name and using their relationship to enforce schools rules differently. However, this was conditional on whether or not such an approach undermined the rest of the school. His concern here was whether pupils had the ability to understand, distinguish between and conduct themselves appropriately in the less formal context inhabited and in part created by the learning mentor, as opposed to the more formal classroom situation:

> So whilst I accept, you know, the [pupil and mentor] being on first name terms and all the rest of it, I think they do a good job and they are able to diffuse things like that (clicks fingers) ... whether it is ... anger management and all the rest of it. They *are* very skilled, *because* of ... their approach and their relationship ... but a teacher is there to teach and you can't have one position undermine another.

The Head Teacher was optimistic about the potential and actual contribution of the learning mentor role at Priory Park High. He commented on one of the mentors' practice specifically which he saw as being 'on the same page' as him with regard to the importance of impact:

> Here, we have an exceptional person, who actually clicks into it and not only will say, 'Do you know what ... [but] I think some strategies we should employ are ...' That to me is exactly what it is about and once that [pupil] engagement is there, then you get onto the learning, because otherwise, you are just going to go round and round and round.

However, alongside the obvious positives that can be identified within this assessment, he also expressed that learning mentors needed to demonstrate a greater degree of accountability as one of many groups of 'stakeholders' within the structure of the school and as a distinct group within the School workforce more widely. Accountability in this context was equated with 'impact' and in reference to the national picture, he believed that there were cases where the role *had* been used astutely, that is, in a way in which the impact could be measured. But he also described some mentor inputs which he had experienced in previous settings as

> [...] pink and fluffy, [because] I couldn't quite grasp what the heck they were there for.

Although not offering any concrete examples to illustrate this observation, he extended this critique to support staff more generally, arguing that they *all* needed to evidence their contribution more explicitly. This, he posited, could be achieved by benchmarking the point at which their support began, then using various means to measure the progress that their intervention had brought about. An example he provided on this point regarded working with pupils who had poor attendance:

> [...] If they come to school, *that's the measure!* If they happen to stay, for some children, more than two hours, *that's a measure* and actually I'd rather they were here than out there ....

Regarding policy initiatives of New Labour, The Head teacher as keen to draw out what had worked:

> So I thoroughly enjoyed Excellent in Cities ... it pulled schools together, it pulled agendas together ... now academies weren't around at the time, ... so within (—), the authority that we worked within, I was on the EIC Board and we actually drove whole city agendas, which was superb.

On this point specifically, he cited how one impact of this coordinated and collaborative approach was that the percentage of young people not in education, employment and training (NEET) had reduced from 15 percent to 5 percent within a year, remarking 'and that to me is a tangible outcome, a hell of an outcome actually'.

However, the Head teacher's assessment was not without its misgivings. Here he talks specifically about how projects (like EiCs) were administered:

> [...] the Labour government brought in a lot of great stuff, but it was strand after strand after strand after strand and do you know what, it got too messy, it became a maze and I think within that maze, people have just got lost in the ether somewhere and that's why there were little pockets of people being employed all over the place.

He questioned the extent to which initiatives were 'thought through' in terms of their longevity, questioning how redundancies were handled once funding ceased. What was also conveyed in this interview was the stark contrast with the political administration that followed New Labour in terms of how *little* intervention was now taking place:

> [...] we were living in this initiative overload era and we have done for actually fifteen years, till recently, when there's only one, Pupil Premium.

The Deputy Head – 'They Have Got Lots of Different Subjects and Then [They] Take That and Almost Do That Teaching Job'

Moving on to another perspective from the SLT, that of the Deputy Head. Like the Head Teacher, the Deputy Head was fairly new in post at the time of the study and was therefore keen to distinguish between what she had observed of the learning mentor role at previous schools and what she saw at Priory Park High. First, focussing on the learning mentor role outside of the school gates, the Deputy Head (like the Head) recognised how the role had the potential to keep the channels of communication between school and home open, however her chosen examples were premised on a more traditional 'teacher–parent' relationship:

> I've seen it work really well where, children have had difficulties and needed to be at home, whether they be medical or, family difficulties ... and the learning mentor has actually liaised between home and school ... you know, [encouraging the pupil to] keep up with course work and revise for exams and things like that and that's needed .... I think it is right that we are positive [about learning mentors] because they are ..., well when they do it well, ... they are talented. They have got lots of different subjects and then [they] take that and *almost do that teaching job.* (Deputy Head, my emphasis)

This description contrasts with that of the Head Teacher's comments which emphasised the role's *lack* of formality, in being something 'other than a teacher' as its very strength. Whereas for the Deputy Head, the worth and contribution of the learning mentor role appeared to be conditional upon how closely it could *replicate* the teacher role.

Within a school setting, the Deputy Head shared some of the concerns expressed by the Head Teacher regarding the tensions that can arise in having differing approaches to working with pupils happening simultaneously. She talked specifically of how the one-to-one intervention could be used as a type of 'perverse empowerment' for pupils, where, in previous settings the role had 'moved away from learning' and become more about supporting young people with behavioural difficulties. In this scenario the learning mentor had ended up as a 'sounding board' or a means of retreat for some pupils. Aspects of the pupil–mentor relationship then became problematic once the mentor was identified by the pupil as someone who was 'on their side'. Here the Deputy Head recalled situations she had observed where learning mentors were apparently

> [...] overriding decisions that had been made about children [and] ... sort of almost siding with the children ....

As a result, staff relationships became fragile, with teachers not feeling supported but rather, undermined by learning mentors. At the same time the Deputy Head was keen to acknowledge the skills-set of learning mentors she had previously line-managed:

> Where they were really good, they did that kind of firefighting with the child, and actually would say 'you know what, I know that you've had a difficulty in that lesson, we are going to quickly work through it, but you need to [go] back or you're going to come and do [the] work with me now, not just sit and get out of the lesson'.

Her concern regarding the learning mentors at Priory Park High was whether the one-to-one interventions that they undertook took during lessons were 'visible enough':

> [...] maybe it is because I'm either in classrooms or meetings or whatever, [but] I don't see so much of what they do outside of breaks and lunch-times.

It is interesting that the mentor's actions in the 'Angry Year 11 Girls' situation (presented in Chapter 6) exemplifies what the Deputy Head describes above as good learning mentor practice involving as it did, a recognition of pupil difficulty followed up with conflict resolution and a swift integration back into the classroom. The fact that she was unaware of this incident and interventions like this would suggest that the visibility of the mentors' work was indeed an issue.

One way in which the Deputy Head's view did differ to both the Head teacher and the DPC (whose contribution is examined in the following section) was that she did not see the learning mentor approach as particularly unique. Rather her view was that *every* member of staff should build relationships with children and on this point implied that this was an area that the school needed to work harder on. Whilst agreeing that the mentor role did afford more time to do this, she strongly believed that teachers also had opportunities to make those types of relationships with pupils *if they chose to do so* through (for instance) allowing pupils to stay in their base room at lunch and break times and using this as a social time to chat or eat packed lunches together, rather than attending to other duties like marking work.

The Director of Pastoral Care

Unlike the Head and Deputy Head, the DPC had spent her entire professional career at Priory Park High, joining the school 24 years earlier as a 'probationer' (now termed 'NQT'[1]). At the time of the ethnography, the DPC role was organised around two strategic areas: 'Attendance' and 'Behaviour'. By focussing on each in turn, it is possible to gain a more nuanced picture of the school's pastoral activities, and how the learning mentor role fitted into this. The remit of managing 'Attendance' entailed whole-school statistical monitoring alongside targeted interventions with 'offending' pupils to ensure that the school performed above the national average. This being an inspection measure on which it had previously required improvement.[2] Despite the school moving back into a 'Good' category in its most recent Ofsted inspection, the DPC believed that 'Behaviour', as her other key area of responsibility, was one which the school needed to show continued improvement in, explaining:

> We have been judged as 'Good', now our next step is to be judged
> 'Outstanding', so we need to have a behaviour that follows suit ....

In addition to leading on these two areas, the DPC oversaw all the varying pastoral interventions (including the learning mentors), as well as line-managing other provision deemed as 'Inclusion'. This encompassed the school's on-site pupil referral centre, the 'Inclusion' room (the internal exclusion provision) and the behaviour support team in their everyday work of on-call duties and working with pupils targeted for behaviour modification programmes. Given the nature and scope of her work and the documentation of increasing numbers of non-teaching staff into schools reported in Chapter 1, it felt pertinent to ask about the ratio of pastoral/inclusion staff to teaching staff at Priory Park High. The response given to this question caught me a little off-guard as the following interchange illustrates:

---

[1]Newly Qualified Teacher.
[2]It is relevant to note that according to the Local Authority's own strategic Children's plan, poor school attendance was a city-wide phenomenon.

DPC: I don't know what the ratio is. Do you?

JB: (somewhat taken aback) Er not off the top of my head I don't.

DPC: No I don't either, because I don't deal with the teaching and learning, that's somebody else's role.

She went on to say that the school had 'a lot of pastoral people' and she was aware of 'what was going on' in this field of activity.[3] Despite her comment that teaching and learning were the responsibility of another person, I nevertheless pressed on, wanting to know if she felt the school had struck an appropriate balance between the two areas, but her response served only to underline, yet again, a separation between the pastoral (her business) and the curricula (not her business) which apparently rendered her unable to comment on the relationship between the two. In effectively bringing a close to this question she stated: 'Like I said, I don't know, because that's not an area I am involved in'.

The Learning Mentor Role – '*A Bit of Everything*'

Initially, the DPC said it was hard to describe the learning mentor role at that time because it was in the process of changing. In the early days it had apparently involved 'a bit of everything', but was predominantly made up of one-to-one work for 'emotional and social reasons'. Overall, her perspective was that the role was 'completely linked' to wider changes that the school was going through both past and present; so for a time, the mentors had been much more involved in working with pupils with behavioural issues particularly during the latter part of the *Excellence in Cities* era (2001–2008) when the team had been larger, 'much larger than the behaviour support team in fact'. This had led to a grey area in terms of who should manage the learning mentor provision and direct line-management had switched, more than once, between varying middle managers who held both Inclusion and pastoral responsibilities before finally going back to herself as overall pastoral manager. Now that behaviour was no longer perceived as 'the first barrier' at Priory Park High she expressed that the learning mentors were in a position to focus much more on the academic and learning side, returning in some ways to their original remit as it was conceived in government circles. Contradictory to this pronouncement however, she went to explain that the mentors now also performed other roles which meant they no longer '[had] a proper caseload' thus limiting their time and availability for one-to-ones which focussed on the academic side. Here she gave the example of Paul's

---

[3]The actual staff breakdown at the time of the study which was drawn manually from school documentation after this interview took place was as follows: *SLT* – 9; *Teaching* (including Year Progress Leaders) – 78; *Pastoral Support and Inclusion* (including Year Managers) – 34; *Other* (Administration; Technicians including IT support) – 29.

increasing time spent visiting feeder primary schools and putting on school open day events for Year 6 pupils, which although she referred to as 'transition' (an area that learning mentors have traditionally been involved with) could also be interpreted as the school marketing itself in order to restore pupil numbers back to what they were prior to its poor Ofsted judgement some years earlier. I raised the issue of redundancies as a possible further impact on the mentors' workload but her only comment was that whilst these were regrettable, the decision was effectively a fait accompli:

> Well we have lost a full person with a full caseload, plus other things ... which [have] had to be redistributed or abandoned. Unfortunately that's the way things go, no matter which area of any job, you know, if you lose staffing, you lose staffing.

'... They Have Got That Special Relationship That Nobody Else Will Have ...'

Despite these changes to and pressures on the ability of the mentors to provide a service, the DPC remained positive about what she saw as their unique approach. This is illustrated in the following extract which makes a direct comparison with the behaviour support role, referred to here as the 'Positive Behaviour Team' due to a rebranding of their title at the time the interview was conducted:

> My thoughts on [the] learning mentors is that they are invaluable in the sense that they have got that special relationship that *nobody else will have*. The Positive Behaviour Team would not have the kind of relationship with the kids as the mentors have, because the mentors' role is not to sanction or impose sanctions, whereas the Positive Behaviour Team is; therefore they [the mentors] *have that completely separate view, like they are kind of separate from the school*, even though they work in the school .... and that is because that relationship is different, [and] ... the pupils who we know will not respond to authority or rules or whatever, are better off working with the mentors because of that. (my emphasis)

The DPC expressed some concerns with how the mentors' work was understood within the wider school staff and put this down to the mentors not advertising their work 'loudly enough' as well as a failed initiative led by her:

> We did start last year working on 'what are your roles' ... I made a list and I wanted that list to be put up everywhere in the school for everybody to see.

When asked if this publicity exercise had been intended for pastoral roles in general, I was told it had only related to the mentor role because:

[...] everybody else knows what everybody else is doing, but the mentors ... not enough people knew what their role was.

Ultimately, this advertising campaign had not happened and when I asked why, she simply shrugged and said she did not know.

SLT Perspectives – Incoherencies, Inconsistencies and Disjunctures

It is clear that some incoherencies and inconsistencies were present in terms of how the learning mentor role was understood by these key members of the SLT. First, the potential of the learning mentor role *beyond* the school gates was noted by both the Head and Deputy Head Teacher, but from different positions. For the Deputy Head, the learning mentor was at their best when they facilitated learning in the home, in effect 'almost doing that teaching job'. For the Head Teacher, it was precisely because learning mentors were *not* teachers and therefore not part of the school 'establishment', that they had the potential to do successful outreach work in marginalised communities and access complex and 'difficult' family situations, building relationships where others had tried and failed. This notion of the learning mentor as a type of credible 'go-between', building bridges between a school and the community/ies is a recurring issue, observed first within educational news media articles in Chapter 1 where it was presented uncritically as a positive aspect of the role, then later on in Chapter 4 with the experiences of 1960s American educational paraprofessionals termed explicitly as 'community agents' (Stewart, 1971).

Moving the focus to inside the school, the data generated with SLT indicate how staff roles were shifting and changing in line with the requirements placed on the school to develop a more explicitly performance-driven culture. For example, the Head Teacher viewing the interventions offered by the mentors as part of a wider move to not only take up, but *take away* from teachers the pastoral demands that arise in a school; particularly an all-inclusive institution such as Priory Park High. But in this handing over of pastoral 'territory' to support staff, both the Head and the Deputy Head expressed concerns about how the different approaches of the mentors might undermine teaching and learning, illustrated by the Head Teacher's comment that '... a teacher is there to teach and you can't have one position undermine another'. In contrast, the DPC did not get as far as recognising the potential conflict in this interplay of the pastoral and the academic; in part because she simply did not see the latter as part of her remit so was unable and/or unwilling to anticipate or act on tensions which might arise. This disjuncture is evidenced even more starkly at the middle-management level which forms the next chapter.

One of the clearest disjunctures to emerge from the data presented in this chapter were the Head Teacher's assumption regarding the level of autonomy that the mentors had in their day-to-day work. This contrasted with the Deputy Head's view that the role and its associated activities were not visible enough despite the range of interventions that were described in the previous chapter, all of which illustrated what she described as effective mentor practice. Rather it was the DPC, as the learning mentors' current line manager, who had the most accurate picture of the *actual* activities that made up the role in its current incarnation. The DPC willingly subscribed to the notion of the mentor role as offering a qualitatively different working relationship with pupils to that of other staff but unlike her colleagues in SLT, regarded this unconditionally as a positive feature. Perhaps the Deputy Head's concern regarding staff relationships becoming fragile due to teachers potentially feeling undermined by learning mentors, was not considered by the DPC as from her standpoint, her work (and the work of those she managed) inhabited only the pastoral domain, which she considered as a separate entity from the academic.

A further disjuncture arises when considering the Head Teacher's view that learning mentors needed to evidence the impact of their work more explicitly. Placed alongside the DPC's comments that the mentor role involved 'a bit of everything' and was constantly changing according to wider issues faced by the school (initiated by external forces like Ofsted judgements), gives rise to the question: how is this evidencing to be done? This point becomes even more pertinent when the additional issue (detected in many of the accounts) of how the boundaries between the work of learning mentors and other support roles was becoming increasingly blurred. For example, the Head Teacher made reference to how the mentor role could quickly and effectively diffuse pupil outbursts of anger whilst the Deputy Head was aware of how in the past, learning mentors had been used in a Behaviour Support capacity in all but name and with varying degrees of success. However, their respective comments were largely made in reference to other school contexts and it was the DPC who again (through sheer length of continuous service) held the most accurate picture of this issue in relation to Priory Park High. On this point she set out a marked difference between the two roles as they were *currently* organised within the school, describing the behaviour workers approach as 'more punitive' and 'sanction-based' and one therefore which definitely would not work if taken up by the mentors who she described as having a unique and 'special relationship' based on not 'imposing sanctions'. When pressed on the question of why the school currently had more behaviour support workers than mentors in terms of who decided the allocation of roles, she initially named the Head Teacher but then qualified the above situation as just one decision within the staffing structure as a whole which '... SLT and the governors work on together'. Curiously, the DPC constantly referred to SLT in the third person, as 'they', not 'we' as if it was a group she did not see herself a part of. Whilst this does not explain why initiatives such as the wider publicising of the mentor role had not taken off, it suggests how the DPC was positioned within the SLT, having a place in name but evidently not a great deal of influence within the hierarchy.

This chapter has demonstrated that differing views of and prescriptions about the effectiveness of the learning mentor role were apparent amongst those members of the SLT who were willing to share their insights. These ranged from seeing the learning mentor role as a quasi-teacher, to one which performs best when given free rein to carve out its own identity – as long as this doesn't undermine the core business of the school, attainment and results. The uniqueness of the mentor–pupil relationship as a tool to engage disaffected young people was also contested. In the next chapter, the discussion moves to the middle-management level of the school hierarchy to examine to whether and to what extent similar inconsistencies in the purpose and construction of the learning mentor role are apparent.

Chapter 9

View from Middle Management: The Multi-faceted Learning Mentor

In the previous chapter clear inconsistencies in senior leadership views of the learning mentor role emerged. The Head teacher's perspective that the learning mentor approach should be different to that of the teacher contradicted the Deputy Head's view that learning mentors were at their best when they closely resembled the teaching role albeit operating in a peripatetic fashion. All three senior leaders identified further issues such as the extent to which other staff understood the learning mentor role; the visibility of their work at Priory Park High and whether paraprofessionals in general did enough to evidence the effectiveness of their interventions.

In this chapter, we continue to look at how the role was viewed and understood from the standpoint of others within the school hierarchy, in turning to middle management. The discussion is organised around two key positions: the Progress Leader and the Year Manager, positions which are designated to each school year. The Progress Leader (PL) was typically from a teaching background and although they continued to have some teaching responsibilities their main role was to monitor the academic attainment of the cohort and line manage the Year Manager. The Year Manager (YM) typically came from a non-teaching background and working in conjunction with the Progress Leader, oversaw pupil issues that were deemed more pastoral in nature. They were also required to monitor attendance and behaviour and make contact with parents if the school had concerns about a pupil that were not related to their academic progress. The two main participants in this chapter are the Year 11 Progress Leader and the Year 7 Year Manager.

The Progress Leader

Path to Priory Park High

The Year 11 PL provided a valuable longevity of scope to the study as through holding posts in other schools, she had over the course of 15 years, witnessed the development of the year leadership role from its earliest days and before the

Propping up the Performative School: A Critical Examination
of the English Educational Paraprofessional, 119–128
Copyright © 2022 by Jo Bishop
Published under exclusive licence by Emerald Publishing Limited
doi:10.1108/978-1-83982-242-120221009

introduction of non-teaching staff to work at this middle-management level. As such, her experience of year leadership before coming to Priory Park High had included monitoring both academic progress and wider pastoral issues; a significant undertaking which had perhaps not surprisingly resulted in burn-out and her eventual departure from her previous school:

> I was Head of Year's 7 and 8 then the whole of Key Stage 3 … it was a different set up to how it is here; I had no non-teaching person to work with me and it was just far too much for one person to keep their head around and [the school] weren't able to shift how they managed that … so that's when I looked for another job.

The increasing separation of the academic functions of schooling from wider pastoral concerns have become more pronounced since the mid to late 1990s (Calvert, 2009; Power 1996), with a greater emphasis being placed on what is arguably now seen as the core business of a school – that of results. Within this high stakes culture, the worth of pupils is measured by their academic attainment (the **BANKERS** at Priory Park High – Chapter 5), both potential and actual, whilst 'barriers to learning' are deemed as problematic especially if they have an adverse impact on academic outcomes. The way in which roles were allocated at Priory Park High, evidenced this increasingly formalised separation between the pastoral and the academic and can be observed in the following extract where the PL describes how her role differed to that of the YM:

> The attendance and behaviour part is done by the Year Manager who is non-teaching, and they deal with that. [The] Progress Leaders' focus is their [the pupils] academic progress … I line-manage the Year Manager and *we come together to put the child back together* and see where, if, there are barriers to learning or where we can support them if they are struggling. (my emphasis)

This explanation of role allocation could be critically interpreted as a fragmented rather than a holistic approach because the pupil is metaphorically 'dismembered' according to whether their need is 'academic' or 'pastoral'. Furthermore, it seems to confirm and align with the comments made by the Director of Pastoral Care when she stated in the previous chapter '*I don't deal with the teaching and learning, that's somebody else's role*'.

On the other hand, given how patchy and/or inconsistent 'good' pastoral care of pupils was in the past (Best, Jarvis, & Ribbins, 1980; Calvert, 2009 and Williamson, 1980) this clear separation of roles could arguably provide a better experience and outcome for the pupil who is in need of support with issues other than the academic. From a learning mentor perspective this 'dismembering' of pupils was strongly contested, described as 'colleagues taking a snippet of *their* perception of a young person's situation' according to 'their own agenda'. In the longer extract that follows Angie is very vocal in distinguishing the learning mentor approach from that of Middle Management claiming that mentors endeavoured to…

[...] not to be a piece from the side, we are actually ... in the middle there *with* that child ... [asking] where is that young person at, *right now?* Yeah, we know where we would like them to be [academically] and how we would like them to be [pastorally], but where are they at *now?* How do *they* perceive things? Because that [starting point] is more important than what anybody else thinks. (Angie, LM)

Thus, the mentor's desire to take a holistic approach in their work with pupils is underlined once again here. Furthermore, it is possible to detect an advocacy function to the role – 'we are actually ... in the middle there *with* that child ... [asking] where is that young person at, *right now*'.

Nevertheless, putting the mentors' qualms to one side, the PL felt confident that by working in conjunction with the YM, her role did achieve a 'holistic view of the child *and* the curriculum'. Perhaps this belief was borne out of a (relative) comparison with subject teachers whom she described as 'more insular'; a situation which she believed had come about as a result of them having to increasingly 'protect' their subject area. This was due to the change that had taken place at the time of the study where a device had been introduced as a means to measure a school's academic progress in which pupil achievement was measured across eight qualifications taken from a DfE approved list (DfE, 2017) referred to as 'Progress 8' alongside 'Attainment 8'. This essentially involved the tiering of subjects into a curriculum hierarchy with differing values being placed on subjects and teachers having to make a strong case for the survival of their discipline if not automatically considered within the approved list.

Understanding the Learning Mentor Role – Ensuring Pupils are 'Learning-ready'

When asked about their understanding of the learning mentor role, the PL's response was to see it primarily as one which supported her own role of ensuring academic attainment.

We would hope that they [the mentors] would be including and focussing on [the pupils] academic progress, or monitoring what the student thought they might need support with or how they felt about it: they might be doing very well with it but not feeling confident about it, you know it's getting into those things. Talking to them about their organisation and their preparation; have they got equipment, planners, and a place to work at home?

Here, the mentors' contribution is seen first and foremost as ensuring a young person's readiness to learn. The mentor's role is to coach the pupil on their time and self-management and assess the practical context in which their learning takes place outside of school. It is worth noting that no acknowledgement is given to the fact that this may be outside of the control of both mentor and young person, however the PL does give a nod to wider affective issues that the pupil may be experiencing such as a lack of confidence.

In terms of how teachers viewed the learning mentor role and specifically interventions which required a pupil's removal from class, the PL confidently expressed that teaching staff understood why pupils went to the mentors and that there was some flexibility for teachers in this:

> They know that they can say 'no not today, not this lesson, you could have them this time next week but they are in the middle of a controlled assessment' and the learning mentor will switch it round if needs be ....

On this issue of taking pupils out of certain classes, she believed that teachers of non-core subjects[1] probably saw some of the interventions connected to extra support with Maths and English as more problematic, given that these involved a greater number of students being absent from certain classes. She further identified a distinct part of the learning mentor role as working in partnership with and as 'back-up' to teachers, with mentors ensuring that pupils completed work set by teachers. In her view, learning mentors were now widely accepted by teachers and seen as a 'completely embedded thing' that is 'necessary' and 'just the way a school works'.

The extent to which these sentiments were shared by teaching staff is questionable as the following examples show. Learning mentors certainly felt that their work was often (wrongly) characterised as time out of formal learning for 'a cup of tea and a chat'. Here Marie, who to remind readers, had worked in a number of paraprofessional roles including learning mentoring, recalls how some teachers resented her taking pupils out of class despite being instructed to do so by either a PL or a YM:

> [...] they would think that you were just, you know, mollycoddling them or [mimics teacher] 'Oh you know, she just takes them down there and gives them a hot drink and toast' and so didn't sort of always quite understand what we [mentors] were trying to do.

Teacher understandings of what the mentor role entailed were certainly mixed as a brief diversion into this data will now show. On the one hand, those teachers who agreed to be interviewed were generally positive in their remarks but at the same time often lacked a contextual understanding of what actually happened in the pupil–mentor one-to-one interventions. Here, a teacher starts by expressing empathy for the pupil experience in terms of both what formal learning entails and the more pressing issues they might be dealing with:

---

[1]At the time of study 'core' subjects were English, Maths, and Science and it was extremely rare for pupils to be taken out of these sessions for a one-to-one mentor interventions.

[...] I think that there is a school of [thought amongst] staff – and it will be in a lot of schools – that just don't see it [the learning mentor role] as being of value, because they might just see a 'naughty boy' ... but me personally when I see Angie with someone I think 'well ... that kid's obviously not capable of sitting in a room for an hour with another 30 kids looking at a board' ... and who is?! I couldn't do it! I couldn't go back to being a student – it's hard. You've got all these other things going on in your life [and] the least important thing is sitting listening to Miss So and So talk about tectonic plates when you're thinking 'I don't want to go home because ... my Dad's knocked seven shades out of my Mum this morning'. I don't believe that school is the biggest part of a child's life. It is for some people but there are bigger things going on and I do understand that kids need that extra provision. Sometimes they do need a cup of tea and ... just to talk. (Drama Teacher)

But then later comments:

I have to be honest ... I don't entirely understand what goes on in those rooms [the mentor base] ... in the same way that no one understands what goes on in here at all! [Laughs whilst gesturing to the studio theatre we are seated in] but they are different members of staff that ... are qualified to do different things .... (Drama Teacher)

Interestingly, in the second excerpt the teacher draws on her own experiences and positioning in the school acknowledging that her lack of 'insider' knowledge about the mentors' work was down to a wider phenomenon of people tending not to understand *any* school activities that lay outside the attainment of core and/or traditional subjects. Therefore, she could relate to the mentor's feelings that their work was trivialised because as a Drama teacher she had experienced this too.

The issue of how the mentor's one-to-one interventions impacted on teachers' work *was* called into question, particularly for teachers of non-core subjects who felt they had to accommodate these disproportionately. As such their comments certainly did not reflect the flexibility or indeed autonomy suggested by the PL above, as illustrated here by a teacher of Food Technology:

Teacher:　I never know when students are going to be taken out of my lesson, so that's really bad and I know that they [the mentors] will try and not hit the same lesson, but then they are told not to hit the core as well, and ... I am not important! (laughs).

Jo:　Is that what it feels like? [Teacher interjects: yeah, yeah]

Jo: And who decides about not withdrawing pupils from certain subjects? Where is that decision made?

Teacher: I don't know.

Along with the frustration of the practicalities of pupils being removed from her classes (and seemingly unaware of who had the authority to make this decision), this teacher also expressed a desire to know more about which strategies were being adopted with those children being removed, be that by a learning mentor or a behaviour support worker, so that as a teacher she 'could then follow up with, [...] some kind of positive reinforcement as well'. This desire to work collaboratively across the academic and pastoral divide is clear to see and would support those arguments set out by teacher authors like Purdy (2013) who in believing that the 'pastoral' is an integral part of teacher identity, implores their colleagues not to abandon these elements of their role despite the removal of these via the remodelling agenda discussed in Chapter 2.

When comparing the views of the PL to those of the teachers, there are clear disjunctures in terms of the rationale for and nature of one-to-one interventions, and moreover how these were accommodated by staff. The PL portrayed teachers as not only seeing withdrawals from their classes as unproblematic but also as something that they had a degree of control over. But this ready acceptance was not discernible in the teachers' own accounts; rather a sense of frustration at being required to support an intervention which some felt they were disproportionately targeted for. Nevertheless, the data presented here demonstrate that there was certainly a desire amongst some teachers to support the mentors in their work, tempered by a frustration that they were not told what an intervention might entail or how they could reinforce that once the pupil returned to their classroom. Furthermore, some teachers felt less valued/less important than those of 'core' subjects which leads to a questioning of whether the academic/pastoral split that has taken place in English education is too simplistic in its analysis.

The Year Manager

A decision to enter the teaching profession is often conveyed as following a sense of vocation. In contrast, support staff often come from non-teaching backgrounds and their reasons for seeking employment in a school, as illustrated in Chapter 4, are more pragmatic, often rooted in finding employment that fits around family responsibilities. The Year Manager's path to employment at Priory Park High was one such case as it was connected to her need to find a job which allowed a continuation of her everyday work as the sole carer to her children after the end of her marriage.

When asked to explain her role as Year 7[2] Manager the participant homed in on the support she provided for those pupils finding the transition to High School challenging:

---

[2]Year 7 is the first year of high school and for pupils usually aged 11–12 years.

[The Year Manager's role is about] … how we can support that particular student to attend school, to *be happy* in school, to *be safe* and to *achieve* in school. (my emphasis)

Her words provide a highly pertinent example of adopting what Frost (2011) has termed 'outcomes speak' and any readers who may have been practitioners at the time of the *Every Child Matters* policy will have quickly recognised some of the five outcomes in this account.[3] As noted in Chapter 4, an institutional ethnographer would explain the participant's use of 'outcomes speak' as an example of 'institutional capture' (Smith, 2005, p. 156), indicating when certain language is used which subsumes or displaces descriptions based on experience. In developing this notion further, another institutional ethnographer talks of '*intentional* institutional capture*' (Eastwood, 2006, p. 193, my emphasis) a process whereby people, recognising that they must work within conceptual frames of the organisation in order to appear 'credible', self-consciously translate their own 'interests' (i.e., the activities which arise from their position in the institutional complex) into institutional discourses. Moreover, their participation is actually circumscribed by the appropriate terminology, as well as their role in that process. Chapter 4 sets out the strategies that can be employed in listening for 'institutional capture' when initially conducting interviews, and furthermore, as a means to see beyond it when listening to interview recordings and reading transcripts. In employing this approach, I was able to ascertain two main strands identified by the Year 7 YM which organised her day-to-day work. These were: ensuring the smooth transition of pupils from primary to secondary school (and in doing so) establishing a relationship with pupils' families where possible and if necessary. These two situations also provided the basis of what proved to be her very positive account of the learning mentor role and as such the discussion will now explore each one in turn.

First in relation to transition, visits to feeder primary schools were undertaken jointly by the YM and one of the learning mentors, (usually Paul) and these took place with more frequency and a greater sense of urgency once the Schools Admissions process had ended and pupils had been formally allocated to Priory Park High. During these visits each person performed a distinct role: the learning mentor would meet with the pupils for an informal chat based on the 'circle time' format.[4] Here the mentor would facilitate a discussion in which Year 6 pupils were invited to explore their hopes and fears around their imminent move up to Secondary School. At the same time, the YM would meet separately with the primary school staff in order to gain their perspectives on the new intake. As with

---

[3]For those not familiar the Every Child Matters five outcomes as noted in Chapter 2 were: Stay Safe, Be Healthy, Enjoy and Achieve, Make a Positive Contribution, and Achieve Economic Well-Being.

[4]This is a nurturing approach which originated in Primary schools and was then used in Secondary Schools for pupils deemed vulnerable in their transition to High School. Group sizes are typically small so that all members can participate, with a particular onus on the promotion of oral communication and the development of listening skills.

other aspects of the mentor role that I witnessed during the study, this work of supporting pupils in their transition from primary to high school was typical of mentors in other contexts (Bishop, 2011). This also offers a further explanation as to why pupils went on to view learning mentors differently to teachers and other support staff given that their first direct experience of secondary school staff was via this relaxed and fairly unstructured time where the adult in authority was introduced to them by his first name rather than 'Sir' or 'Mr —'.

Understanding the Learning Mentor Role as Their Pastoral 'Eyes and Ears'

The YM continued to offer very positive accounts of the learning mentor role premised on how they supported her in her work:

> I have to praise them because without the learning mentor, my job would be so much harder. You know, basic things from helping the student with hygiene, right up to the academic side of things, you know, helping them with their homework, helping them with self-esteem ... it's a massive, massive area of different things that they can help the child and support [me] with.

Interestingly, this summary of mentor activities chimed with the Director for Pastoral Care's earlier observation that the learning mentor role encompassed 'a bit of everything':

Despite the Year Manager role being designated as the pastoral lead, the Year 7 Manager asserted that the mentors were actually 'more the pastoral carers' in comparison to her own role which was essentially about 'managing' significant numbers of pupils:

> I, as a Year Manager, have to deal with every single child, whether it's ... a student who's highly academic or a student who has severe SEN [Special Educational Needs] issues, whatever it could be, I need to know everything about that particular child. Now currently I've only got a hundred and sixty eight students in my year group. Other Year Managers have got two hundred and sixty students ... So it's really, really vital that we've got an additional person there to actually help us with whatever situation comes along ... and just [to] be that friendly face, to actually say [to pupils] 'right ok, how can I help you?'

She continued this theme in her description of the mentors as the 'eyes and ears' of the YM in that 'they identify a lot of the problems for us as well'. Given the significant number of pupils (although in the view of the YM 'only' 168), that she was required to keep track of it is not surprising that the learning mentors were perceived as the staff who were actually 'doing' the pastoral care and as such felt that their role provided a qualitatively different type of relationship/avenue of support for pupils:

> It's completely different. Whereas the students would have a lot more respect for myself, as in 'Miss —' and they know that I've got a little bit more authority, they [pupils] actually refer to the mentors ... by their first name and it's more of a ... (thinks) ... a role of like a friend ... I mean with a Year Manager role, they [pupils] do still come to you and talk to you about personal things. But with the mentor role, *it's more of a friendship relationship, than it is an authority kind of relationship* (my emphasis).

Her observations are remarkably similar to those many facets of the learning mentor role identified by the pupils in Chapter 7, namely her perception of the mentor as a 'friend' to pupils and once again, a staff/pupil relationship that differs to others in the school. This praise was not wholly unqualified however in that she also identified a group of pupils who relied on the mentors to 'be there twenty-four seven for them'. This she deemed problematic as it gave her the (additional) task of saying to pupils 'actually yeah, they [the mentors] are there for you, but we are here for you as well and this is what we need you to do'.

As identified above, the other area which the YM saw as key to her role was in establishing a relationship with pupils' families; something which had increased out of necessity over the last few years due to what she saw as a greater number of families facing complex issues which led to them being under the gaze of outside agencies. When asked to clarify these 'issues' she cited poverty, drink and drug addictions and parents being younger and/or not coping with aspects of parenting. This suggests that although Year Managers did indeed form relationships with parents, these were not necessarily positive and/or freely entered into. An example is given here where the YM is talking about the difficulties in supporting parents who resisted the often assumed notion of a home–school partnership:

> [...] because a lot of parents who come from certain areas ... think that school is where you palm your child off ... [speaks as a parent] 'let them deal with behaviour, let them deal with the attendance, because it's our time now, we can do what we need to do' you know? And it doesn't work that way [so] it is breaking down that particular barrier to say 'actually no, we need to work together, this is your child, yes we are looking after your child in school, we are trying to help your child achieve, but we need your support as well ...'

In situations like this, the YM (like the Head teacher previously), saw the mentors as offering the potential to be seen by parents as someone different to her role, at one point overtly framing the mentor and herself within a 'good cop/bad cop' scenario. This was more likely to happen in situations where parents might be in conflict with the school over a decision or course of action regarding their child. So in following directly on from the quote above she went on to express:

> [...] and that's where mentors come in really handy because they can come out with us to do home visits ... they can come into meetings [in school] with us, with a parent there and say 'actually look, we're not all bad guys, this is the reason why we [the mentors] are here ...'

A Shared Middle Management Perspective of the Learning Mentor Role?

It is clear that both the Progress Leader and Year Manager's understanding of the learning mentor role was developed entirely from how it was positioned in relation to their own work. Both saw the learning mentor as 'in service' to their position but with each one placing a different onus which was determined by their own specific area of responsibility. Thus, for the PL, the role of the mentor was primarily to ensure that the correct conditions were in place for the pupil to access formal learning. In contrast, the YM saw the learning mentor as the 'face' of pastoral care; the mentor's role being to build the actual relationship with pupils, because this was something which the YM was not always afforded the time to do. The YM also saw them as conveying the 'friendly face' of school to parents as and when required. Placing the two accounts alongside one another this separation of the academic and the pastoral at middle-management level becomes even more explicit.

This and the previous chapter have shown that despite senior/middle management and some teaching staff viewing the role and contribution of learning mentors in a generally positive light, there were also a number of inconsistencies and contradictions in how the role was understood and what the mentors were expected to do. It is therefore important to ascertain how these varying mis/understandings translated into the learning mentors' experiences of their work and day-to-day management. This then will form the focus of the next chapter.

Chapter 10

Mentors Talking Back

The previous two chapters indicate that there were different and contradictory perspectives amongst and across senior and middle management regarding the role and functions of the learning mentor. This chapter explores how these misunderstandings translated into the learning mentors' experiences of their work. The discussion is organised around the issues which the learning mentors identified as their key frustrations in carrying out their day-to-day work. These can be summarised as: the problematic nature of 'official referrals'; how little information they felt they were given about the pupils they were tasked with supporting and the time-limited nature of these interventions. The final part of this chapter looks at their broader experiences of line management including challenges that were experienced in securing opportunities for professional development.

The Problematic Nature of 'Official Referrals'

The way in which official referrals were organised and conducted was previously set out in Chapter 6. To remind the reader, a member of middle management, usually a Year Manager or a Progress Leader would identify a pupil deemed to have 'barriers to learning' and refer them to the mentors' case load, leaving it to the mentor to contact the pupil and make the introductions. Although this aspect of the mentors' work included meetings of a one-off nature (such as the example of the student sent by a teacher to complete her college application) they more commonly involved up to six sessions. It was possible to observe many positive elements in the varying examples given in Chapter 6, for example, one-to-one's which complemented other provisions; those responding to a pupil's changed conduct or demeanour; or those representing an attempt to prevent a student moving closer to temporary exclusion. However, the mentors also disclosed concerns about whether the one-to-ones were always utilised as a genuine attempt to support pupils, suggesting that there were other agendas at play. Indeed, as the ethnography continued they became more vocal in their concerns about how official referrals were organised, the 'conditions' in which they were required to work and the expectations placed upon them.

Propping up the Performative School: A Critical Examination
of the English Educational Paraprofessional, 129–141
Copyright © 2022 by Jo Bishop
Published under exclusive licence by Emerald Publishing Limited
doi:10.1108/978-1-83982-242-120221010

Ever-changing Systems

One reason for the learning mentors' discontent was the frequency with which the system for organising one-to-one's changed. Early on in the ethnography, Paul had initially conveyed a seemingly straightforward and 'glossy' process of how official referrals came about:

> *Paul*: If we've been given a referral, we're given a sheet .... on the top, there's the [pupil] name, form, issues as to why this student has been referred to us. And then we're kind of given a blank canvas and we put a programme together of what we think would suit that particular individual ... and that's based on experience.

> *Jo*: So in that sense you make all those decisions?

> *Paul*: Oh absolutely, oh yes. Senior leadership basically say 'get on and do your best with this student' which is good. You know, there's no written rule 'you have to do this, you have to do that'. You are left to your own devices.

Although, his account suggests that the mentors had a degree of autonomy in deciding what to do within the intervention, it was a piece of datum that I eventually interpreted as an example of 'institutional capture' as opposed to an authentic experiential account (see Chapter 4 for a definition and explanation of these methodological concepts). In formal interviews held early on in the study, Paul initially gave sanitised or official explanations of learning mentors' work, perhaps because he wanted to give a good account of Priory Park High to me the outsider. What emerged in later more informal discussions involving all of the mentors were the tensions and conflict that actually existed around *who* referred the pupil and *how* that selection was carried out. Firstly, Angie described the referral process in one of its (many) iterations as amounting to little more than a 'bun fight' where Year Managers met with a panel which included the Director for Pastoral Care and in a one-hour meeting slot were required to argue their case for pupils who they thought might benefit from an intervention; in effect competing with one another as to which pupils got the finite number of referrals. The learning mentors were not invited to these forums unless they made a strong case to attend. Then, in the latter part of the study, it became apparent from attending a Monday morning staff briefing that a reorganisation of pastoral staff had taken place so I consulted the mentors to ask if and how this impacted on the process of official referrals. Paul's response, given below, could not have been in more contrast to his earlier explanation:

> What process? Seriously, I would settle for a scrap of paper with a name on it at this point.

Lack of Input, Lack of Information, Lack of Knowledge

The mentors were also frustrated with the lack of input they had into these decisions, a situation that was illustrated earlier in the case of Sally (Chapter 7) who Angie requested to see officially but who was instead referred to the behaviour support team to undertake an Anger Management programme. This time it is Marie, who evidences how this aspect of the mentors' work was handled by her immediate line manager during her time as a mentor:

Marie: You could maybe mention that you'd seen something that you felt needed picking up on, but on the whole, they [pupils] would just get referred to you, with very little detail of what the problem was. There was a high level of secrecy that I found frustrating at times. I know there is child protection and all that kind of thing, but sometimes ....

Jo: So might child protection have been the reason for the secrecy?

Marie: [nods]

Jo: But that wouldn't be necessarily shared with you? They (line-managers) would just say 'we think this person could do with a mentor'?

Marie: [Agrees] ... and there would be general issues [of concern] like you were supposed to get a form, you never did. So basically you would just meet with the child and assess it for yourself really.

Marie felt that such a position had both benefits and drawbacks describing the mentoring job as 'a double edged sword':

Marie: You were left mostly to your own devices and at times, that can be good, but I felt some of the time, I would have needed, you know, some more guidance or help or support from upper [middle] management.

The limited amount of information given about the pupils referred for support was identified by all of the mentors, with the withholding of child protection information being identified as a particular thorn in their side. Here Paul talks of his experience:

It is hard because we are coming at it blind. We might do or say the wrong thing. I once asked a kid I was mentoring if maybe they could seek support from their dad who as it turned out had left the

family home due to child protection issues. I felt so bad to that kid
but angry that nothing had been said to me.

Angie (also present in this conversation) talked about how these issues then
had an impact on their work more generally:

> [...] And how many times do we get pupils coming in [to the men-
> tor base] saying they are upset. They don't want to talk; they just
> need a hug and a tissue, someone to mop them up. I 'get' the sensi-
> tive nature of child protection issues; I accept it is a thin line but
> how sterile do they want us to be? They want us to toe the line but
> they don't work our reality!

The learning mentors felt that being in possession of confidential information
at Priory Park High, somehow equated with power and position in the school
hierarchy in that the more you knew, the higher up you were. Correspondingly, a
lack of information denoted a person's more lowly position and from the mentors' perspectives was used as a means to keep them there. Thus, the withholding of information had come about in part because access to staff development
appeared to equate with opportunities for promotion and as such were guarded,
over-zealously so in some cases. The origins of those situations disclosed above
had come about some years earlier before the creation of the Year Manager role
(and thus more formalised systems of pastoral care), when the mentor role still
involved 'doing a bit of everything' (as described earlier by the Director of Pastoral Care) and reinforced by Angie who when reminiscing about the early days
of the mentor role remembered them 'scurrying around what were to become the
pillars of the *Every Child Matters* initiative' and trying to carve out a position for
themselves. At this time (early to mid-2000s), the mentors had approached their
line manager to request enhanced Child Protection training which they felt was
an important part of their ongoing professional development. Their request was
turned down due to this type of training being seen as more 'relevant' to other
staff which the mentors interpreted as a means to keep them '... in their station'.
Some years later when it had become the norm for Child Protection training to be
rolled out to the school workforce more generally, the mentors again experienced
frustrations in terms of their manager's interpretation of how this information sat
alongside other policies like Data Protection, this being given as a reason, once
again, to withhold child protection information from the mentors. As Paul said:

> [So now] we have had child protection training; we have had Data
> Protection training and when there are issues and concerns, we
> know that we don't speak with lots of people – I get all that. But
> with your immediate colleagues it is like 'you have given me a
> young person, you have said there are child protection concerns,
> but you have not told me what they are; yet you expect me to work
> with that young person'. That shows exactly what you think of me
> as a professional.

In actuality, many learning mentors in other schools did eventually take on more child protection responsibilities and in some cases became the legally required nominated 'Safeguarding' person, a role which had previously been the reserve of the teaching profession (Bishop, 2011).

The Time-limited Nature of One-to-One Interventions: '... And That Would Be Hard – Telling the Child That I Couldn't See Them Anymore'

The time limit imposed on their formal one-to-one interventions was another source of frustration expressed by the learning mentors. Here Marie articulates their collective experiences on this issue:

Marie: We would meet maybe every other week with the Inclusion manager, to talk about the cases and then they [the panel] would suddenly decide that particular pupils didn't need mentoring anymore. You wouldn't really .... well you could object, but on the whole, they would decide. They would say 'well I think six to eight weeks is fine'. I always felt it wasn't long enough; six weeks and you are only just getting to know somebody, building up for them to trust you. So that I found really frustrating, not having enough time, it was like half doing a job and that was a bit, you know, I felt that was a bit annoying.

Jo: [clarifies] But you didn't actually have any influence or sway over how long you could see them for, that wasn't a decision you could make?

Marie: Well somebody would say 'oh I think they're doing well now, I think they should come off' and you would say 'well no, that is because I am still supporting them, I'm trying to step back a bit, they are doing well, but there could be a fall around the corner' and they would say 'oh no, there's somebody else who's more needy, so they've got to come off now' and that would be hard, telling the child that I couldn't see them anymore. Well you didn't, you did carry on seeing them, you know? So as time went on, your workload got bigger and bigger because once you had mentored them, you would always have them kind of thing. I mean that should be, they [pupils] should always know that they can come to you if they need to. But yeah, I had to sometimes be inventive of how I saw people because they [middle managers] would say 'no you can't see them anymore'.

This account is invaluable in that it encapsulates the contested process of the mentor intervention in its entirety, demonstrating not only how mentors' assessments of pupils in their care were overridden, but also their reaction to this in continuing to offer support unofficially to the pupil anyway which has obvious implications for workload over time. Marie's account also indicates the pressures which members of middle management were under in moving pupils through the support systems as from their perspective there was always another pupil 'waiting in the wings' deemed to be in greater need of support. Marie, who as explained earlier had 'acted up' in the position of a Year Manager, was able to offer a key insight into the work that this involved. She recalled how initially she saw this as an opportunity which she assumed would entail a greater degree of pastoral input with pupils, as well as meeting and making relationships with their parents. However once in role, the reality turned out to be somewhat different:

Marie: I was quite surprised ... you're dealing mostly with negative things with the children, time seems to be spent dealing with problems that have arisen and also some menial tasks that I felt that we were too well paid to do, if you know what I mean, I don't mean it was beneath me, but ... I felt that if you had more time for positive things, then the negative stuff wouldn't happen.

Jo: Could you give an example of something that you felt was quite menial?

Marie: Like giving out detentions, writing out the slips, finding the kids, giving the slips to the kids, you know ... it would take ages and then they wouldn't turn up and then you'd have to go back to the data sheet and fill it in, ... you were doing it with the same kids though. To me it was pointless, it wasn't working. Surely you'd have been better getting them kids to talk about ... more like you would as a learning mentor, to stop it from happening, so you didn't have to do that.

The lack of actual pastoral work involved in this role was a key factor leading to Marie's decision not to make the move from TA to Year Manager a permanent one, even though the opportunity arose to do so:

Marie: I felt that it wasn't a role for me full time. There is a lot of admin, a lot of paperwork, a lot of people wanting stuff there and now and I just thought ... I don't actually need to do this. Yes I would like to earn more money and respect, but ....

Marie's take on the Year Manager role was extremely frank and without a trace of the institutional capture that had been apparent in other accounts gathered early on in the fieldwork. Perhaps this was because Marie was no longer acting up as a Year Manager so some time had passed which enabled her to reflect on this period. It is important to note that her account above reinforces the views of the Year 7 YM who expressed that she needed the learning mentors to do more of the hands-on pastoral work because the bulk of her work was spent managing and monitoring significant student numbers.

Like Marie, Angie was not unsympathetic to the pressures that Year Managers were under to move pupils rapidly through the referrals system, stating that she had 'a soft-spot for their reality'. When asked to clarify further, she acknowledged their heavy workload and the pressure on them from *their* immediate line-managers to 'come up with the goods'. However, this did not mean that she was wholly in support of their approach or would not call out what she considered to be poor practice. One such example proved to be a critical piece of datum in evidencing how the learning mentors' lack of status led to their exclusion from key events. This is recounted below and provides an extremely illustrative example of the mentor's position within the school.

Daniel, the Meeting and the 'Missing' Learning Mentor

Daniel was a Year 10 pupil who Angie had supported both officially and unofficially for a significant period. Based on numerous observations of their interactions Angie and Daniel's relationship could be described as 'straight-up'; Angie was constantly but good-humouredly challenging Daniel about aspects of his behaviour or poor choices he had made, in her words 'always bending his ear about something'. For his part, Daniel responded well to Angie most of the time and demonstrated a desire to engage with her and a respect for her that was not usually extended to other staff. Angie's work with Daniel had also involved one or two home visits enabling the beginnings of a relationship with his mother whose previous reluctance to engage with the school was seen as a problem by middle managers. Daniel's home life was complex in that one of his parents and an older sibling held numerous criminal convictions and had served custodial sentences, so their presence at home was sporadic. Although often reticent to talk openly about his situation, Daniel did on a handful of occasions, disclose to Angie that he feared for his future, expressing a kind of fatalism given the path that others in his family had taken and his own record of temporary school exclusions.

Angie suspected that Priory Park High's real agenda for Daniel was one that would eventually result in his permanent exclusion, a decision that she felt strongly was not the answer, particularly considering Daniel's perspective on and insight about his situation. She saw the school's stance of trying out varying interventions with Daniel as disingenuous and merely 'going through the motions' in order to provide an evidence trail that they had 'explored every avenue' before his permanent exclusion. Moreover, she was critical of how little or no thought was given to how this could undermine her work with him. The situation described above culminated in an incident where Angie had been walking past the schools 'board room' – the facility used to hold formal meetings – and, glancing through the glazed panel in the door caught sight of Daniel, his mother, and older brother seated at the table having a meeting with his Year Manager and the Director of Pastoral Care. She recalled that her immediate reaction had been 'oh that's good' as this was the first time that Daniel's mother had actually been into the school. However, this had been followed with a mixture of puzzlement and anger, as to why she hadn't also been invited to, or even told about the meeting given that she was the member of staff who had been the most involved with Daniel's family to date. Angie spoke about this incident later that day:

> *Angie*:   I had done the initial home visit and filled out all the paper-work ... but hadn't been invited to the meeting!
>
> *Jo*:   Why do you think that happened?
>
> *Angie*:   Maybe the Year Manager was overworked and just didn't think, I like to think it wasn't malicious ... maybe we [the mentors] are an afterthought or maybe we are still thought of as like on the TA side ... you know 'Oh we don't need them, we can just do this'.

Despite these eventual uncomfortable reflections on her exclusion from this meeting, Angie had, at the time, made a swift decision to intervene in order to ensure that Daniel did have someone present who could ensure that his viewpoint was put across. As such when reading Angie's further account of what happened, there appears to be a clear intent on her part to act as Daniel's voice or witness to his reality:

> Anyway ... I made sure I put myself in there! I just walked in and sat down. That boy is not going to be able to voice in that meeting how shitty and upset and low he's been feeling. He was just sitting there with his head down waiting to get a 'bollocking,[1] he's not going to speak up and express that. ...They [pastoral and middle managers] need to know ... and if they don't know how can they help him? And that can be forgotten about, it [pastoral interventions] is about helping someone.

Once again, it is possible to see the different motivations at play and at odds here. Angie views her role as being primarily *'about helping someone'* but recognises that other agendas and pressures are present, leading to outcomes which she considers to be harmful to pupils that some staff have deemed problematic but in her view are vulnerable and in need of support. From the perspective of the middle managers, Angie's intervention could have been seen as an attempt to undermine their actions in calling the meeting. Nevertheless, the mentor felt strongly that there was no path back for Daniel if he was excluded. Indeed, the negative

---

[1]A colloquial term for a severe reprimand.

outcomes for young people in this situation in relation to accessing further education, training and employment, as well as the increased risk of entering the criminal justice system (Bryson, 2010; Department for Education, 2018b; Ogg & Kaill, 2010; Vincent, Harris, Thomson, & Toalster, 2007) suggest that her fears were well founded.

Angie expressed that situations like the one above came about primarily because those that directly managed the mentors had never themselves worked in these roles. As such they lacked a genuine understanding of what the learning mentors did during what she termed their 'grass roots hours', which she saw as vital in building up a relationship and 'giving a good type of practice and service'. Seeing her role in this way is clearly at odds with how it had been envisaged by others and perhaps explains the reason for her exclusion from the meeting with Daniel. This sentiment was expressed many times during the study, no more so than her earlier comments where she rounded on her line-managers in relation to their 'sterile' stance on child protection matters leading to her earlier exclamation of: 'They want us to toe the line but they don't work our reality!'

Unofficial Interventions: Unseen, Unacknowledged?

One way in which the mentors resolved the dilemmas and frustrations set out above was to consciously take a more agentic approach to their work. This was implied by Marie's earlier comment that in relation to time-limited interventions 'you did carry on seeing them, you know?' Thus never far from the surface of mentors' accounts of their work was the extent of their unofficial interventions, as illustrated in Chapter 7 by Josie who sought support when experiencing her parents' separation and subsequent reconciliation and Sally, whose concern for her mother was not fully acknowledged by the school. This gives rise to the question of whether the middle and senior managers were aware that these two work practices of official and unofficial interventions co-existed. Both the Head and Deputy Headteacher expressed the importance of the mentor role not undermining the teacher's role, along with a wider concern expressed amongst staff that pupils should not be able to 'misuse' mentoring interventions. It could be argued however that this is the reality: the role *at one and the same time* supported teachers in contributing to resolving barriers to learning and ensuring the swift return of pupils to class (as in the Angry Year 11 girls); but the very existence of both role and its physical space, the Mentor Base, was offering something that pupils could agentically turn to which in itself had the potential to undermine the teaching role. It is that 'messiness' or incoherency which is often the end result of having support roles like the learning mentor situated alongside the teacher. The contested and contradictory ways in which the Mentor Base was seen at varying points in the study particularly illuminated this issue, as seen here in this Progress Leader's comment:

> What we do have to put our foot down with every so often is the learning mentor base becoming a haven where the students decide they can go down there and hide from their lessons and

their work and their teachers ... you know when things get over-whelming for them, which yes in a way we've encouraged that by providing the support ... but we have to discourage them from doing that when it's not really necessary or when they are doing it too often and [need to] talk about what the problem is as opposed to just going and hiding from it. [Also] when they [pupils] are doing it because ... they are being a bit lazy or today they are tired or overwhelmed or have missed a deadline or just because they haven't organised themselves ... But then for other students we use it almost for that purpose where it is a haven for them at certain times in their school career because of what's going on at home or because they just need it ....

This rather confusing narrative conveys how the Progress Leader veers between seeing the value of the mentor base as means of support – just as long as some pupils don't use it too much! She provides clear examples of how some pupils 'misused' certain aspects of the mentoring provision but at the same time recognises that for others, the support provided by the mentors in the base, represented something of a 'life-line'.

Experiences of Line Management

Over the period of the ethnography, the mentors recounted numerous incidences where they felt they had been overlooked by their immediate managers both in relation to their more typical day-to-day work *and* when critical events took place. During the earlier part of the study, the school implemented a second round of redundancies as a direct result of losing funding after the Ofsted inspection (previously noted in the school pen picture presented in Chapter 5). As a result of this process the mentors were one of the staff groups targeted for cuts and were required to attend an interview as a means to decide which two of the three would remain. In the weeks leading up to the interview it was possible to observe visible changes in the dynamics of the mentoring team as they struggled to support one another whilst fearing for their own job and future at the school. For ethical reasons I withdrew from the team during this period. The outcome was that Cheryl was unsuccessful in retaining her position and for a number of weeks was facing the very real prospect of redundancy. At the eleventh hour she was redeployed into another newly emerging paraprofessional role, that of Parental Advisor and from this point on she became extremely withdrawn in terms of her contact with myself as researcher. A few months later, there was a further staffing restructure which was not communicated very clearly to the two remaining mentors, leaving a question mark in their minds over what their role would actually be. Angie in particular viewed this as the final straw:

In December, our line management changed. Again. Or you know, was passed on to another hand although it's still a little bit blurry ... I said [to middle management] 'Look what's going on? Last year, we lost a colleague … we weren't even asked our opinion, we were told how things would be, then we started back and no one's even met with us! Yeah we've got thick skin but how do you think that makes us feel? What type of professionalism is that? Is there something that we are missing here, do we [both] need to start looking for another job?'

As has already been shown, some of the frustrations expressed by the mentors were based on an uncertainty and therefore anxiety about how their work was perceived and understood by others in the school. This became even more evident when a further Ofsted inspection took place during which the Headteacher actively arranged for one of the inspectors to meet with Paul and observe a one-to-one intervention. Within Paul's animated retelling of his Ofsted experience, his surprise and pleasure at being singled out by the Headteacher was evident:

[…] even though we have said it would be nice if people at least pretended to take an interest in our work … the Senior Leadership Team were confident about sending inspectors to see us ….

Appraisal and Continuing Professional Development

The mentors' dissatisfaction with how they were line-managed could also be evidenced when discussing their opportunities for formal appraisal and continuing professional development (CPD). In one incident a new appraisal system had recently been introduced in which staff were required to complete their own personal develop review under the guidance of their line manager. Angie and Paul did not receive any information about the new system so were surprised when late one Thursday, they were contacted by their line manager instructing them to submit their reviews promptly due to the submission deadline being the very next day. Concerned about not having had any guidance about something that could potentially impact on their career path and pay, they had gone to talk to the member of staff who was the school lead on this. He in turn expressed concern that they had been 'left out of things'. In their frustration, the mentors decided to boycott the official process and their line manager ended up completing and submitting their individual reviews on their behalf.

In a further example, it is possible to contrast one mentor's experiences of seeking further professional development with teachers pursuing the same objective. As noted in Chapter 2, an up-skilling of the schools workforce had led to the then Department for Education and Skills (DfES) commissioning the development of National Occupational Standards (NOS) and a qualification framework for Learning, Development and Support Services (DfES, 2004). For learning mentors, the first step into this was a national training programme which involving constructing a portfolio of evidence-based work. This then led on to a Foundation Degree (FD) written by the LEA, in partnership with a local Higher Education provider for those wishing to continue their professional development. Angie had completed the national training programme relating to the NOS whilst working at a previous school and already possessed a Higher National Diploma (HND), an academic qualification which is equivalent to the FD. Exploring her options, she asked her immediate line-managers if she could enrol to do an MA in Youth and Community Studies which included a professional youth work qualification, reflecting the wider trend of having a multi-disciplinary base in school settings (Calvert, 2009; Nathan, 2011). Making the case that her attendance on the course would have a limited impact on the school in terms of time away from the job (missing one half-day a week for approximately half the school year) and funding (she was intending to self-finance), Angie asked to be supported to undertake the course. The initial response from her line-managers was less than enthusiastic, declining her request that one of them take on the role as her nominated practice supervisor, this being a requirement of the course. Formal confirmation of whether she could or could not do the course was not given despite numerous requests. Feeling frustrated at this lack of clarity, Angie made a direct approach to the then Headteacher who granted permission for her to undertake the course. She then doggedly approached three teachers with whom she felt she had informal but good working relationships in the hope that one of them would be willing to undertake the supervisory role mentioned above. This rather drawn-out process was one I explored further with Angie:

> *Jo*:   Was it a bit stressful? I mean doing something that you knew you didn't have your manager's support and approval of, in terms of actually applying for and then doing the [MA] course?

> *Angie*: It was weary ... but you know summat [something] I was like ... for the microphone, I'm sticking two fingers up! (Gestures) Do you know what I mean? But if I had to wait on them to make a decision, I'd still be waiting!

When asked if the process at this time was as arduous for teaching staff wishing to undertake further courses for *their* CPD Angie laughed bitterly exclaiming 'Hell no!'

It was never made clear to Angie by her immediate line-managers as to why this course was not seen as an appropriate path to pursue in their eyes. Also unclear, is why the apparent indecision on the part of her line-managers was eventually and rapidly overridden by the Headteacher, an act which throws further confusion on the notion that paraprofessionals cannot easily access the upper echelons of the school hierarchy. What *is* clear is that Angie faced but overcame, her own 'barriers to learning' in her desire to take on CPD.

This chapter has demonstrated how the contradictions and incoherencies previously found in senior and middle-management views of the learning mentor role, impacted the day-to-day work of this paraprofessional group. The mentors reported frustrations regarding how little information was shared with them regarding the pupils they were tasked with supporting as well as the time-limited nature of these interventions. Access to training and continuing professional development was also identified as a further area of concern with obstacles at middle-management level that appeared to be based on the mentors' lack of professional status. Moving forward, an important question to consider is whether these issues occurred because of the newness/experimental nature of the learning mentor role or whether they are in fact characteristic of all paraprofessional roles. The penultimate chapter seeks to address these issues.

Chapter 11

View from an 'Older' Paraprofessional Group

The data presented in this chapter were generated through discussing the work knowledges of two Higher Level Teaching Assistants (HLTAs), Cath and Pat. The initial premise for including the HLTAs and TAs in the study was to gain their perspectives and understandings of the learning mentor role. However, when talking about the work of the mentors, they made a series of comparative references to their own work and it became apparent that their standpoints as 'longer-serving' paraprofessionals who pre-dated the notion of a 'schools workforce' (Calvert, 2009) offered many parallels with the learning mentors' experiences. This was particularly pertinent in relation to how their role had initially been perceived and understood by teaching staff. The discussion starts in outlining the current roles performed by the HLTAs, Cath and Pat. In addition, Marie, who at the time of the study was working as a Teaching Assistant (TA), but, as previously noted had also worked as a learning mentor and Year Manager, also makes a significant contribution in this chapter.

Current Roles and Specialisms of the HLTAs: Cath and Pat

We first met Cath in Chapter 5 during our tour of Priory Park High in the school pen picture. Cath's main responsibility was to run the Pupil Nurture Centre (PNC) which as previously explained, supported pupils who, for a variety of reasons were deemed to be vulnerable and would struggle in larger mainstream classes. Cath had started her working life as a teaching assistant working with pupils deemed to have challenging behaviour prior to the role of 'behaviour support' becoming as established and formalised to the extent that it had by the early 2010s. She described her work activities in the PNC as:

> Looking at pupils a bit more closely, giving them time to talk … just getting an overall view of the pupil really, not just in terms of learning but the whole picture …. So although pupils will work in

Propping up the Performative School: A Critical Examination
of the English Educational Paraprofessional, 143–158
Copyright © 2022 by Jo Bishop
Published under exclusive licence by Emerald Publishing Limited
doi:10.1108/978-1-83982-242-120221011

there [the PNC] and bring work from other lessons it's also giving us a chance to have time to talk and to do other things as well, maybe put some programmes of work in ourselves ....

Cath felt strongly that this was a positive approach as it ensured that each pupil had a connection with a member of staff as soon as they started attending the school. This was seen as particularly beneficial for pupils entering the school as a result of a managed move who might present with more challenging behaviour and would therefore benefit from this personal approach; an observation which has been echoed in the wider literature (Vincent, Harris, Thomson, & Toalster, 2007).

As well as the PNC, Cath had recently been appointed to run a new provision called the Key Stage 3 (KS3) Learning Centre. This intervention had come about to replace a previous system known as the 'withdrawal room'; a place where pupils were taken if teachers felt that they were disrupting others learning but which overtime was felt to be ineffective. As Cath explains here: 'It was recognised that it was ... the same group of pupils there most of the time ... particularly out of Year 9'. Thus, the KS3 Learning Centre was designed as an intensive catch-up mechanism for those pupils that had 'gaps in their learning' from the previous year, whilst trying to keep pace with the current demands of the curriculum. Despite heading up both provisions Cath disclosed that she had not '... got a new contract or anything so I don't know what my title is yet' suggesting that the school's approach to appointing HLTAs was in a state of flux and/or that their job titles and the contractual obligations that accompanied them were not as explicitly set out as those for teaching staff.

Moving now to Pat who was ran the ASDAN provision. Readers may remember that her path to Priory Park High was examined in Chapter 5 when discussing IE's 'generous definition of work'. Here it was noted that her employment choices were inexplicably bound up with the need to find a job which fitted around her work as a parent. However, as the excerpt below shows, this pragmatism is only part of the picture as throughout the ethnography, Pat talked passionately about her work of supporting pupils, especially those who had a particular type of barrier in accessing the curriculum:

Pat: I've always been involved in the nurture groups and the access groups. So it's the kids with moderate learning difficulties, severe learning difficulties and autism.

Jo: Is that something that you just kind of fell into or something you found out that you like and are good at?

Pat: It was a case of we had one boy [at the school], who was severely autistic ... speech and language problems, communication difficulties. He communicated by the odd word and grunts ... and I just fell in love with him; he was a handful, but he was wonderful to support, and so I went on then

to look at 'Asperger's Syndrome' and ... 'Teenagers' ... the
reaction with the hormones and everything else to these
'isms' so to speak, you know? And found a little niche there
that I really enjoyed doing.

The fact that both Pat and Cath managed provisions which supported those
pupils who were situated *outside* of mainstream class settings is important to
note as it raises questions about existing understandings of the HLTA/TA which
depict these roles as predominantly classroom-based (Cruddas, 2005).

In Chapter 5, I underlined the importance of looking beyond institutional
capture or discourse to gain an accurate understanding of people's work activities when interpreting data. If I were to go no further than the participants' own
descriptions of the provisions that they were tasked with running, they would be
understood, somewhat uncritically, as the different facets one might expect to see
in the day-to-day functioning of a mixed ability, all-inclusive school. However,
once attention is paid to the actualities of their work it is possible to explicate how
the institutional order *creates* the conditions of individual experiences (McCoy,
2006) which specific to this study are those whose work entails supporting young
people who for varying reasons are on the margins of mainstream provision.
Thus, as the work knowledges of both HLTAs unfolded, it became ever clearer
that a number of striking parallels could be drawn between *their* accounts and
those of the learning mentors. The key issues to emerge were: the importance
of the staff/pupil relationship, the pastoral elements that were integral to their
work tasks and their starting points in relation to their work as paraprofessionals.
These issues will now be discussed in turn.

The Importance of the Staff/pupil Relationship – 'I Wanted to Have That Relationship With Young People That Maybe You Don't Always Get as a Teacher'

Cath's response to the question of what she enjoyed about her work was immediate and emphatic:

Spending time with the young people really, that's the most
important part of my work. And also that it's very varied so
it changes all the time ... because I never really wanted to be a
teacher, I didn't want to stand in a classroom and do ... (pauses
and thinks) I wanted to have that relationship with young people
that maybe you don't always get as a teacher, and I like the challenge of doing something a bit more ... a bit more difficult ...
I think (laughs a little).

Similarly, the positive regard that Pat had for the pupils she worked with was
clearly conveyed and not just through her earlier comments regarding the pupil
who she described as a 'handful, but [...] wonderful to support'. When recalling

some of the pupils she had worked with when first appointed and was at that time relatively inexperienced in a school setting, it was evident that Pat had significant insight into the time, patience, and empathy that was required to establish a relationship in the first place. Particularly, as she explains in this account, with those pupils who were initially extremely hostile to any offers of support:

> I was in a class where I was pushed in at the deep end because they were so short staffed and it was exam time as well. I came in at the beginning of May, so it was straight into GCSEs ... So I was put in the bottom set English, Year 11, and there was a group of kids at the back, these girls, and they were just horrible [smiles]. They were foul mouthed, their every other word was 'f***ing' and they were rude ... if you walked near them to see if they wanted any help they would say [mimics] 'oh miss, your breath stinks!' and this kind of thing. I didn't give up ... I'm a stubborn little mule! I thought 'no, you are not going to get rid of me that easily'. So the more they persisted in telling me my breath stank, the more I used to pull up my chair and see if they needed any help; and eventually it got through to them that I wasn't there to put any barriers in the way, or to take the mickey out of them. I did really want to help ... and then you get talking to the individuals and you see the barriers that they've got ... and then you really get to know the kids.

This is reminiscent of Cheryl and Angie's comments in Chapter 6 about not allowing pupils' hostile behaviours and/or verbal outbursts to become the primary focus of their interactions with them. Pat's resilience and patience in seeing beyond the behaviours displayed by the pupils meant that she could develop a deeper understanding of the young people she supported. In our discussions she went on to cite numerous barriers that pupils encountered including for some a reluctance to acknowledge that they had a learning disability/difficulty in the first place, due to the stigma that they perceived to be attached to this. The 'barriers' she refers to in the account above were personal issues faced by some, specifically one of the 'horrible' girls above who eventually disclosed to Pat a recent suicide in the family – an event that her younger brother had not coped well with by disengaging from school and turning to heavy drug-use, much to the concern of his older sister – Pat's pupil. In her recounting of this situation, Pat spoke directly about the area this pupil was from, having lived there herself as a child, specifically how she saw it as representing both positive and negative elements in their lives:

> [...] in some ways [it is] a fantastic community because they look after each other; but in other ways, it becomes the norm for them to be out on the streets doing the drugs because ... that's their life.

This apparent knowledge of locality offered a further parallel with the assumed notion that learning mentors were somehow more known or embedded in the local community than their teaching counterparts (and the US paraprofessionals before them). It also ties in with the Headteacher's earlier observation of some school staff having a greater ability to access, (through patience, time, understanding or even their own biography) the 'places, people and contexts that perhaps other school staff could not.

HLTAs/TAs Delivering Pastoral Care within Their Provisions

Turning now to how pastoral elements were shown to be integral in the work of HLTAs and TAs, we start with perceptions of the spaces that their interventions took place in as these provide another aspect of the data which offered parallels with the mentor experience. Like the Mentor Base and Breakfast Club, the PNC was characterised as an inviting and nurturing place but, unlike the mentor-led provisions, it was not open access. Here, Cath explains this point further:

Cath:	We get loads of kids going 'can I come in the PNC?[Mimics young children] Do you know what I mean? … little faces at the window … [laughs]
Jo:	And why do you think they want to do that? What is their perception of what you do?
Cath:	I think they think we have a nice time [Mimicking pupils again] 'oo are you giving them a cup of tea! Can I have a cup of tea too?' Do you know what I mean? Like we have quite a lot of kids [coming to the PNC] who don't have breakfast for example … you know there's a bit of that really so those not coming to the PNC think it's someone nice to be with for a bit and it's a bit of a chill out … and I think they see that probably with the mentors as well.
Jo:	And what do you say to them then when they ask to come in?
Cath:	We just say 'no you can't sorry' and they say 'if I'm naughty can I come in?' and I say 'no if you were naughty you would definitely not come in!' I think … very few kids don't appreciate coming in [to the PNC], very few. One or two, perhaps quite high achievers who say 'Why am I in here? Is it the stupid room?'

Although pupil perceptions do not figure in this chapter to the extent that they did when discussing the Mentor's work previously, it is interesting that some pupils saw provisions like the PNC (above) and the Mentor Base when used to hold one-to-one interventions (expanded on below) as something for the 'other', characterised by stigmatising comments like: 'Is this the stupid room?' This is ironic given that such provisions originate from an agenda based on notions of inclusion. Marie also noted this reticence to engage with support mechanisms on the part of some pupils during her time as a learning mentor:

> [There is a] perception [amongst] what you class as the academic 'good' kids [that] think they [the mentors] are just here for the naughty kids ... if you've got a mentor, it means you are naughty and that's what they think about somebody that has a mentor [so] sometimes pupils would want to be quite secretive about them having a mentor. They didn't want their friends to know ... you had to meet with them in secret.

Returning to the HLTAs, Pat was also keen to convey what she very definitely saw as the pastoral dimension of the TA role along with other elements which could be likened to the mentoring interventions:

> I think the majority of TAs have a part-mentoring role; we all key-work certain kids, so we've got children that have got whatever difficulties they have in class and we are kind of responsible pastorally for them. So we meet with them, however often we can; sometimes it's easy because you are doing class work with them, so you can have a chat, find out what's going on in their lives or whatever. So we do kind of have that ... little bit of a rapport there with them.

It is accounts like these which raise the critical question of whether the job title of a support role actually matters if, in effect, they are all providing support and care. However, Marie's work knowledge forms a key piece of datum here having held the unique position of being employed *simultaneously* on part time contracts as both TA and learning mentor. Her comments below suggest that there were clear differences between the two roles and performing both at once presented problems for her and the pupils:

> [It] was quite difficult because half the time I was a mentor and half the time I was a teaching assistant. The kids were a little bit confused as to why I was in the class or not, and then I found a pull because I knew there were children that would need me and I was in school, but I couldn't, I couldn't help them at that time because that was my teaching assistant time.

A further parallel revealed in these discussions was the familial aspect of the relationship; however, rather than this perception coming from pupils as it did in relation to the mentors, it was Pat explaining how in her early days as a TA, she had drawn on her skills and experience as a parent in order to build relationships with pupils:

> [I would] think from a parent point of view because that's where I was at that time, I was like their parent.

It was also made apparent earlier that autobiographical aspects of her background were utilised as a means to build relationships with some pupils on the basis of what she perceived as shared experiences. In this excerpt she returns again to where she had lived when growing up:

> [...] And you say to them [pupils] 'look, pack it in, you're talking to someone who's already converted, I've lived there, I've been in that council estate ...' But yes, you have got to find ways to break down those barriers and it's ... by just carrying on and trying and trying ...

Starting Points in Relation to Their Work as Paraprofessionals: 'I Didn't Realise That Ordinary People Could Help Ordinary Children Just as Much as We Do ...'

The way in which the work of TAs had been perceived by teaching staff in its early days provided a direct parallel with the experiences of the learning mentors. For Cath this was in relation to how she felt some teaching staff had viewed 'the pupils that I work with' and how this had a knock-on effect to her own sense of identity and status:

> Well I've done it for 12 years – worked with pupils with mostly behavioural difficulties. When I first started, the issue was kind of brushed under the carpet *and you felt like you were under there with them*, but now it's changed and I think people have a different view of it really. (my emphasis)

She believed that this change in attitude had come about due to the time and effort put in by both herself and her line manager in going directly to teachers, to encourage them to develop an understanding of some pupils situations 'and some of the difficulties they experienced at home' and then crucially, showing teachers the work that pupils had done whilst being supported by the TAs outside of their class sessions:

> And I think once staff [teachers] have seen what we've actually achieved ... for example in PNC in the last couple of years, we've had Year 10s and 11s who have done their GCSE course work with us [and] I think staff have been ... impressed that we have managed to get that sort of work out of pupils and ... at that level as well. We have actually taken some kids ... for a whole year and got them through Maths GCSE and things like that. So I think that's made a difference ... that they can see that we are not just kind of patting [pupils] on the head and giving them a cup of tea, *we are actually getting some real learning work out of it* and this is really where the Key Stage 3 room has sprung up [a recognition that] we can get some real work out of the pupils we work with. (my emphasis)

Pat also recognised this lowly position that was occupied by TAs, but her account of her early experiences was far more agentic. Not only did she compare her own (employment) transition to adulthood unfavourably to that of her two siblings (who had entered the teaching and legal professions, respectively), she also reflected on how her own time at school had gone on to affect her earlier views of who did, and more tellingly did not, work in schools:

> I wish I had done it [the TA role] years and years ago [but] I left school and ... I did alright with my O-Levels[1], I passed everything that I took, but I was never an academic ... I think my view of school was a bit coloured because ... I didn't realise that ordinary people could help ordinary children just as much as we do, you know?

In further contrast to Cath who had cited the attitudes of some teachers as being a significant obstacle to her work being valued, Pat believed that in some instances it was the reluctance of TAs' themselves to 'change with the times' referring to some as 'the old wood', who 'just wanted to come in and be classroom assistants' and not step-up to the then new TA role which she described as 'being a pastoral role and getting to know the children'. This view of how the TA role had developed was also recognised by Marie although she did not share Pat's assessment of their peers:

> I mean it's like when the Teaching Assistants have gone from being called ... Learning Support Assistant, 'LSAs' and they'd be mums whose children went to the school, you know? We've stepped up, not that there was anything wrong with them, but you know, we've moved on and a lot more is expected as a Teaching Assistant, much more, which is good. Whereas now, there's more striving towards working together with the teacher.

Despite how the TA role had developed, Marie expressed that she avoided getting into direct conflict with other staff due to a fear of not appearing professional coupled with a belief that staff occupying lower positions in the hierarchy found it difficult to challenge those higher up:

> One thing that I'm not very good at although I've got better at it is conflict with other people. I really struggle with it, having to say to somebody 'I don't like how you did that' or 'I don't agree with that'. If something's happened in a classroom that I've been unhappy with, I find it difficult to go back and talk to somebody about it ...

---

[1]The predecessor qualification for school leavers to the GCSE.

Once I had clarified that the 'people' cited here were in fact teachers and middle managers, Marie distinguished between younger teaching staff (who she felt could see the benefit of having a TA in the lesson) and their older counterparts. She also identified that middle managers could and did undermine the actions of those teachers and TAs who might be seeking a more equitable working relationship. Here she recalled a recent incident where a TA in the school had been reprimanded by a Progress Leader for following a teacher's instruction to sign the report card of a pupil she had been working with, pointing out that this was not part of the TA role. Marie felt that the overriding position of TAs which she saw as being located at the foot of the school hierarchy, was one which defined them:

Marie: I don't feel that there's any professional ... [pauses and searches for a word].

Jo: [offers] recognition?

Marie: [nods] ... [Because] as Teaching Assistants, we are the lowest paid members of staff probably in the school ... I think that, you know, they [middle and senior managers] feel that we are at the bottom of the pile. Often most of the Teaching Assistants do it because they love the job, it wouldn't really be for the pay because you could earn more in Tesco's or wherever really [laughs].

Although Marie presents her own lack of confidence and the lowly position of TAs in the school hierarchy as separate issues, I argue that they were very much connected. If a group of staff are used to carrying out instruction-based tasks they are not going to feel comfortable when 'suddenly' given more autonomy in drawing on their own assessments of pupils; especially when there is a perception or fear that to do so may be deemed as an inappropriate action by a higher authority.

The accounts given thus far paint a puzzling picture. As a support role, TAs are much more long standing and arguably therefore established in the fabric of a school and the mind-set of teaching staff. In many cases they have taken on further education and training to achieve HLTA status, enabling them to run interventions that were previously seen as falling within the domain of the teaching profession. Yet they continue to struggle with their professional identity and their place in the school hierarchy, not to mention remaining as some of the lowest paid members of staff.

HLTAs Perceptions of the Learning Mentor Role

The discussion now turns to consider whether HLTAs and TAs had, as fellow support staff, a more nuanced understanding of the learning mentor role than the senior and middle managers presented in previous chapters. Both HLTAs were noticeably more forthright and confident in conveying their understandings of the work of learning mentors. For example, Cath described them as 'a significant adult for pupils to go to in crises or [at] other times' to which the mentor would respond as a 'sort of coach' in talking things through with pupils. She also identified their signposting function in providing pupils and/or their families with connections to other services should that be necessary. One of the ways in which she distinguished the role from her own was how it tended to be 'much more mobile' compared to her work which took place in one of two classrooms. Like the Headteacher, she was also aware of the nature of the contact that mentors had with parents describing it as a 'friendly link' with school and contrasting that with her own form of contact with parents which was likened to more of 'a sort of teaching role'.

But even when questioned specifically about the learning mentor role, it was striking that Cath continued to draw on her own experiences as a TA. For example, when asked how she felt the role was perceived by other staff in the school, she observed a similar shift in attitude from the negative to the largely positive which is illustrated here:

Jo: And how do you think the learning mentor role is perceived in school by other staff?

Cath: I think it is … good. When I first started it was awful!

Jo: Was it?

Cath: Yes … and my role as well, I think people used to think 'oh they [mentors and pupils] just sit about, drink cups of tea, have a few sweets then pat them on the head and off they go'. I honestly think that that was the idea … Because it was all new, having people in school who were not teachers or teaching assistants [but] even teaching assistants … when I first got here, they used to have their lunch in a different room [from teaching staff] – how weird is that? … Whereas now it is a lot different; they [learning mentors] are more accepted … they have managed to get pupils in for exams … I think once teachers see that they have got a hand in learning through what they are doing then that's something they are more comfortable with. That is what they know and they think '… they are actually doing something that is helping' … but I don't think a lot of them [teachers] have seen it beyond that really. I don't think they see that other part of what they do that much.

In this excerpt, Cath indicates that the school struggled initially to understand the purpose of the learning mentor role and this reminded her of her own early days at Priory Park High, where the idea of a non-professional being given responsibilities for pupil's learning was very new. This demarcation of the paraprofessional from the professional was further underlined by the designation of separate staff rooms for each group. At the time of the study this arrangement no longer existed and the TAs could be observed as a distinct group seated together in the shared staff room every break and lunchtime. This (no doubt well-earned) downtime further illustrated how the TAs time with pupils was structured around timetabled sessions of formal learning whereas for the mentors, pupil-contact happened across lesson *and* break times.

As we delve further into this ethnography, it is possible to seen an increasingly common perception of interventions that take place outside of the classroom characterised as 'sitting about and drinking cups of tea' thereby trivialising them and obscuring their potential impact. To counter this, Cath provides further evidence regarding the contribution of the mentors in her observation that they helped ensure pupils were physically in school to sit their exams which in turn reassured teaching staff that their work is of value. Thus, the mentors are portrayed, like the TAs before them, as a group who have had to 'prove their worth' to teaching staff in terms of delivering the learning and achievement 'goods' on which the progress of the school is assessed and which clearly have a currency within the school context. However, lacking in currency and therefore less visible are the more pastoral dimensions of the learning mentors' work vis-á-vis Cath's belief that teachers are not able or willing to see beyond the academic to 'the other part of what they do'.

Similarly, Pat conveyed a good understanding of the learning mentor role, describing it as someone who was there for pupils having difficulties and thus providing 'another pair of ears'. She was also one of the few members of staff who was aware of the Breakfast Club as an intervention that was bound up with the role (possibly because it was on the same corridor as the provision she ran). It was notable that when talking about the approach of the mentors in building relationships with pupils she drew on, and likened the role to her own youth work experience as a Duke of Edinburgh Leader[2] implying once again the informal and voluntary elements of the role. She was also keen to highlight the nature of the support provided by the mentors insomuch as it took place *outside* of the classroom. Having identified this distinctive aspect of the mentor role she went on to question if this was actually the most effective way for learning mentors to carry out their work:

> It makes me wonder if the children who have got a learning mentor might perform better in class if the mentor was there to support them … as well as outside on the social and emotional aspects of things … because they must only see one side and then get reports from teachers … and in fairness, there are still some teachers that, if a kid's tarred with a bad brush, then they are never going to be any different in that teacher's eyes. They [teachers] don't give them

---

[2]This is a voluntary youth awards programme founded in the UK in 1956 by the late Prince Philip, Duke of Edinburgh.

second chances and poor 'Johnnie' because he swore at them once, they're never going to forgive him as long as he lives, until hell freezes over; he is still going to be [mimics teachers] 'that nasty boy that swore at me' and you know that's an adult wrong really, that should be righted.

Once again, the visibility of the mentors is raised as an issue in this account. Whereas Cath had an understanding of the mentors' role as 'much more mobile' in that, unlike many staff roles, they were not always going to be carrying out their work in a particular place at a specific time, Pat asks whether they should actually spend more time in the classroom if only to verify whether a teacher's perception of a pupil is correct. This questioning of *where* mentors might be most effective was also shared by Marie who when working as a mentor had drawn on her experience as a TA and taken it upon herself to go into class sessions to conduct pupil observations. Here she explains her rationale for doing so:

> Because I'd been a TA, I did [as a mentor] like to go into lessons with them, I found that really useful to be able to see what they were like, or their perception of [mimics the pupil] 'oh this teacher hates me and I don't do anything wrong'. So I'd think 'right, ok, I'll come in and see what's happening' … and because you weren't in that conflict with them, like the teacher was, it was easier to point out things that they might be doing that could be frustrating for the teacher. They would often confuse 'the teacher hated them' as opposed to 'the teacher doesn't like their behaviour' … well they [pupils] do, don't they! You know, [role plays a pupil/mentor interaction] 'She hates me!' 'No she doesn't, she just doesn't like how you behave. It's not the same thing at all'.

Thus, when in post as a learning mentor, Marie utilised classroom observations as *one of many* strategies in working with young people and challenging their perceptions and behaviours. This is a different position to Pat who is essentially questioning how effective the mentor's role can be when they are not linked explicitly to the key site where teaching and learning takes place, that is, the classroom. It also shows the value of one person experiencing different roles as in Marie's unofficial approach of fusing the more effective aspects of both the mentor and TA role in working as a type of hybrid.

These accounts also indirectly revealed how the HLTAs perceived power differentials between pupil and teacher as seen in Pat's desire to advocate for young people who may have been labelled or 'tarred with a bad brush' which she viewed categorically as an 'adult wrong' in need of remedying. This empathy with, and desire to support pupils where teachers had been too heavy-handed, bore another striking similarity with the mentors' perspectives and approach noted in previous chapters.

HLTA Explanations for 'Divisions' Between Teaching and Support Roles

The final issue under discussion relates to how the experiences of both TAs and HLTAs suggest that divisions or 'camps' were seen to exist between teaching and support staff. Pat's explanations as to how this had come about were based on her belief that the practices of support staff afforded them greater opportunities to really know the pupils:

> [Support workers] do have a bit more empathy with the children ... I mean there are no excuses for rudeness and swearing and things like that, but you can have an understanding of it when you know the kids and I think as a learning mentor or a support worker, you do get that, you know? [Emphasises this point] *You do!*

Her following comment implied that the reason for this was that teachers at Priory Park High were now facing ever greater pressures to deliver on the academic side given the recent Ofsted history resulting in a judgement of 'Special Measures' and as a consequence, falling pupil numbers:

> I think the teachers probably do [empathise with the pupils] but they have just got so much else on their minds anyway, with the finances and the situation they are in and pressure that they are under to deliver ....

And later on:

> Getting results, getting them through their exams ... that's more what the teacher focus is going onto, which is *the business side of the school* rather than ... *the pastoral care ... side.* (my emphasis)

Cath also pointed to how the teaching role had changed due to increased divisions between the roles of support and teaching staff. But rather than link these to the school's recovery after a poor Ofsted, she saw it as the consequences of previous policy agendas discussed below which had led to a 'hollowing out' of the pastoral dimension:

Cath: I think over time ... some of the onus on *the whole child* has been taken away from some form tutors and I think that's coming back, now that they're taking on that job of ringing up parents and talking and thinking a bit more about the children they've got in their class.

Jo: And you think it was missing for a while in school?

Cath: Yeah! I think it was kind of ... the mentors used to work in a room with me – we all used to work together at one point, and I think *we always felt like we were taking that on* ... you know *it was kind of left with us in a way*, well not just us, but ... a handful of people ... and because teachers are so busy as well and they have got all the data and whatever to do I think actually spending time with their kids ... [trails off] ... and really it should be the whole school that takes it on, shouldn't it? You know *everyone*.

Jo: I remember reading that one of the purposes of *Excellence in Cities* and the subsequent creation of roles like the learning mentor was that it 'freed up teachers ... [Cath interjects and we both say] ... to teach!'

Cath: But it's not just about teaching ... I don't see why you would come into a school just to teach when you are with young people ... there's more [to it] than that isn't there? But I think people have realised that now. They have a form period time, although they [SLT] are putting quite a lot of learning stuff back in that! But ... I would like to see people [teachers] just play games with their class or you know doing something like ... [pauses and thinks]

Jo: Something that is not all about learning?

Cath: Yeah!

Jo: And did you just say that you think this is coming back again?

Cath: I think it is just that everybody felt, you know, that they needed to take that onus back on again ... of *caring* for the child and I think that is important ... it is like ... you know that saying 'it takes a village to bring up a child' well I think it takes a school to bring up [a child] ... and that's the whole school. Not just a couple of people ...

This rather lengthy extract has been included in full as it identifies a number of issues which are key to this discussion. Cath starts by questioning the ethos of the school in terms of how it cares for its pupils. She is convinced of the need for a whole school approach, but wider policy initiatives had ended up channelling school staff into respective 'camps' and effectively separating the academic from the pastoral as seen in her comment: 'it was kind of left with us in a way'. To explain further, her previous training and qualifications were undertaken during the era of New Labour which as discussed in Chapter 2 envisaged, and talked positively of, a burgeoning 'Schools Workforce'. Cath herself had undertaken the *National Programme for Specialist Leaders of Behaviour and Attendance* instigated in 2007 by the then Department for Children, Schools and Families[3]; an initiative that formed part of the Social Inclusion agenda. She also referred to the *Every Child Matters* agenda and the *Learning Mentor National Training* as part of this discussion. However, in her view qualification and policy initiatives like these had effectively led to a 'giving up' or jettisoning of teacher-responsibility for the care of pupils. The loss of this relational element for teachers clearly comes out in this discussion countered by Cath's enthusiastic promotion of the need for a 'whole-school' approach. Earlier, in Chapter 8 the Deputy Head had offered a similar viewpoint in her observation that the staff–pupil relationship was an area the school needed to tackle. Comments like these suggest that the school had indeed struggled with this issue of who should 'do' the caring. This was further evidenced by Cath's observation that whilst form tutors were being handed back some pastoral time as a means to re-establish that building of relationships with pupils, SLT were 'putting quite a lot of learning stuff back in that'. This suggests that the function of form time was ill-defined and when seen as a forum to 'do' pastoral care was under threat.

The tension between the academic and the pastoral was clearly an issue in the school at the time of the study. This was borne out not only by Cath's comments above but further observations in the field. For example, on one occasion I attended a meeting in the Board Room and spotted multiple copies of an article published in the teacher CPD section of the *Times Educational Supplement* entitled 'Rapport is the key to re-engaging students' (Maddern, 2012). It advised teachers to (amongst other things) 'show teenagers respect, and let them know they are cared about and understood' and to 'ensure students develop a relationship with a trusted adult who can help them to keep on track with their learning', advice which strongly illustrates the 'seen' and 'unseen' mentor approaches outlined in earlier Chapters. Although I was unable to discover who had disseminated this article, its presence suggested that some staff in the school were thinking about and trying to promote a teacher–pupil relationship that went beyond a purely 'learning for results' function.

Like the learning mentors, the HLTAs recognised the difficulties experienced by teachers in imbricating the pastoral and academic strands into their everyday practices but more fundamental questions about the *purpose* of education were also raised in their accounts. Cath's rhetorical questioning of why someone would come into a space where there are young people, 'just to teach', is an observation which reflects the impact of this stripping down of the teaching role to focus solely on academic results. This has in turn, recast schools as exams factories (Hutchings, 2015) and performative institutions. Cath's plea that 'there is more than that [to school] "isn't there?"' reminds us that school should also be seen as a

---

[3]This Department was replaced by the Department for Education after the change of government following the 2010 General Election.

place that engages with broader understandings of pupils and 'their lives outside of the classroom' (Martin, 2016, p. 4).

Similar *and* Different Paraprofessional Experiences

This chapter has shown that there are a number of common denominators in paraprofessional experiences but tangible differences as well. The early experiences of the HLTAs suggest that schools have struggled to understand and integrate new forms of working not fitting the pedagogical model of 'teacher and learner' for some time. This is not therefore unique to the learning mentors. Furthermore, the work of both groups of paraprofessionals has been wrongly characterised and misunderstood by teachers which has led to a feeling of inferiority but conversely, a desire to 'prove their worth'. Perhaps most striking were the similarities in their respective approaches to supporting pupils. Both HLTAs and learning mentors talked of the pupils in a way which demonstrated that they were sensitively attuned to the needs of those young people who found themselves at the margins of school provision. The relationships that resulted further suggested that these staff had a more nuanced understanding of pupil experiences than their teaching colleagues.

The mentors and HLTAs/TAs both recognised the pressures that teachers were under to deliver results and how this limited their ability to include pastoral elements into their everyday interactions with pupils. For some support staff there was also an awareness of the extra-local when pointing to the impact of previous policy initiatives on theirs' and teachers' roles. Here their comments suggested that *compared* to teachers, their everyday work placed them *outside* of that performance-driven culture. The extent to which this might be so is a critical issue which will be discussed in the concluding chapter.

There were however important differences to note as well. The activities comprising the HLTA/TA role meant that the purpose of their work was less likely to be questioned, misunderstood, or misinterpreted. This is because provisions like the PNC and ASDAN embodied something that teachers, Progress Leaders and senior leaders (the latter two of which come from professional teaching backgrounds) could recognise and relate to in terms of their own work activities. Thus, although not under the gaze to the same extent as, for instance, teachers of 'Banker' and 'RAP' pupils, the work of HLTAs/TAs was more embedded into the academic endeavours of the school compared with that of learning mentor provisions and interventions. For their part, pupils were clear that the roles were qualitatively different and when a member of staff (Marie) was employed as a TA and learning mentor simultaneously, the result was confusion for pupils and a feeling of being conflicted and 'pulled' for that member of staff. This suggests that the degree to which schools actually think about the impact of different areas of learning and pastoral support being positioned alongside each other is questionable. In the final chapter, we will return to the issues raised by this data.

Chapter 12

Discussion and Conclusion

The ethnography of a learning mentor team presented in this book has enabled a detailed example of the work of paraprofessionals in an English state secondary school at the start of the twenty-first century. It has shown that the experiences of such workers are not dissimilar to earlier paraprofessional groups be that in an English context or, those working in comparative societies some 50 years earlier.

The purpose of this final chapter is to take a meta view of the experience of and understandings about paraprofessional work – both historical and contemporary – and in doing so consider a number of fundamental questions that this type of work gives rise to. For example, whether it is possible to identify a number of potentially progressive elements within a model of the paraprofessional workforce regarding on the one hand, a more diverse workforce (in terms of social class and ethnicity) thereby providing children and young a greater number of relatable adult role models being present and accessible within a school. Furthermore, whether such roles offer a space outside of the 'performative gaze' in which workers can work more creatively and in a more child-centred way. Conversely, there are also potential downsides to consider such as the paraprofessional experience being one of enduring lower pay, status and job security. Moreover, whether the work merely represents a form of 'warehousing' or social control over those pupils perceived as the 'drop-outs', the 'disruptive' and the 'deviant'? The discussion will now offer a critical analysis of these and other issues.

Drawing Parallels Between Policy Agendas in Their Construction of the Educational Paraprofessional

As shown in Chapter 3, paraprofessionals have existed within, and made contributions to earlier systems of formal education in other advanced capitalist nations. Accounts of campaigns to eradicate poverty through the employment of the 'indigenous poor' (Pearl & Reissman, 1965) and real-time documentation of the paraprofessional experience (Stewart, 1971) enable a comparison of how paraprofessional roles have been understood and utilised in an earlier time. It is clear that in both the USA and England, paraprofessional roles have been

Propping up the Performative School: A Critical Examination
of the English Educational Paraprofessional, 159–174
Copyright © 2022 by Jo Bishop
Published under exclusive licence by Emerald Publishing Limited
doi:10.1108/978-1-83982-242-120221012

created via projects that had explicitly political overtones and were predicated on the notion that the background of the paraprofessional contributed a type of organic skill set which supposedly enabled them to act as a 'bridge' and/or 'broker' between institution and community. Starting with a consideration of 'Policy Climate', Table 4 expands on these parallels offering examples where appropriate:

Table 4.   Parallels between Earlier Accounts of Paraprofessionals and Contemporary Experiences.

USA Mid 1960s Policy Climate	UK Early 2000s Policy Climate
'War on Poverty' realised through the Economic Opportunity Act 1964, gives rise to federal programmes such as *Head Start*, providing the impetus for new initiatives like 'New Careers for the Poor'	New Labour's policy agenda premised on the identification and elimination of risk and the centrality of work giving rise to new forms of working through initiatives like *Every Child Matters*
Compensatory Education based on the belief that a human potential for learning could be sharply curtailed by poverty	'Compensatory' initiatives (like the learning mentor role) are implemented to ensure that underachievement in areas of deprivation is 'eliminated and never excused'
Objectives	Objectives
To resolve unemployment and enable social mobility	To encourage 'employability' through up-skilling sections of the working class
To eradicate poverty amongst the 'indigenous poor'	To utilise employment (accompanied by a system of working tax credits) as a way out of poverty
Based on a Belief That:	Based on a Belief That:
The utilisation of 'community agents' (Stewart, 1971), that is, those persons only 'one step removed' from the client will improve services (HARYOU cited in Pearl & Reissman, 1965, p. vii)	The utilisation of people whose own biographies of school and 'growing up' offers a form of empathetic support to some young people that professionals might struggle to deliver
Underpinned By:	Underpinned By:
A policy goal of on-the-job education and training of paraprofessionals in collaboration with higher education institutions (not realised)	The creation of academic and vocational qualifications at Levels 3 and 4 which were validated by new government bodies as part of a Lifelong Learning agenda (now defunct)

New Public Management Giving Rise to a System of Performativity

Although many shared characteristics can be seen between the two policy eras above, one key development which differentiates each one is the implementation of new approaches to managing public services since the 1980s (Hood, 1995). Previously introduced in Chapter 2, the term 'New Public Management' (Newman & Clarke, 1997) initially signalled a move away from traditional bureaucratic methods towards systems characterised by performance management, performance measurement and monitoring, an emphasis on 'outputs' (which involves the close control of behaviour to maximise efficiency) and, a distrust of traditional professionals (Hudson & Lowe, 2004; Mahoney & Hextall, 2001). The backdrop to these changes has arisen from two key developments: first, an increasingly globalised economy as nation states became ever more aware that the growth of their economies depended on the notion of a 'universal consumer' of its goods and services; thus, the performance of education systems needed to be shaped in a way that permitted international comparisons (Elliot, 2001). This has been underpinned by the second development – the notion of a 'knowledge economy'. Here 'knowledge' and 'education' are treated as business products which can be exported for a high value return. This is then reflected in the changes to the economies of the UK (and many other industrial nations in that the nineteenth and twentieth centuries) that were traditionally based on manufacturing but now characterised by one 'where we compete on brains, not brawn' (Tony Blair, cited in Ball, 2008, p. 17). The impact of such changes should not be underestimated:

> The stakes are high. Throughout the world governments are attempting to reform their education systems in the face of national and global change. In many advanced industrial societies', where both economic and natural resources are in decline, investing in human capital now constitutes a central platform of economic and education reform. (Gleeson & Husbands, 2001, p. 1)

Earlier chapters documented how New Labour invested in the lives of poor children and young people through a host of new social and educational policies such as *Every Child Matters* and *Excellence in Cities*. But these investments were not given unconditionally and it is this which enables an understanding of what has changed when comparing and making sense of policy enactments in the two eras under consideration. In return for such investments in the New Labour era, workers had to accept a far greater degree of monitoring and micromanagement of their activities, in effect, the introduction of a new culture which has been termed 'performativity' within educational contexts (Ball, 2003; Jeffrey & Troman, 2012). Chapter 2 set out how the seeds of a performative culture were sown within an English context, starting with the Conservative's Education Reform Act of 1988 (Perryman, 2012) and then proceeding with a much firmer and confident resolve under New Labour (Elliott, 2001). To remind the reader of the three distinct strands of performativity: the pervasive culture of targets and auditing; a regime of regulatory mechanisms and a general marketisation of the environment (Bright, 2012). In Chapter 2 some attention was given to how performativity has impacted on teachers at the macro level with reports of creativity being stifled and confidence eroded, not just changing what the teaching role was but fundamentally, the persona of the individual who carried it out.

Given that the majority of this literature has tended to interrogate the shaping of subjectivities amongst 'professional' practitioners (see e.g., Murray, 2012), the extent to which performativity impacts on educational *para*professionals is less well known. For example, a key driver of performativity for teachers is performance management which has given rise to a discourse described as having deeply 'totalising' characteristics. Within this, teachers are presented as units of labour to be distributed and managed and whose structural characteristics (such as their ethnicity, gender and class) are deemed largely irrelevant, provided that they comply with certain specifications and meet particular working criteria. But what happens when structural characteristics *do* take centre stage? As seen in the case of both the 1960s US paraprofessional and the early 2000s English paraprofessional, ethnicity, gender and class, (and in some cases an amalgamation of all three) come to be viewed as *the* 'qualifying experiences' needed to undertake a paraprofessional role. In contrast with teachers, the structural characteristics of paraprofessionals are not irrelevant but actually become *the* totalising characteristics referred to above; whether that means being cast as a 'bridge' between school and community due to an assumed possession of local knowledge, or as a role model who is tasked with raising the achievement of certain groups of young people whose engagement in education is a cause for concern. Both examples are predicated on a belief that each group – the paraprofessional and the child/young person – will have similar experiences through a shared biography of place and community/family experiences.

Positioning and Understanding the Place of a Paraprofessional within a Performance-based Culture

It is therefore vital that a more holistic analysis of the impact of performativity is undertaken; that is, one that considers *all* staff groups present in a school. One aspect of such an analysis is the need to consider the degree of visibility given to different work activities. This is because performative cultures presume that the performance of core activities within organisations can be made transparent to the public's gaze on a continuous and sustainable basis via the aforementioned technologies of audit. Within schools the core activities are deemed to be those teaching and learning activities that lead to qualifications as measurable outcomes. Adopting an ethnographic approach enabled myself, as researcher, to investigate the issue of visibility in relation to paraprofessional staff. Thus, what follows is a series of diagrams (labelled Figs. 1–4) which map the work activities of staff groups at Priory Park High, taken as an example of a typical all-inclusive English state secondary school. In line with the ethnography the primary focus of this analysis is on the learning mentor role and the mapping is based on accounts of 'work knowledge(s)' which, to remind the reader, is a term used in Institutional

Ethnography to denote a person's experience of and in their own work, meaning what they do, how they do it and what they think and feel. It also refers to the implicit or explicit coordination of their work with that of others (Smith, 2005).

1. Understanding a School's Activities as 'Core' and 'Peripheral'

The first diagram illustrates how the school's overall activities can be designated as either 'core' or 'peripheral'. During the ethnography, it became apparent that the school was organised around a curriculum/pastoral split, a situation not untypical in English state schools (Power, 1996). In practice this meant that the activities and staff associated with the curriculum attained a higher status, more secure conditions of employment and a more transparent and accessible career path than those whose focus was deemed more 'pastoral'. This was reminiscent

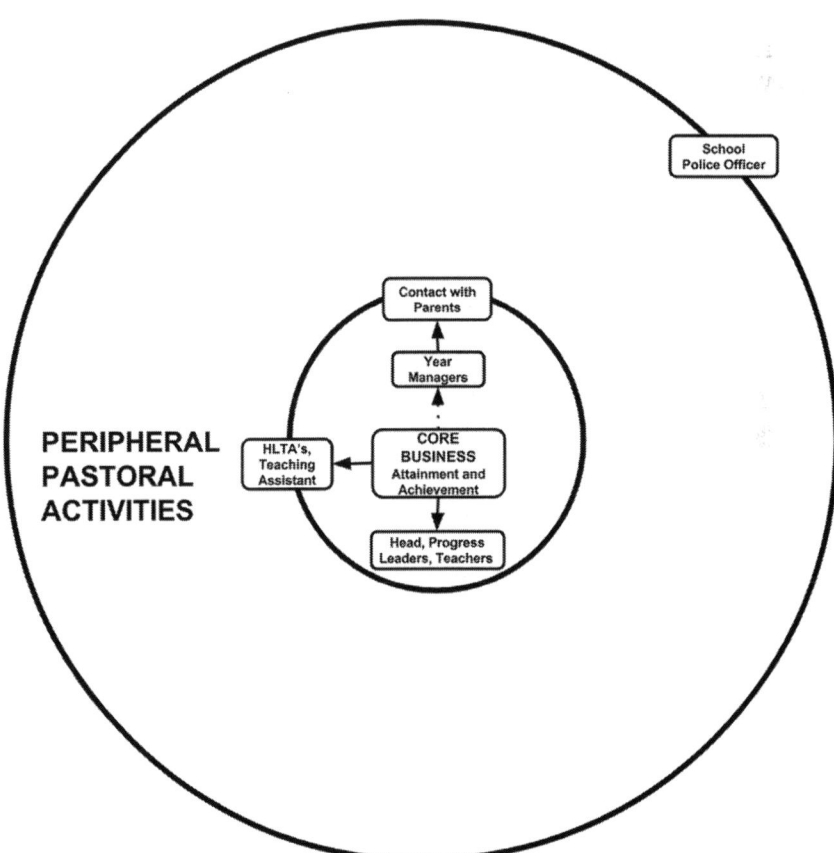

Fig. 1.   Understanding the School's Activities as 'Core' and 'Peripheral'.

of the notions of core and peripheral labour that emerged from debates around labour flexibility since the early 1980s (Pollert, 1988). For the core, the model rests upon the assumption of a direct relationship between primary employment conditions and the business concept of an organisation's 'core activity'. In contrast, the periphery provides a 'numerical flexibility' in which workers are employed in less secure or irregular ways. Thus, the first 'map' set out above takes as its premise that the core business of the school is attainment and achievement realised through the teaching and learning components of school activities (Fig. 1). This is particularly significant in Priory Park High, given its (then) recent Ofsted judgement of a school that 'Require[d] Improvement'. The core workers inhabiting the inner domain are the Headteacher (and other senior leaders), the Progress Leaders (those teachers with responsibility for overseeing that attainment levels were secured for each Year) and of course the teaching workforce as a whole. To pre-empt accusations of an overly simplistic analysis it should be acknowledged that the core could be further broken down into subjects according to status, meaning the 'contribution' of different areas of the curricular to a school's academic success and what governments have deemed as more or less desirable at different times. This was illustrated by the comments of the Teacher of Food Technology in Chapter 9 who referred to 'the core' as a set of subjects which she understood her own area as very much outside of and therefore lacking in value and status.

Returning to the first 'map', the broken line connecting up to the Year Managers denotes that whilst their work activities helped to 'shore up' the core business of attainment, their primary role was to oversee the pastoral 'business' of the school in terms of monitoring attendance, contacting parents, identifying pupils perceived to have 'barriers to learning' and referring them on to mentoring or behavioural interventions. HLTAs and TAs are depicted as 'hovering' between the core and periphery as on the one hand they are predominantly class-room based, supporting the teaching and learning activities of the core business and in the case of provisions like the Pupil Nurture Centre, ensuring that some pupils are 'exam-ready'. However, the experiential accounts of HLTAs whose provisions were situated outside of the core, demonstrated that they too had a different relationship with pupils to that of teachers, with their work being characterised by numerous pastoral elements. Although not figuring in this particular ethnography it is worth noting the presence of other peripatetic workers, such as the school's police officer who can be seen hovering on the boundary poised to intervene in sometimes dramatic fashion, as and when required.

2. Mapping the Learning Mentor 'Seen' Activities

From this point on, the diagrams are intentionally presented as a 'layering' of work activities. This second 'map' (Fig. 2) locates the learning mentors within the core–periphery structure in terms of depicting the *official* version of their activities (see top left), described here as '"Seen"' Mentor Activities' and expanded further in the accounts of Breakfast Club, the Mentor Base and perhaps most significantly their one-to-one work arising from official referrals (all appearing

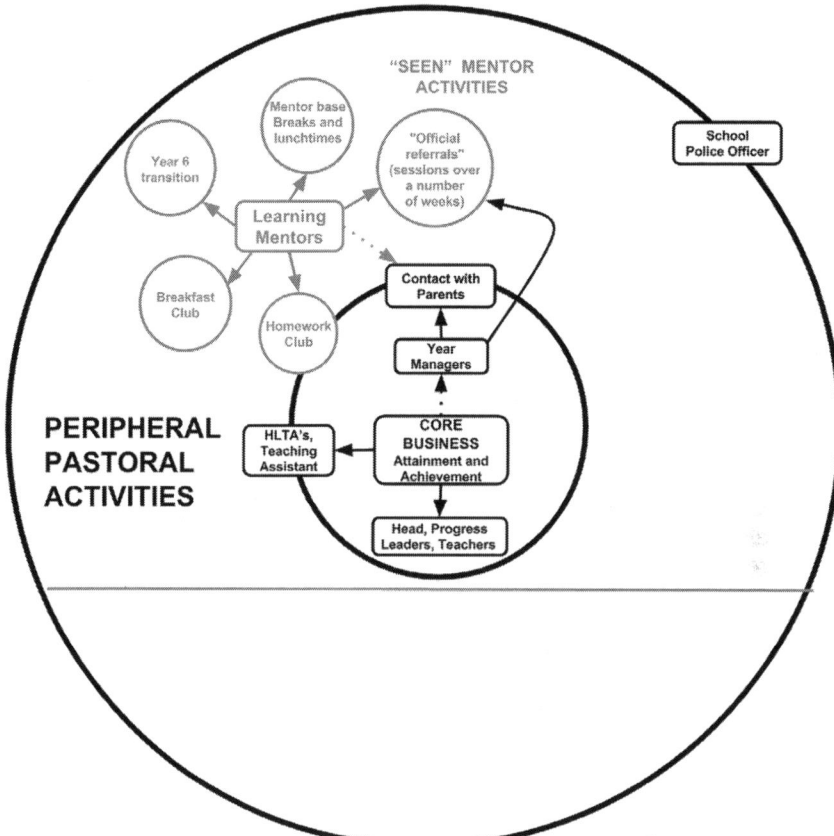

Fig. 2.   Mapping the Learning Mentor 'Seen' Activities.

in Chapter 6). The broken line connecting to parents symbolises two key issues: first that the role was seen as enabling a more informal means to engage parents, particularly those deemed as hard to reach. But once established, this was an area of mentor work that could be taken over or which they could be excluded from at any point. The example of Daniel and Angie recounted in Chapter 10 illustrates both of these situations.

The insecure and precarious nature of the employment relationship is also a feature of operating in the peripheral domain as most if not all paraprofessionals are employed on a term-time basis or may find their role in the ascendancy or descendency depending on whatever policy initiative is in vogue. Thus, readers may remember that the learning mentor who was served a redundancy notice in the study, ended up being redeployed at the 'eleventh hour' into another temporary policy-driven role of 'Parental Advisor'. Here it is possible to identify a further parallel with the paraprofessionals of 1960s America who also had to negotiate the ever-present threat of project monies and inevitable job loss.

It would appear that although paraprofessionals past and present are initially 'hired as their brother's keeper' (Austin, 1972, p. 61); they ultimately have to look out for themselves.

3. Mapping the Learning Mentor 'Unseen' Activities

Whilst, the 'Seen' domain outlined above illustrates an understanding of how the learning mentor role was practised through 'official knowledge', that is, how the school presented and made sense of this role, the third 'map' (Fig. 3) depicts the significant amount of work that could be observed as falling into the domain of 'Unseen' Mentor activities (see bottom centre). By this I do not mean that this aspect of their work was *literally* invisible but more the lack of recognition (and thereby value) that was ascribed to it by those operating from within the core. This aspect of the map is illustrated by the observations, interviews and informal discussions with both mentors and pupils in Chapter 7 which tell of spontaneous

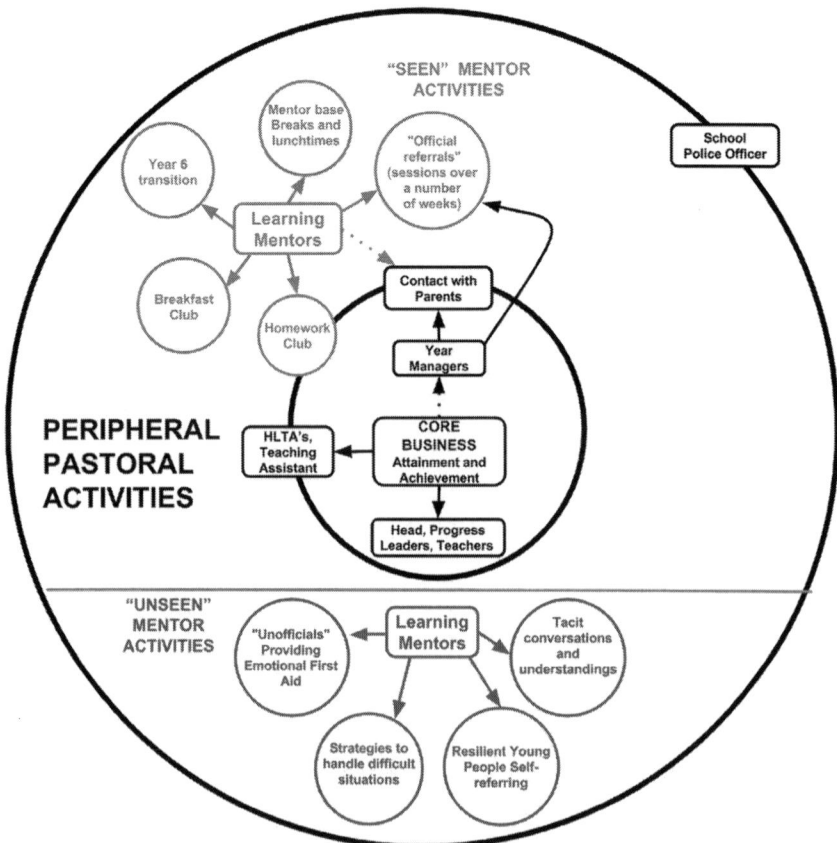

Fig. 3.   Mapping the Learning Mentor 'Unseen' Activities.

one-off interventions; the application of 'emotional first aid' and what I refer to as 'tacit conversations' with pupils regarding how they negotiated and handled problematic aspects of their formal learning or balanced their schooling with significant events going on at home (such as Josie and Sally also recounted in Chapter 7). The many incidents and accounts of pupils' independently self-referring to the mentors, and/or pupil–mentor relationships which continued once they had been formally ended by the middle managers underlined the essential but marginalised position of this aspect of the mentor's work.

4. Other Paraprofessional Groups Active in the Institutional Process

People's experiential accounts can act as 'doors' which may be lead to further work knowledges thereby providing a means by which to look at another angle of a particular story. Thus, through hearing about the experiences of members of a particular group, the researcher can identify the relations that are to be explored by looking particularly at how their work is articulated to and coordinated with others active in institutionalised processes (Smith, 2006). One of those 'particular stories' was that of the behaviour support workers whose work activities are set out in the fourth 'map' (see centre right in grey scale).

The behaviour support team is positioned in a similar way to the HLTAs and TAs as hovering between the core and periphery. This is because aspects of their role like being 'on call' directly supported the activities of teaching and learning by swiftly withdrawing pupils whose behaviour or actions were deemed as disruptive. However, the remainder of their work activities, such as containing pupils who are excluded from class or withdrawing them from lessons to attend anger management sessions, are less 'seen' and therefore located in the periphery.

On more than one occasion, the senior leadership team required learning mentors and behaviour staff to work more closely together due to a reorganisation of pastoral provisions; a move that was viewed as problematic by each group. Here a behaviour support worker illustrates this resistance in the following comment:

> [...] with the mentors, they're known by their first names ... but we aren't known by our first names and because we do the sanction-based side of things and they [pupils] see that ... so we've got that kind of authority as well. We are different, our team [behaviour support] is different to how teachers would work but we are very different to how the learning mentors would work; but we couldn't ... do how they work ... it wouldn't work, it wouldn't!

In a similar vein, the mentors viewed the behaviour support duties like 'on-call' (corridor patrol and withdrawal from class) as completely alien and anathema to their role, seeing these types of interventions as undermining a relationship painstakingly built over a period of time and with a large degree of voluntarism on the part of the pupil. Thus, whilst the distinction in both philosophy and approach of the learning mentors and behaviour support workers were clear to

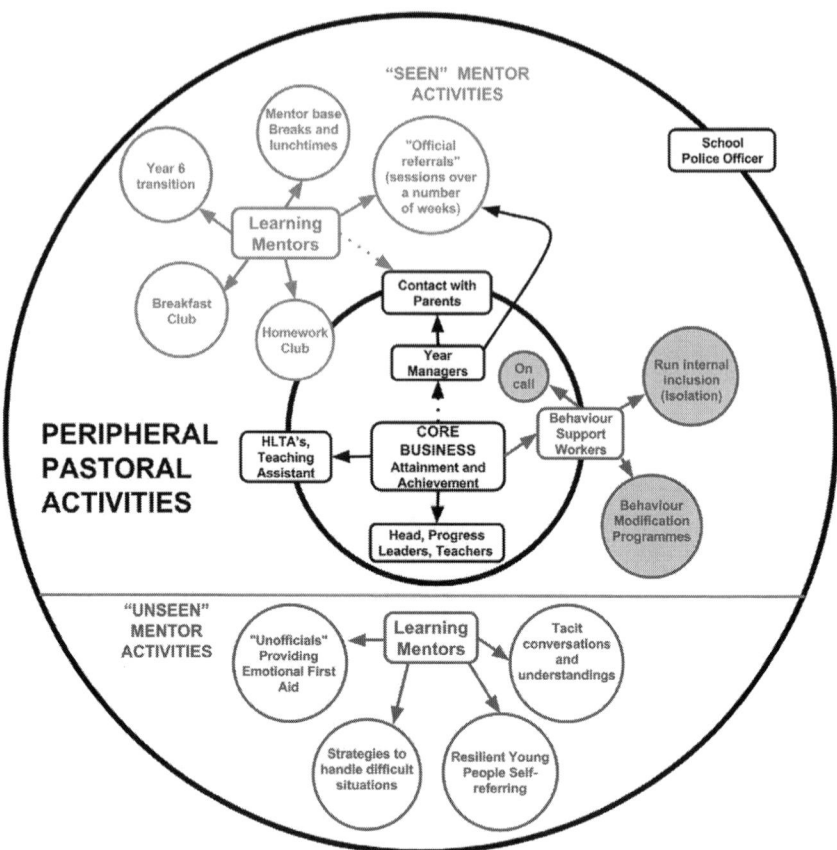

Fig. 4.   Other Paraprofessionals Active in the Institutional Process.

each group (and myself as an 'outsider') they were continually referred to generically as 'our pastoral provisions' by senior and middle management with seemingly little thought as to how they might work alongside each other. I return to this issue further below when commenting on the development of pastoral care systems within performative systems.

Through this mapping of the varying work knowledges, the problematic of the study emerged: *that the needs of the most marginalised young people were being attended to by the most marginalised group of staff – the learning mentors.* Earlier chapters demonstrated how their marginality occurred through varying ways: how their work was perceived and often misunderstood by staff – particularly those operating in the core; how it was organised and (mis)managed by their own line managers; how many of the interventions carried out by the learning mentors and other paraprofessionals were driven by third party agendas be that 'readiness for learning' or behaviour support. In a wider sense this analytic exercise reveals and makes visible the IE notion of the 'relations of ruling' in that the data illustrate how a performative culture drills down and impacts the minutiae of everyday interactions, particularly on those situated outside of the core business of progress and results. However, it is equally important to acknowledge that the conscious choice of learning mentors to sometimes work in a more unofficial and liminal way did enable young people to develop a greater understanding of their own situations with both groups operating outside of official structures and processes. This poses a key question of how such helping relationships develop and operate within the context of a performance-based culture and more specifically whether it is possible for paraprofessionals to operate *outside* of the performative gaze. It is to this issue that the discussion now turns.

How Helping Relationships Develop and Operate within the Context of a Performance-based Culture

There are a number of real consequences when a school's success is viewed as synonymous with narrow performance measures. As illustrated by the quotes set out in Chapter 2 when first examining the notion of performativity, teachers can be reduced to classroom technicians charged with the delivery of an instrumentalist curriculum (Wilkins, 2015), whilst pupils are reconstructed purely in terms of what they contribute to the school's academic endeavour. This was clearly evidenced in Priory Park High's designation of each Year 11 pupil as either 'BANKER', 'RAP' or the irrelevant 'other' (i.e., young people who were unable to access the standard offer of attaining five GCSEs). One step up the hierarchy, we saw how the middle-management view of children and young people becomes fragmented according to their specific area of responsibility be that academic achievement or pastoral well-being. This shift is taken as read by school leaders, reflected in the Headteacher's observation in Chapter 8 of learning mentor interventions not just 'taking up', but actually 'taking away' from teachers the pastoral demands that arise in a school. But this view of formal education fails to see schools as key spaces of childhood thereby downplaying or ignoring significant aspects of children's transitions and the social, emotional and, cognitive development which is a part of these. This state of affairs leads ultimately to partial understandings of children and young people's educational experiences (Frost, 2005; Martin, 2016). In contrast, the nature of the work undertaken by paraprofessionals has the potential to enable a wider concept of 'childhood' and in keeping with the themes of their work taking place in 'seen' and 'unseen' domains the discussion will now critically explore how this might happen.

Analysing Mentors' Work in the 'Seen' Domain

The ethnography revealed how the learning mentor approach led to qualitatively different relationships with pupils, as compared to those experienced by staff based in the core where more formal activities did not always allow for these types of 'critical friend' or 'familial' relationships. One interpretation is to see paraprofessional roles like the learning mentor as an informal educator, or in an English context, a form of school-based quasi youth work. By that I am referring to a person operating in a role primarily outside of the classroom who is able to have a clearer picture of the broader context surrounding the child or young person. Because of this, they have the potential to facilitate young people's learning in a wider sense be that dealing with conflict and managing relationships both school-based and familial; or strategising to make a 'success' of their schooling. It is important to note that 'success' has a much broader definition in this context, representing anything from achieving academically to avoiding permanent exclusion – and any number of scenarios in between. In essence, the key focus of their work is assisting a child or young person in their social development and for that reason it has to be seen as having great value in a wider educative sense.

But this work should not be regarded uncritically as the interactions that took place between paraprofessionals and pupils clearly involved a number of complex interactions and are therefore open to a number of interpretations. For instance, whilst the work of learning mentors could be interpreted as a type of social pedagogy, it could also be perceived as a modern-day example of 'pastoralization'. This term, conceptualised by Williamson (1980) just over four decades ago, refers to a structural device where the relationship-forging skills of the (then) teacher but the (now) paraprofessional, are used to reduce the resentment/dissatisfaction felt by those pupils unable to benefit from 'product' teaching and who may rebel against its constraints. I propose that the mentors' official, 'seen' interventions, that is, those that were orchestrated by a third party working within a more rigidly performative agenda did contain elements of pastoralisation in that they were based on the notion of getting a child or young person 'learning ready', in order that they could cope with the demands of a performative system. But, despite the fact that they were supposedly official constructions of support, the amount of non-school issues that pupils brought to these meetings means the work of the learning mentors could be more usefully understood as 'picking up the pieces within a performative system' rather than its official description of 'removing barriers to learning'.

The notion of engagement mentoring (Colley, 2003a) as outlined in Chapter 2 offers further possibilities in gaining a critical understanding of learning mentorship if, like pastoralization, it is interpreted as a device that seeks to transform the 'dispositions' of young people but with an emotional cost to each party. Colley argues that the power relations implicit in engagement mentoring are far wider than those which may exist within the mentoring dyad itself because the 'players' within the 'field' are not just the mentors and mentees but extend to those who set up and organise mentoring schemes. As noted above, in IE terms, these are the 'relations of ruling' at play, that is, governments and policy-makers who conceive and produce the textual discourses on which mentoring programmes are predicated. Examples from Priory Park High and other studies of learning mentorship (Jones, Doveston, & Rose, 2009) indicate that the learning mentors did indeed struggle to synthesise their personal and/or professional values with the demands and structures of the institution in which they were situated. This interpretation of mentoring re-affirms an earlier call for a serious evaluation of the practice given that has its origins in the developmental relationship of one individual with another, but is now being 'structured, directed and redefined to satisfy institutional as well as individual needs' (Gay & Stephenson, 1998, p. 54).

Analysing Mentors' Work in the 'Unseen' Domain

However, neither 'pastoralization' nor engagement mentoring can fully explain those interventions which were carried out by learning mentors with their 'unofficials' in the *unseen* domain. Accounts of pupil–mentor interactions contained in Chapter 7 demonstrate that these did enable a genuinely open and interactive educational process that was based on lived experiences and informed by the personal values and beliefs of both mentor and mentee. In this domain, it was indeed possible to witness the conditions for respectful practice. However, we return once again to the key issue of invisibility; although such interventions were powerful *and* empowering, they were also unnoticed and unacknowledged within the wider institution. As has been noted above, this issue of the invisibility and peripherality of the mentoring team is a key finding of the study but the reasons as to why it happened are varied and complex. One interpretation could be that this aspect of the mentor's work is a product of incremental change. By this I mean that although the policy which created learning mentors is now defunct, the role has endured, albeit in response to local and extra-local situations such as whether a school continues to fund the role through its own budgets or whether it remains within the governance of the local authority. In relation to the latter, this is however becoming a minority experience for English schools due to the policy dominance of an academisation programme (Thomson, 2020). But the nature of mentors' activities within the unseen domain could also be explained as a conscious decision of these workers to construct their work *outside* of the performative gaze as this enabled them to work in ways that by-passed formal structures. This freedom to act intuitively was clearly of benefit to the mentors and has also been bemoaned by some teachers as a loss to their role (Purdy, 2013) – a debate which continues to this day as illustrated by headlines like: *Teachers' jobs are academic and pastoral. You can't split the two* (Jarmy, 2019). It might also explain why some aspects of the learning mentor role were trivialised and/or seen as less important by those whose work was so relentlessly monitored within the context of performativity.

But it is equally important to consider that the decision to operate in the unseen domain was due in part to the frustrations expressed by the learning mentors regarding how aspects of their work was organised and imposed upon them. Therefore, rather than interpreting this as an aspect of 'creative professional identity' as proposed by Rhodes (2006), I argue that this is better understood as a form of 'Psychic Stretch'. Not however as it was originally envisaged within the context of the 'New Careers' project where practitioners experienced 'immense personal strain' due to being pulled between the demands of the agency and the demands of their community. Within this book I rework 'Psychic Stretch' to describe the 'disjuncture' experienced by the mentor when they had to align what the school decreed as the best 'solution' for a young person, with what they felt the most appropriate course of action to be. Thus, in situations like wanting to override decisions about which pupil should be seen for a one-to-one intervention or making time to continue a mentoring relationship unofficially because it had been 'pulled' by middle managers, the learning mentors expressed a feeling of being pulled in two directions, attending on the one hand to the varying and complex needs of pupils, whilst trying to meet the expectations of middle managers who, in turn, had their own performative agendas to adhere to. In managing this disjuncture, it would appear that the learning mentors had to adopt a form of bifurcated consciousness (Smith, 1987) in inhabiting simultaneously, the official and unofficial domain and thus successfully doing their job. The other meaning originally given to the notion of 'Psychic Stretch' was how the paraprofessional had to negotiate the expectation that in order to maintain their integrity and skill as an indigenous worker they were expected to question practices within professionally-led institutions. This translates less well into a present-day context of performativity given that the mentors were never employed to offer a counter narrative to official school discourses of 'Achievement' above all else. That said, such views were frequently expressed in the unseen domain through tacit conversations with pupils (and also to myself as researcher).

Whether through choice or design, the liminal spaces occupied by the learning mentors contribute to establishing a broader understanding of educational paraprofessionals who can be identified as one of many twenty-first century occupational roles that inhabit an undefined space and have an air of impermanency. Such roles are subject to the vagaries of policy and whatever initiatives happen to be in vogue. Thus, the learning mentor can be understood as both a descendent of the community agent created by the 'New Careers' project in 1960s America *and* a product of more recent initiatives such as workforce remodelling and the increasing popularity of youth mentoring in England during the early 2000s. Such developments exemplify how approaches are recycled again and again, leading to paraprofessional roles which, although given different titles, are designed to prop up or fill the gaps within more formal structures.

What the Enactment of the Learning Mentor and Other Paraprofessional Roles Tells Us About How Practices Previously Conceived as 'Pastoral' are Evolving

The accounts of paraprofessional work set out in this book also show how conceptions and practices of pastoral care have been changing since the late 1990s. This is due in part to a more diverse schools workforce which has come about through policies such as the remodelling of the teaching profession and a series of early intervention, social justice initiatives. But to achieve a 'complete' picture of the changes initiated by these policies it is important to understand how they sit alongside an understanding of schools as performance-based cultures.

State education is currently based around the 'standard school offer' (Martin, 2016) which is premised on the narrow idea that school is a path to academic success (assumed to take the form of A levels) and then University. As graduates, many teachers will themselves have gone through the standard offer which simultaneously reproduces middle class values whilst stereotyping the working class 'other' (Smart, Hutchings, Maylor, Mendick, & Menter, 2009). For varying reasons there are a significant number of pupils who cannot engage with the standard offer. New Labour recognised this and devised a 'compensatory offer' through policy initiatives like *Excellence in Cities*, Extended Schools and *Every Child Matters*. In order for it to be actualised, the compensatory offer relied on groups of less-qualified, more peripheral staff; all the better if people taking up these roles had similar class or ethnic backgrounds to those young people under the gaze of these provisions. In the literature this was exemplified in the idea of learning mentors interfacing between schools and communities (Jones et al., 2009) and illustrated in several ways in this study from Paul's path to Priory Park High as a working-class man of African-Caribbean origin to Pat's 'realisation' that 'ordinary people' had the skills to help 'ordinary children'. Thus, key participant groups in this study, as well as examples given earlier from the wider literature (Odih, 2002; Rhodes, 2006), suggest that pastoral care work continues to be extremely feminised and in some schools has become noticeably racialised. Not surprisingly, those who work in such provisions have lower pay, lower status and less career progression.

When schools are driven to be so fixated on the core aspect of their business, represented above as the standard offer, there is a danger that the processes and practices making up 'pastoral care' become marginalised (Tucker, 2013). This was illustrated in the ethnography through the pupils receiving official referrals to a number of pathways in the school which were operating in 'silos' and often conflicting with one another in both ethos and practice. As such, a question posed some years ago regarding whether a school's existing 'pastoral teams' were simply 'ineffective groupings' which made little corporate contribution to 'the pastoral endeavour' (Best, Jarvis, & Ribbins, 1980, p. 150), would appear to still hold currency. Other critiques from this era also resonate in the present day:

> In some cases new labels have been attached to old systems, but generally neither material provision nor educational thinking and practice has been applied to providing the resources and techniques needed to meet the very wide range of individual needs within the comprehensive school. Thus what happens is that the problems of the individual child become apparent through the pastoral system. (Williamson, 1980, p. 176)

It would appear that many of the issues that were identified by commentators in the 1980s remain unresolved. I argue that 'pastoral care' is still a problematic, 'slippery' and diffuse concept (Calvert, 2009) some 40 years after seminal critiques offered by those authors cited above. It continues to be viewed as a separate enterprise from a school's academic endeavours with the more recent increased presence of staff other than teachers only serving to underline this continuing split. Within current 'how to' texts aimed at pastoral leaders this is no longer questioned but accept as the norm (Nathan, 2011) which has in turn, resulted in tensions and boundary disputes over 'who does what'. The ethnography reinforced this point because the demise of *Excellence in Cities* coincided with the school being judged poorly in terms of behaviour which led directly to the *reduction* of learning mentors and the *expansion* of the behaviour support workers. Although some would argue that each approach is needed, seemingly little thought was given to what the impact would be when the learning mentor, which had been previously described by the Director of Pastoral Care as representing an 'invaluable' and unique relationship for pupils to access, was replaced in large part by another role, based predominantly around sanctions and the correction of behaviour. Thus, due to a combination of changing government policy agendas and tightening school budgets, one support role was in the ascendency whilst the other was in decline. This example illustrates how the terrain of pastoral care continues to be fought over according to wider school agendas and increasing job insecurity. In the study it was illustrated by different paraprofessionals being pitted against one another which played out in observable simmering tensions and sometimes explicit hostilities. It also reinforces the findings of other studies which document the difficulties that paraprofessionals face when attempting to put down 'professional roots' in terms of permanence and career/pay progression (McCann, Granter, Hyde, & Hassard, 2013).

So how should education systems move forward in relation to the employment and contribution of education paraprofessionals? In the short term, I ask that researchers see beyond the classroom and the staffroom as traditional sites of school research and remember that more hidden spaces exist which are worthy of exploration. In short, including paraprofessional experiences will ensure a more complete picture of academic considerations and analyses of school life. In making this request, I reassert the earlier call for 'respectful attention' (DeVault, 1991, p. 4) to be paid to the experiences of those doing marginalised work in schools. This will hopefully achieve a more nuanced understanding of how these varied approaches impact on children and young people as pupils, and schools as institutions.

In the longer term a more transformative course of action is needed. Short-term policy initiatives based on the assumption that it is possible to 'educate your way' out of social problems fail to acknowledge the "work of learning" that takes place outside of school and which requires a significant level of resources which are simply not available or achievable to many families (Ball, 2010, p. 158). Where the political will for such social justice initiatives does exist, there needs to be a greater degree of permanency to the paraprofessionals who are tasked with delivering them. The 'rise and fall' story of the learning mentor presented in this book, demonstrates that when new roles are conceived and then grafted onto schools *as they are currently imagined*, the outcome is little more than a crystallisation of paraprofessional roles as the inferior 'other'. The increasingly diverse nature of the English schools workforce that has been witnessed in recent years, does offer the potential for a more culturally credible and therefore relevant school experience for greater numbers of young people in terms of both *who* they see around school and what type of support they can access. But for this potential to be realised there needs to be a radical shift in the dominant discourse of what constitutes 'learning' and a move away from the idea of schools as institutions of purely academic endeavour. Thus, in this re-imagining of education, the pastoral endeavour, which I define as the supporting and 'critical friending' of young people during their transition to adulthood, becomes the concern of everyone, not just the marginalised few.

References

Allison, E. (2008). A brave face: Despite deprivation and tragedy, the pupils of Gorton Mount primary find much to smile about. *The Guardian* [Online] 4 November. Retrieved from http://lexisnexis.com/uk. Accessed on March 9, 2012.

Andrews, D. (2006). 'Non-teachers' moving into roles traditionally undertaken by teachers: Benefits and challenges – For whom?. *Pastoral Care in Education, 24*(3), 28–31.

Austin, M. (1972). The professional and the paraprofessional: Manpower and educational implications. In M. Austin, M. J. Lickson, & P. Smith (Eds.), *Continuing education in social welfare: School social work and the effective use of manpower* (pp. 58–65). Tallahassee, FL: Florida State University.

Bailey, B., & Robson, J. (2004). Learning support workers in further education in England: A hidden revolution?. *Journal of Further and Higher Education, 28*(4), 373–393.

Ball, S. J. (2003). The teacher's soul and the terrors of performativity. *Journal of Education Policy, 18*(2), 215–228. In Ball, S. J. (Ed.). (2006). *Education policy and social class: The selected works of Stephen J Ball*. World Library of Educationalists (pp. 143–156). Abingdon: Routledge.

Ball, S. J. (2008). *The education debate*. Bristol: Policy Press.

Ball, S. J. (2010). New class inequalities in education: Why education policy may be looking in the wrong place! Education policy, civil society and social class. *The International Journal of Sociology and Social Policy, 30*(3–4), 155–166.

Ball, S. J. (2017). *The education debate* (third edition). Bristol: Policy Press.

Ball, S. J., Maguire, M., & Braun, A. (2012). *How schools do policy: Policy enactments in secondary schools*. Abingdon: Routledge.

Barber, M. (2007). *Instruction to deliver: Fighting to transform Britain's public services*. London: Methuen.

Barker, I. (2008). Assistants are now a force to be reckoned with. *Times Educational Supplement*, July 11.

Bartlett, S., & Burton, D. (2020). *Introduction to education studies*. London: Sage.

Barton, G. (2010). Backroom brigade is 'frontline' force's secret weapon. *Times Educational Supplement*, February 5.

Batsleer, J., & Davies, B. (2010). *What is youth work?*. Exeter: Learning Matters Ltd.

Belgutay, J. (2016). Twenty children a day exclude for racial abuse, official figures show. *Times Educational Supplement*, August 8. [Online] Retrieved from http//www.tes.com. Accessed on March 12, 2013.

Bell, D. (2003). Education action zones and excellence in cities. *Education Review, 17*(1), 11–15.

Best, R., Jarvis, C., & Ribbins, P. (1980). *Perspectives on pastoral care*. London: Heinemann Educational Books Ltd.

Bird, C. (1980). Deviant labelling in school: The pupils perspective. In P. Woods (Ed.), *Pupil strategies: Explorations in the sociology of the school* (pp. 94–107). London: Croom Helm.

Bishop, J. (2011). Learning mentors eight years on – Still removing barriers to learning?. *Research in Education, 85*, 30–42.

Bishop, J. (2017). *Removing barriers to learning or picking up the pieces? An ethnography of the learning mentor in a performance-based culture*. Unpublished Ph.D. thesis, School of Education, University of Huddersfield.

Bishop, J. (2021). Educational paraprofessionals: Underpaid, undervalued and now over here. *British Journal of Educational Studies*, *69*(2), 197–216.

Bishop, J., & Sanderson, P. (2017). Marginalized, misunderstood, and relatively unseen: Using institutional ethnography to explore the everyday work of learning mentors in an English state secondary school. In J. Reid & L. Russell (Eds.), *Perspectives on and from institutional ethnography* (pp. 125–145). Bingley: Emerald Press.

Blair, T. (1997). Prime minister Leader's speech at party conference, Brighton, October 6. Retrieved from http://www.britishpoliticalspeech.org/speech-archive.htm?speech=203

Bochel, H., Bochel, C., Page, R., & Sykes, R. (2005). *Social policy: Issues and developments*. London: Pearson, Prentice Hall.

Bolton, S., & Boyd, C. (2003). Trolley dolly or skilled emotion manager? Moving on from Hochschild's managed heart. *Work, Employment and Society*, *17*(2), 289–308.

Brendtro, L., & Ness, A. (1983). *Re-educating troubled youth*. New York, NY: Aldine De Gruyter.

Bright, G. (2012). 'It's not a factory!' Performativity in education and support provision for marginalised and excluded youth in a UK former coal-mining community. In B. Jeffrey & G. Troman (Eds.), *Performativity in UK education: Ethnographic cases of its effects, agency and reconstructions* (pp. 217–239). Painswick: Ethnography and Education Publishing.

Brook, P. (2009). The alienated heart: Hochschild's 'emotional labour' thesis and the anti-capitalist politics of alienation. *Capital and Class*, *98*, 7–31.

Bryson, P. (2010). Alternative education, equity and compromise: Dilemmas for practice development. *Child Care in Practice*, *16*(4), 347–358.

Burgess, S., Briggs, A., McConnell, B., & Slater, H. (2006, September). *School choice in England: Background facts*. CMPO Working Paper Series No 06/159, Bristol, University of Bristol.

Calvert, M. (2009). From 'pastoral care' to 'care': Meanings and practices. *Pastoral Care in Education*, *27*(4), 267–277.

Campbell, M., & Gregor, F. (2004). *Mapping social relations: A Primer in doing institutional ethnography*. Walnut Creek, CA: AltaMira Press.

Cheminais, R. (2009). *Effective multi-agency partnerships: Putting every child matters into practice*. London: Sage.

Clark, A. (2004). The mosaic approach and research with young children. In V. Lewis, M. Kellet, M. Robinson, S. Fraser, & S. Ding (Eds.), *The reality of research with children and young people* (pp. 142–156). London: Sage Publications Ltd.

Clayton, T. (1993). From domestic helper to 'assistant teacher' – The changing role of the British classroom assistant. *European Journal of Special Needs Education*, *8*(1), 32–44.

Colley, H. (2003a). *Mentoring for social inclusion: A critical approach to nurturing mentor relationships*. London: Routledge Falmer.

Colley, H. (2003b). Engagement mentoring for 'disaffected' youth: A new model of mentoring for social inclusion. *British Educational Research Journal*, *29*(4), 521–542.

Colley, H., & Guery, F. (2015). Understanding new hybrid professions: Bourdieu, illusion and the case of public service interpreters. *Cambridge Journal of Education*, *45*(1), 113–131.

Conradie, L., & Golding, T. (2013). *The short guide to working with children and young people*. Bristol: Policy Press.

Constable, D., & Roberts, M. (2003). *Handbook for learning mentors in primary and secondary schools*. London: David Fulton Publishers.

Cruddas, L. (2005). *Learning mentors in school: Policy and practice*. Stoke-on-Trent: Trentham Books.

Currie, J. (2001). Early childhood education programs. *Journal of Economic Perspectives*, *15*(2), 213–238.

Dean, H. (1999). Citizenship. In M. Powell (Ed.), *New labour, new welfare state?* (pp. 213–233). Bristol: Policy Press.

Denscombe, M. (1980). Pupil strategies in the open classroom. In P. Woods (Ed.), *Pupil strategies: Explorations in the sociology of the school* (pp. 50–73). London: Croom Helm.

Department for Children, Schools and Families (DCSF). (2009). Internal Exclusion Guidance. Retrieved from https://dera.ioe.ac.uk/712/1/DCSF-00055-2010.pdf

Department for Education. (DfE). (2017). Progress 8 and Attainment 8: Guide for maintained secondary schools, academies and free schools. Retrieved from https://www.gov.uk/government/uploads/system/uploads/attachment_data/file/497937/Progress-8-school-performance-measure.pdf. Accessed on March 12, 2017.

Department for Education. (DfE). (2018a). *School Workforce in England.* https://www.gov.uk/government/collections/statistics-school-workforce

Department for Education. (DfE). (2018b, March). *Creating opportunity for all: Our vision for alternative provision.* London: HMSO.

Department for Education and Employment. (1997). *Excellence in schools.* White Paper. London: DfEE.

Department for Education and Skills. (2001a). *Schools achieving success.* Cm 5230, TSO.

Department for Education and Skills. (2001b). *Good practice guidelines for learning mentors.* Nottingham: DfES.

Department for Education and Skills. (2003a). *Raising standards and tackling workloads.* London: DfES.

Department for Education and Skills. (2003b). *Every child matters.* Cm 5860, TSO.

Department for Education and Skills. (2004). *Every child matters: Next steps.* Nottingham: DfES Publications. Retrieved from https://dera.ioe.ac.uk/4973/7/EveryChildMattersNextSteps_Redacted.pdf

Department for Education and Skills. (2005). *Supporting the new agenda for children's services and schools: The role of learning mentors and co-ordinators.* Nottingham: DfES.

DeVault, M. (1991). *Feeding the family: The social organization of caring as gendered work.* Chicago, IL: University of Chicago Press.

DeVault. M., & McCoy, L. (2002). Institutional ethnography: Using interviews to investigate ruling relations. In J. Gubrium & J. Holstein (Eds.), *Handbook of interview research* (pp. 751–776). London: Sage Publications.

Dorling, D. (2010). *Injustice: Why social inequality still persists.* Bristol: Policy Press.

Dorling, D. (2011). *So you think you know about Britain?.* London: Constable and Roberts Ltd.

Drury, E. (2013). Making the leap from teaching assistant to teacher: Teachers who first worked as TAs share their stories of rising through the ranks, *The Guardian*, June 26.

Dunning, C. (2018). New careers for the poor: Human services and the post-industrial city. *Journal of Urban History*, *44*(4), 669–690.

Eastwood, L. (2006). Making the institution ethnographically accessible: UN document production and the transformation of experience. In D. E. Smith (Ed.), *Institutional ethnography as practice* (pp. 181–197). Lanham, MD: Rowman and Littlefield Publishers.

Edmund, N., & Price, M. (2009). Workforce re-modelling and pastoral care in schools: A diversification of roles or a de-professionalisation of functions?. *Pastoral Care in Education*, *27*(4), 301–311.

Egan, G. (2002). *The skilled helper: A systematic approach to effective helping.* Los Angeles, CA: Brooks/Cole.

Egan, G. (2005). *The skilled helper: A problem-management and opportunity-development approach to helping.* Los Angeles, CA: Brooks/Cole.

Elliott, J. (2001). Characteristics of performative cultures. In D. Gleeson & C. Husbands (Eds.), *The performing school: Managing, teaching and learning in a performance culture* (pp. 192–209). London: Routledge Falmer.

Field, H., & Gatewood, R. (1976). The paraprofessional and the organization: Some problems of mutual adjustment. *Personnel and Guidance Journal, 55*(4), 181–185.

Fontana, A., & Frey, J. (2005). The interview: From neutral stance to political involvement. In N. Denzin & Y. Lincoln (Eds.), *Qualitative research* (3rd ed., pp. 695–728). London: Sage Publications Ltd.

Freedman, M. (1993). *The kindness of strangers; adult mentors, urban youth and the new voluntarism.* San Francisco, CA: Jossey-Bass Inc.

Frost, N. (2005). *Professionalism, partnership and joined-up thinking: A research review of front-line working with children and families.* Sheffield: Research in Practice.

Frost, N. (2011). *Rethinking children and families: The relationship between childhood, families and the state.* London: Continuum.

Frost, N. (2014). Children's services: The changing workplace? In P. Foley & A. Rixon (Eds.), *Changing children's services: Working and learning together.* Bristol: Policy Press.

Gans, H. (1962). *The urban villagers: Group and class in the life of Italian-Americans.* London: Free Press.

Garner, R. (2013). Must do better: 200 secondary schools on Government 'hit list' after failing to reach target for GCSE passes. Retrieved from http://www.indpendent.co.uk. Accessed on November 12, 2013.

Gay, B., & Stephenson, J. (1998). The mentoring dilemma: Guidance and/or direction?. *Mentoring and Tutoring, 6*(1/2), 43–54.

Gentleman, L. (2009). Social policy in the noughties: 10 years of change and controversy, *The Guardian,* December 16.

Gewirtz, S. (2001). Cloning the Blairs: New labour's programme for the re-socialization of working class parents. *Journal of Education Policy, 16,* 365–378.

Giddens, A. (1998) *The Third Way: The renewal of social democracy.* Cambridge: Polity.

Gillies, V. (2016). *Pushed to the edge: Inclusion and behaviour support in schools.* Bristol: Policy Press.

Gleeson, D., & Husbands, C. (Eds.). (2001). *The performing school: Managing, teaching and learning in a performance culture.* London: Routledge Falmer.

Goldbart, J., & Hustler. (2005). Ethnography. In B. Somekh & C. Lewin (2005). *Research Methods in the Social Sciences* (pp. 16–23). London: Sage Publications.

Grahame, P. R. (1998). Ethnography, Institutions and the Social Organisation of Knowledge. *Human Studies, 21,* 347–360.

Harris, A., & Allen, T. (2009). Ensuring every child matters: Issues and implications for school leadership. *School Leadership & Management, 29*(4), 337–352.

Hendrick, H. (2003). *Child welfare: Historical dimensions, contemporary debate.* Bristol: Policy Press.

Hochschild, A. (2012). *The managed heart: Commercialization of human feeling.* London: University of California Press.

Hodgson, A., & Spours, K. (2013). Middle attainers and 14–19 progression in England: Half-served by New Labour and now overlooked by the coalition?. *British Education Research Journal, 40*(3), 467–482.

Hood, C. (1995). Contemporary public management: A new global paradigm?. *Public Policy and Administration, 10*(2), 104–117.

Hudson, J., & Lowe, S. (2004). *Understanding the policy process: Analysing welfare policy and practice.* Bristol: The Policy Press.

Hutchings, M. (2015). *Exam factories? The impact of accountability measures on children and young people.* London: National Union of Teachers. Retrieved from teachers.org.uk

Jarmy, C. (2019). Teachers' jobs are academic and pastoral. You can't split the two. *Times Educational Supplement,* London, May 31.

Jeffrey, B., & Troman, G. (2004). Time for ethnography. *British Educational Research Journal, 30*(4), 535–548.

Jeffrey, B., & Troman, G. (2012). *Performativity in UK education*. Gloucestershire: E&E Publishing.

Jeffrey, B., & Woods, P. (1998). *Testing teachers: The effect of school inspection on primary teachers*. London: Falmer Press.

Jewell, S. (2010). *Shaping the future: On the job: Meet the workers*. Retrieved from http://www.guardian.co.uk. Accessed on March 9, 2012.

Jones, K., Doveston, M., & Rose, R. (2009). The motivations of mentors: Promoting relationships, supporting pupils, engaging with communities. *Pastoral Care in Education*, *27*(1), 41–51.

Katan, J., & Etgar, T. (1998). "New Careers for the Poor": A review of the career of an innovative idea. *Social Security*, *5*, 127–141.

Kerry, C. (2002). Support staff as mentors: A case study of innovation. *Education Today*, *52*(3), 3–12.

Kirkman, S. (2004). *A shortfall in the cure-all?*. Retrieved from http://www.tes.co.uk. Accessed on January 8, 2010.

Kvale, S., & Brinkmann, S. (2009). *Interviews: Learning the craft of qualitative research interviewing*. London: Sage Publications.

Lee, C. (2011). *The complete guide to behaviour for teaching assistants and support staff*. London: Sage Publications.

Lepkowska, D. (2004). Excellence boon to primaries. *Times Educational Supplement*, December 17.

Levinson, D. J., Darrow, C. N., Klein, E. B., & Levinson, M. (1978). *Seasons of a man's life*. New York, NY: Random House.

Levitas, R. (2005). *The inclusive society? Social exclusion and new labour* (2nd ed.). Basingstoke: Palgrave Macmillan.

Lewis, K. C. (2004). Instructional aides: Colleagues or cultural brokers?. *The School Community Journal*, *14*(1), 91–111.

Lewis, V., Kellet, M., Robinson, C., Fraser, S., & Ding, S. (2004). *The reality of research with children and young people*. London: Sage Publications Ltd.

Maddern, K. (2012). Rapport is the key to re-engaging students. *Times Educational Supplement*, October.

Maddern, K. (2013). A day to celebrate the 'unsung heroes' of education *Times Educational Supplement*, July 12.

Mahoney, P., & Hextall, I. (2001). Performing and conforming. In D. Gleeson & C. Husbands (Eds.), *The performing school: Managing, teaching and learning in a performance culture* (pp. 174–191). London: Routledge Falmer.

Mansaray, A. (2006). Liminality and in/exclusion: Exploring the work of teaching assistants. *Pedagogy, Culture & Society*, *14*(2), 171–187.

Marshall, H. (2006). Professionalism and the whole primary school factors aiding and impeding the work of the learning mentor. *Support for Learning*, *21*(4), 194–198.

Martin, D. (2016). *Whatever happened to extended schools?*. London: UCL Institute of Education Press.

McCann, L., Granter, E., Hyde, P., & Hassard, J. (2013). Still blue-collar after all these years? An ethnography of the professionalization of emergency ambulance work. *Journal of Management Studies*, *50*(5), 750–776.

McCoy, L. (2006). Keeping the institution in view: Working with interview accounts of everyday experience. In D. E. Smith (Ed.), *Institutional ethnography as practice* (pp. 109–126). Lanham, MD: Rowman and Littlefield Publishers.

Miles, M. B. (1979). Qualitative data as an attractive nuisance: The problem of analysis. *Administrative Science Quarterly*, *24*, 590–601.

Miles, M. B., & Huberman, A. M. (1994). *Qualitative data analysis* (2nd ed.). Thousand Oaks, CA: Sage.

Morrison, N. (2008). *Catch them when they fall*. Retrieved from http://www.tes.co.uk. Accessed on March 9, 2012.

Mortimore, P. (2013). *Education under siege: Why there is a better alternative*. Bristol: Policy Press.

Moss, G., Webster, R., Harmey, S., & Bradbury, A. (2021). *Unsung heroes: The role of teaching assistants and classroom assistants in keeping schools functioning during lockdown*. London: University College London, Institute of Education.

Murray, J. (2012). Performativity cultures and their effects on teacher educators' work. *Research in Teacher Education, 2*(2), 19–23.

Naidoo, R., & Muschamp, Y. (2002). A decent education for all? In M. Powell (Ed.), *Evaluating new labour's reforms* (pp. 145–165). Bristol: The Policy Press.

Nathan, M. (2011). *A pastoral leader's handbook*. London: Continuum.

Newman, J., & Clarke, J. (1997). *The managerial state: Power, politics and ideology in the remaking of social welfare*. London: Sage Publications Ltd.

Odih, P. (2002). Mentors and role models: Masculinity and the educational 'underachievement' of young Afro-Caribbean males. *Race Ethnicity and Education, 5*(1), 91–105.

Ogg, T., & Kaill, E. (2010). A new secret garden? Alternative provision, exclusion and children's rights, Civitas.

Ofsted. (2003). Excellence in cities and education action zones: Management and impact, HMI 1399.

O'Grady, C. (2006). *What's my job … lead learning mentor*. Westminster. Retrieved from http://www.tes.co.uk. Accessed on March 9, 2012.

Peace, R. (2001). Social exclusion: A concept in need of definition? *Social Policy Journal of New Zealand, 16*, 17–35.

Pearl, A. (1974). Paraprofessionals and social change. *Personnel and Guidance Journal, 53*(4), 264–268.

Pearl, A., & Reissman, F. (1965). *New careers for the poor*. New York, NY: The Free Press.

Perryman, J. (2012). Inspection and the fabrication of professional and performative processes. In B. Jeffrey & G. Troman (Eds.), *Performativity in UK education: Ethnographic cases of its effects, agency and reconstructions* (pp. 41–66). Gloucestershire: E&E Publishing.

Philip, K. (2003). Youth mentoring: The American Dream comes to the UK? *British Journal of Guidance & Counselling, 31*(1), 101–112.

Philip, K, & Hendry, L. (1996). Young people and mentoring – towards a typology?. *Journal of Adolescence, 19*, 189–201.

Piper, H., & Piper, J. (2000). Disaffected young people as the problem. Mentoring as the solution. Education and work as the goal. *Journal of Education and Work, 13*(1), 77–94.

Piper, H., & Simons, H. (2005). Ethical responsibility in social research. In B. Somekh & C. Lewin (Eds.), *Research methods in the social sciences* (pp. 56–63).

Pollert, A. (1988). Dismantling flexibility. *Capital and Class, 34*(1), 42–75.

Powell, M. (1999). *New labour, new welfare state?*. Bristol: Policy Press.

Powell, M. (2002). *Evaluating new labour's reforms*. Bristol: Policy Press.

Power, S. (1996). *The pastoral and the academic: Conflict and contradiction in the curriculum*. London: Cassell.

Power, A., & Willmott, H. (2007). Social Capital in the Neighbourhood, Centre for Analysis of Social Exclusion, report 38.

Purdy, N. (2013). *Pastoral Care 11-16: A Critical Introduction*. London: Bloomsbury Academic.

Putnam, R. D. (2000). *Bowling Alone. The collapse and revival of American Community*. New York: Oxford University Press.

Rhodes, C. (2006). The impact of leadership and management on the construction of professional identity in school learning mentors. *Educational Studies, 32*(2), 157–169.

Rhodes, J. E. (1994). Older and wiser: Mentoring relationships in childhood and adolescence. *Journal of Primary Prevention, 14*, 187–196.

Rogers, R. (1961). *On becoming a person: A therapists view of psychotherapy*. London: Constable.

Rogers, R., & Frieburg, J. (1994). *The freedom to learn*. Hoboken, NJ: Prentice Hall.

Rose, R., & Doveston, M. (2008). Pupils talking about their learning mentors: what can we learn? *Educational Studies, 34*(2), 145–155.

Saltzman, H. (1965). The Poor and the schools. In A. Pearl & F. Reissman (Eds.), *New careers for the poor* (pp. 38–54). New York, NY: The Free Press.

Shaw, C., Brady, L., & Davey, C. (2011). *Guidelines for research with children and young people*. London: National Children's Bureau Research Centre.

Silver, H., & Silver, P. (1991). *An educational war on poverty: American and British policy-making 1960-1980*. Cambridge: Cambridge University Press.

Simmons, R. (2017). Mrs Thatcher's first flourish: Organic change, policy chaos and the fate of the colleges of education. *British Journal of Educational Studies, 65*(3), 353–368.

Smart, S., Hutchings, M., Maylor, U., Mendick, H., & Menter, I. (2009). Processes of middle-class reproduction in a graduate employment scheme. *Journal of Education and Work, 22*(1), 35–53.

Smith, D. E. (1987). *The everyday world as problematic: A feminist sociology*. Boston, MA: North Eastern University Press.

Smith, D. E. (1990a). *The conceptual practices of power: A feminist sociology of knowledge*. Boston, MA: North Eastern University Press.

Smith, D. E. (1990b). *Texts, facts and femininity: Exploring the relations of ruling*. London: Routledge.

Smith, D. E. (2002). Institutional ethnography. In T. May (Ed.), *Qualitative research in action* (pp. 17–52). London: Sage Publications.

Smith, D. E. (2005). *Institutional ethnography: A sociology for people*. Oxford: Altamira Press.

Smith, D. E. (2006). *Institutional ethnography as practice*. Lanham, MD: Rowman and Littlefield Publishers.

Smith, G. W. (1998). The ideology of 'fag': The school experience of gay students. *Sociological Quarterly, 39*(2), 309–335.

Smith, M. K. (2009). 'Social Pedagogy' in the encyclopaedia of informal education. Retrieved from http://www.infed.org. Accessed on July 1, 2012.

Smith, G., Smith, T., & Smith, T. (2007). Whatever happened to EPAs? Part 2: Educational priority areas – 40 years on. *FORUM, 49*(1 & 2), 141–156.

Stanfield, R. E. (1973). *The uses of paraprofessionals in the delivery of manpower and social services through public service employment: The Vermont experience*. Vermont: Vermont Department of Employment Security.

Steinberg, R., & Figart, M. N. (1999). Emotional labor since the managed heart. *American Academy of Political and Social Science, 561*, 8–26.

Stephenson, C. (2006). *Case study: The learning mentor*. Retrieved from http://www.tes.co.uk. Accessed on March 15, 2012.

Stewart, B. (1971). *The role of secondary school para-professionals*. Eugene, OR: Oregon School Study Council.

Stoney, S. (2005). Hopeful signs in our inner cities. Retrieved from http://www.tes.co.uk. Accessed on June 26, 2006.

Tabberer, S. (2000). Teenage motherhood, decision making and the transition to adulthood. *Youth & Policy, 67*, 41–54.

Thomas, T. (2007). A year of tackling anti-social behaviour: Some reflections on the realities and rhetoric. *Youth & Policy, 94*, 5–18.

Thomson, P. (2020). *School scandals*. Bristol: Policy Press.

TES. (2009). How do I become … a learning mentor?. *Times Educational Supplement*, April 24.

Tucker, S. (2009). Perceptions and reflections on the role of the teaching assistant in the classroom environment. *Pastoral Care in Education, 27*(4), 291–300.

Tucker, S. (2013). Pupil vulnerability and school exclusion: Developing responsive pastoral policies and practices in secondary education in the UK. *Pastoral Care in Education, 31*(4), 279–291.

Van Maanen, J. (2011). *Tales of the field: On writing ethnography*. Chicago, IL: The University of Chicago Press.

Vincent, K., Harris, B., Thomson, P., & Toalster, R. (2007). Managed moves: Schools collaborating for collective gain. *Emotional and Behavioural Difficulties, 12*(4), 283–298.

Walby, K. (2005). How closed-circuit television surveillance organizes the social: An institutional ethnography. *Canadian Journal of Sociology, 30*, 189–214.

Walford, G. (Ed.). (2008). *How to do educational ethnography*. London: The Tufnell Press.

Wallace, W. (2001). The listeners. *Times Educational Supplement*, March 23. [Online] Retrieved from http://www.tes.co.uk/article.aspx?storycode=344986. Accessed on March 9, 2012.

Wilkins, C. (2015). Education reform in England: Quality and equity in the performative school. *International Journal of Inclusive Education, 19*(11), 1143–1160.

Williams, F. (2004). What matters is who works: Commentary on the green paper every child matters. *Critical Social Policy, 24*(3), 406–427.

Williamson, D. (1980). 'Pastoral care' or 'Pastoralization'?. In R. Best, C. Jarvis, & P. Ribbins (Eds.), *Perspectives on pastoral care* (pp. 171–181). London: Heinemann Educational Books Ltd.

Willis, P. (1977). *Learning to labour*. Aldershot: Gator.

Wolcott, H. (1973). *Man in the principal's office: An ethnography*. New York, NY: Holt McDougal.

Wolcott, H. (1994). *Transforming qualitative data: Description, analysis and interpretation*. Thousand Oaks, CA: Sage.

Woods, P. (1980). *Teacher strategies: Explorations in the sociology of the school*. London: Croom Helm.

Woods, D. (2013). Leadership – Show them who's boss. *Times Educational Supplement*, November 1.

Index

Note: Page numbers followed by "*n*" indicate notes.